For Lynette, the love of my life.

And for Gareth and Tanith, who make me so proud.

It is for our young that we should fight for change.

3 5 7 9 10 8 6 4 2

Ebury Press, an imprint of Ebury Publishing
20 Vauxhall Bridge Road
London SW1V 2SA

Ebury Press is part of the Penguin Random House group of companies
whose addresses can be found at global.penguinrandomhouse.com

Penguin
Random House
UK

First published by Ebury Press in 2016

www.eburypublishing.co.uk

A CIP catalogue record for this book is available from the British Library

ISBN 9781785034756 (hardback)
ISBN 9781785032691 (trade paperback)

Printed and bound in Great Britain by Clays Ltd, St Ives PLC

CONTENTS

CHAPTER 1
BUXTON

The coin hung in the air, daring me to breathe. For a single moment everything just stopped. Then I snapped out my right hand, caught it and slammed it down on the table.

A pause. Two long, deep breaths. Then I lifted my hand away. There it was, heads, the Queen's profile winking up at me.

So, that was that. I was becoming a cop.

'Well, if that's your decision, son, I'm sure you'll see it through.'

The reaction from my family was pretty much as expected. My father believed in the calm, thoughtful path. Every question could be reasoned out, and whoever lost their temper first also lost the argument. Throughout my entire childhood I don't think I remember hearing a single voice raised in anger.

My mum was a bit more concerned.

'The police, Neil? Are you sure that's for you?'

I could understand her anxiety. I had lasted less than a year on my business studies course at Salford Polytechnic before dropping out and coming back home – not exactly a demonstration of commitment or hard-headed practicality. But even at nineteen I knew that moping around, stacking shelves at Marks & Spencer wasn't for me. I wanted something more. I needed to prove myself – I needed adventure.

I had originally planned to find that adventure the standard way teenagers did in 1989: by saving up for a Eurorail pass, and fruit-picking my way around Europe while trying to chat up exotic foreign girls. But then I stumbled on the police recruitment ad at the back of the local paper.

At first the idea seemed completely ludicrous, beyond absurd. But something about it struck deep. I found myself daydreaming about this, more than even the topless beaches of Marseille. The thought grew and gnawed at me, becoming almost a fixation. Somehow, deep down, I knew this was something I *had* to do, that I could never face myself in the mirror if I didn't step up to the self-imposed challenge.

That's how I ended up standing at my desk, flipping a coin, with a police recruitment application and a map of southern France laid in front of me. Tails, I was taking off around Europe. Heads, I'd join Her Majesty's law enforcement.

My girlfriend Sam also seemed bewildered.

'You... a police officer?' she squealed with laughter.

'Yes... I just...' I paused and fumbled, searching for the words, before simply blurting out, 'I just want to help protect people.'

As naïve and silly as I must have sounded, something in my garbled melodramatic phrase struck a chord in our own relationship. Sam and I had met as teenagers. I was at the boys' school, she was at the girls', and our paths crossed at parties and school discos – a fairly old-school story. We had a lot of fun in those early days, sneaking bottles of cider with our little gang, discovering the world together – doing all the things young lovers are meant to do. But I also saw something else in Sam. I often felt there was something vulnerable or melancholy about her, something that needed protection. I tried my best to be there when she needed me, and to support her through whatever she was going through. Looking back, I can see that helping Sam also allowed me to feel a sense of purpose. As a kid I'd spent entire days tearing through all the classic adventure books by Bernard Cornwell, C.S. Forester and all the rest. These were stories of men – and they were usually men – doing the right thing in difficult circumstances. That impulse to do the right thing, to come through in the hour of need, defined my early relationship with Sam, but it was also what propelled me towards the police.

Because, truth be told, most other aspects of my character wouldn't have marked me out as ideal cop material. Aside from reading, my only real obsession was music. I'd burn through every issue of *Melody Maker* and the *NME*, before racing to the local library to find the new records by Black Sabbath or the Smiths, along with the old greats like Jimi Hendrix and the Beatles. A friend of mine told me that smoking hash was amazing for listening to records, so we would occasionally score a bit of dope off someone's older brother, then lie back to listen to the Doors and Yes. As promised, it was pretty amazing.

But this was also the era that saw the birth of the War on Drugs. I watched Ronald Reagan on TV saying that one smoke of crack would get you addicted for life, and believed it without question. Those worlds of addiction and violence seemed a universe away from my friends and me, smoking a bit of weed and listening to rock & roll – but the cowboy-ish, War on Drugs mythology gradually seeped in.

That's where the idea of joining the police really came from. There were bad people out there preying on the weak and vulnerable, and they needed to be stopped. I wanted to fight the good fight – to catch the bad guys and protect the innocent from vicious criminals. Basically, I was young and naïve, and like most young men setting off on an adventure, this became about discovering who I really was.

It took about six months just to qualify for training. The first interview was at home. The police wanted to know what kind of families their recruits came from. I don't think mine could have been any more ideal unless my old man had been a copper himself.

If the mythical 'Middle England family' that politicians fawn over in their focus groups really exists, we were it. Having been sent to the coalmines during the Second World War, my father had worked his way up to become a regional agent for small businesses around the Midlands and north of England. We lived in Buxton, a picturesque market town just at the edge of the Peak District, and while we certainly weren't wealthy, we didn't want for anything either.

In any case, we seemed to pass muster with the Derbyshire Constabulary, and I was invited for further testing.

The first examination was not at all what I had expected. We were split into groups of four and handed a pile of newspaper clippings. We were then told to decide, as a group, which issues were the greatest priorities for UK policing.

This was the summer of 1989 and the country was experiencing the birth of the acid house rave scene. The tabloid press were reacting with typical hysteria, as if a few kids getting loved up and dancing in a field spelled the end of Western civilisation. So, the other guys in my group all put the acid house stories at the top of their list.

Now, this was something I actually knew about. When I had started my business studies course, I had turned up at eighteen-years-old in Manchester, in 1988. This was quite a magical time and place to be alive. I never got into ecstasy, but the music itself had blown me away. A few tokes on a spliff and I could dance all night at the Hacienda with everyone else. One thing I absolutely knew was that ninety-nine per cent of what was written about this scene was bright shining bullshit. It was certainly nowhere near as serious as the other headlines we were presented with in the exam – stories of guns, beatings and real organised crime.

But the other guys in my group were completely adamant, and I realised they weren't about to change their minds. So I suggested a compromise, treating the rave headlines as a medium priority, and we presented our results.

What I learned later was that the examiners didn't particularly care what order the clippings went in. What caught their eye was that my first instinct was to suggest a compromise, rather than just sticking blindly to my position. Above all else, an effective police officer needs mental flexibility. You need to be able to adapt and change at a moment's notice. Out of the twelve people on our examination team, four were selected. I made the cut.

Suddenly everything became very real and very serious. This was it. I really was becoming a cop.

CHAPTER 2

DERBY

There's no nice way to say it: I was crap.

My very first call-out after training was to break up a fight between two groups of known local trouble-makers that was kicking off in a pub car park. I did exactly as I had been trained, placing myself between the gangs and trying to de-escalate the situation. 'Look,' I began, trying to stare down a massive skinhead almost vibrating with barely contained rage, 'I'm sure we can all just calm down and—'

I never even finished the sentence. The guy just pushed straight past me and drove his fist hard into the face of one of the rival gang members. The entire crowd immediately exploded, and the rest of my team had to pile in to break up the melee, sustaining several minor injuries on the way.

That brawl should never have even started. I had failed to project authority. And in a tense situation, a cop who can't assert authority can be more dangerous than no cop at all. Once people lose faith in the *idea* of the police, things can spiral into anarchy very quickly – especially when everyone is a bit pissed.

I just couldn't seem to find my place. The constant split-second decision-making was almost impossible, and I was no good with violent confrontation. I had been brought up to reason things out, to talk issues through and find common ground. This is generally a positive approach, but not much use when trying to break up a pitched battle between pissed-up hooligans outside a pub.

In those first few months, situations that could have been resolved spun out of control. Criminals who should have been caught easily got away, leading to complex and expensive manhunts. And I found myself called into my sergeant's office for dressing-downs and poor performance reviews. I was on the edge of losing my job before I had even really started.

There was also the culture shock. I had moved from Buxton, an unpretentious, pleasant little market town, to Allenton, a grim suburb of Derby, built from mile after mile of funereal post-war council blocks. It was impossible to tell where the grey of the concrete ended and the grey of the sky began. Allenton had the highest crime rate in the county, and from the distress calls we received at the station, the favourite pastime seemed to be domestic violence. I found myself called out over and over again to arrest my own neighbours, only to have to return home there later that evening.

By now, Sam had moved out of her parents' house and was living with a friend in Manchester, so I'd get to go and see her at weekends. But Sunday evening always meant sitting alone back at my digs in Allenton, dreading the cycle in to work the next day.

But the most extreme culture shock didn't come from the neighbourhood – it came from the police force itself.

Very early in my training I was walking across our station car park with some guys from my team when we passed a dog-handler from the Canine Unit standing around with his giant Alsatian. Of course the dog surged forward, barking and straining at the lead. We all jumped back, but the handler, a white South African guy, just laughed and said 'Oh don't worry lads, I've trained him to only bite the nig-nogs.' I was completely stunned. I had never heard anything like that before in my life. This was still the era of apartheid. Hearing *that* sentence, in *that* accent, from someone supposedly fighting on my own side, was nauseating. Even more disturbing was the fact that no one else in the group objected. Everyone just sort of giggled and walked on, accepting that this was just *how things were.*

Of course there were good people in Derby, and they did a lot of important work. But just through sheer overwork, there was also a widespread atmosphere of cynicism, indifference and casual racism. From my very first days there, I'd see my superiors rolling their eyes as if the public were just irritating extra paperwork, or worse, fundamentally bad people.

Perhaps unsurprisingly, as a department our statistics weren't very good at all. With a slight change in the 'just get through the day' mentality, we could have done so much better – not that I was much help with my own bumbling.

I had joined the police to fight the good fight, but I was beginning to realise that I had been very naïve. Now I was crashing hard against real life and the gritty practicalities of the job. When that dog-handler had dropped his 'nig-nogs' line, I hadn't taken some sort of principled stand. I was unsure of myself, and conscious of being the new guy. I didn't want to start calling out cops who'd been on the force for years. These were my new colleagues and superiors, so I kept my mouth shut and got on as best I could. But that didn't feel right either. How did my own silence fit into that self-image as the guy *fighting the good fight*?

I came to the verge of quitting many times. But somehow I knew that just couldn't happen. I had joined the police to prove something to myself. I wasn't going to walk away at the first sign of difficulty. There was always a little voice inside telling me to just grit my teeth, to get through it. It became a point of inner pride that no matter how bad things got, I could take it.

But I also knew that I had to do something to improve the situation.

'Listen Alex, do me a favour mate, I need to get smacked in the face.'

'You fuckin' what?' Alex looked at me like I'd lost my mind.

'Look, I can't keep up here – take me down the gym and teach me some boxing. I need to know how to take a punch. Come on mate, help me out.'

Alex was one of the other recruits who had joined up with me. He was also a talented boxer who had won silver in the Amateurs. I figured this was as good a place to start as any.

The gym was basically a converted garage with a few heavy bags, some Sugar Ray Leonard posters and the smell of stale sweat, but my wish came true – I definitely learned how to take a punch. It was hard going at first, but I was keen and fairly physically fit, and eventually became quite a handy long-range counterpuncher.

The boxing definitely helped my confidence in general, but the improvement in my working life was slow. Halfway through my two-year probation period it was still the same old story: 'Woods, you're with Sergeant Hornby this month,' 'Woods, why don't you go with Sergeant Picknett for a bit.' I didn't need to be a genius to tell that officers were trying to palm me off on one another. I was hanging on by a thread.

Eventually, I was transferred to Sergeant James McCarthy, an older Scottish officer who spoke with a gentle Perthshire lilt. It was McCarthy who first saw something in me. He recognised, well before I did, that I actually might have something to bring to the job. Gradually, he helped me learn to play to my strengths.

I found my stride in the interview room. I discovered I had a talent for extracting confessions from suspects, even hardened criminals who had faced down much more experienced officers.

I could read people. That little flicker of the eye; the way they tapped their foot a little faster when they were getting angry; the little bead of sweat that formed on their forehead as they got nervous or were caught in a lie. Squeezing confessions is a massively useful skill in the police force. If you can convince a criminal to confess at the interview stage, you save everyone the time and expense of a lengthy investigation and trial.

Over time, detectives from CID actually started coming up and saying things like 'Bloody hell, are you the one who got a confession out of *that bloke*? Well done mate, we've been trying to crack him for years.' None of my colleagues in uniform seemed to notice – to them police work just meant making arrests and banging heads together. But it was the CID guys that I really looked up to. If I had a future on the force, I already knew it lay in that direction.

I became Sergeant McCarthy's go-to guy for suspect interviews and witness statements. My detection rate actually grew to become one of the best on the squad.

But while it was a relief to finally find a role, I still didn't fit into the brash, abrasive culture at Derby. As my probation period drew to a close, I knew I would squeak through with the bosses, but I wasn't sure I even wanted the job. So, when I happened to spot an ad for a position in Glossop, North Derbyshire, on the station noticeboard, I told myself I would apply and give it a go in another setting. If I didn't get the position, I would quit.

My acceptance letter from Glossop arrived the same day as the news that I had passed my probation. I folded the letter and stuck it in my pocket with a sigh. It looked like I was still a cop.

CHAPTER 3
GLOSSOP

I reported for duty on my first 6 a.m. to 2 p.m. shift, and found myself thrown straight into a murder inquiry. Someone had been beaten to death outside a rough pub in Hadfield, the neighbouring town.

As the new guy, I was given the job of guarding the crime scene. On any investigation, anyone who enters or leaves the scene must be meticulously logged and follow a very specific path so as not to interfere with forensics. Any tiny mistake and a defence lawyer can have a field day in court tearing apart your laboriously collected evidence.

So, I stood there all day with a clipboard, marking when the specialist units came and went. It's a necessary and important role, but also generally acknowledged as the most boring job in British policing.

But it did give me the opportunity to observe my new department at work. I was blown away. The entire squad acted with painstaking professionalism and attention to detail. To be fair, the guys at Derby would probably have got the job done too, but with the Glossop team there was never a hint of cynicism or arrogance. Questions would come up and I'd instinctively cringe, waiting for someone to crack the inevitable crass one-liner, but it never came. In fact, the team at Glossop conducted themselves with more than just professionalism – they acted with actual care.

This was how I'd imagined police work when I had signed up at nineteen. People were thinking things out, building a timeline of the incident and putting together a suspect profile – all while taking care of some quite traumatised witnesses.

Over the following few weeks my impressions of the Glossop team only multiplied. They quickly tracked and arrested the pub murderer, and consistently showed themselves to be brilliant, principled, hard-working people who cared deeply about the job. For the first time in my life I felt like I was exactly where I needed to be.

Two weeks into my reassignment to Glossop, I was sent out on my first solo foot patrol. It was a busy Saturday night as I paced the town in my clumpy regulation shoes and one of the awful, sweaty rubber macs they made us wear in those days.

Completely by chance, I turned down an alley behind the local club at exactly the right moment to see some big lug raise a brick and smash it through the back window. There was a moment of silence as our eyes locked. I looked at him, he looked at me. Then he turned and ran.

I heard myself shout, 'Stop! Police!'

Of course he didn't stop. No one ever does. I had one split-second of self-awareness to think, 'Oh God, did I actually just say that?' before sprinting off in pursuit.

We raced round the corner and down another alley, before he realised he wasn't getting away. He turned and swung at me. I ducked, taking the blow on my helmet. Then, acting completely on instinct, I sidestepped left, threw my hip into his and slammed him hard onto the ground, exactly as I had been trained. Before I even realised what I was doing, I was snapping on the handcuffs and reading him his rights.

This was an important moment for me. When I threw that big guy to the floor, I had felt a little surge of adrenaline, but no panic. In fact, I had felt weirdly calm, as if the world had suddenly slowed down. It was a big step for me to realise that not only could I keep my cool in stressful situations, but that a cop can apply serious force both ethically and intelligently.

Not only could I do this job, I could do it well.

From that moment I was making arrests of hostile suspects left, right and centre. It actually got to the point where my sergeant had to tell me to cool off. One Saturday night in town I made four arrests, two for common assault and two for criminal damage. In each incident people had been injured, and these arrests were absolutely necessary. But, on the Monday morning, Sergeant Hanford approached my desk. 'Woods, my office please.'

I instinctively cringed, remembering the dressing-downs I had received in Derby.

'So, Woods, these four arrests you made on Saturday evening?'

'Yes sir.'

'You really can't muck about like that, you know.'

'But sir, those were serious crimes in progress.'

'Listen Woods, I know you trained in Derby but that's a big city. If a situation escalates, backup can be there in minutes. Things are different here. Where you were the other night, no one would have been able to reach you. You need to think ahead in these situations, Woods...we don't do your big-city ways around here.'

He raised his eyebrows to inject a little humour; I think we both knew it was odd I was getting told off for doing the job too well. But he was absolutely right, and it was another reminder that good police work isn't about rushing in and bashing heads, it's about thinking ahead and maintaining absolute tactical discipline.

But, sergeants are nothing if not competitive. My record of arrests made my superiors look good. So, despite his admonitions, Hanford made sure I was rewarded. He recommended me for the Advanced Driving Course. In those days courses and specialised training were often given out to reward outstanding work. It's an excellent way to incentivise people and expand their skills. Unfortunately, cuts have now made this impossible. Courses are now only offered to officers who will definitely need them, so Traffic Division might get on the Advanced Driving Course, but it would generally be off-limits to regular PCs.

This is a shame because that course was a godsend for me. It meant I could step up and start manning the Rapid Response car, a whole new education in high-intensity police work. Jez Radway, the officer generally responsible for the Rapid Response car, was one of the most intelligent and principled people I met during my entire time on the force, and became a real mentor. It was Jez who took me aside one day and mentioned that if I wanted to apply for a placement with the Drugs Squad, he would write in support of my application.

This was huge.

Throughout the 1990s Britain was awash with narcotics. The fall of the Berlin Wall and opening of the Eastern Bloc had created a heroin superhighway from Central Asia. Crack had exploded out of the American ghetto and begun squeezing the life out of our own inner cities. Meanwhile, the ascendancy of dance music and the rave scene meant that MDMA, amphetamine and cannabis were the fuel that kept the engine of youth culture running.

This led to massive political pressure on police forces to crack down on the drugs trade. And that meant bigger budgets for Drugs Squads all over the country. A force's Drugs Squad, or DS, were always the guys with the best kit, the flashiest cars and the most experienced detectives. It was where any smart, ambitious young cop wanted to be. But most would have to wait years. Getting the tap was obviously a gesture of approval from the higher-ups – and I jumped at the chance to prove myself.

The initial reception was a little disappointing.

The officers on the Drugs Squad absolutely hated these month-long attachments. This was a tight-knit group of experienced detectives, involved in long, complex investigations. For them, being sent a new regular PC just meant another bumbling plod they had to babysit.

So, I spent my first morning the same way as every single other officer on attachment – they took me out to the car park to show me their radio communications kit, then all had a good laugh when I stuck my finger in my ear as if I was in some Hollywood movie. This is a classic newbie error. Obviously, if you're undertaking surveillance, the last thing you do is walk around with your finger in your ear like a cartoon spook. The equipment works just fine on its own; the finger-in-the-ear routine was just cooked up by film-makers because it looks cool onscreen.

By now I had learned to expect a ribbing from the more experienced cops, and took it with a laugh. That afternoon though, everything became extremely serious, as I got my first taste of the DS at work.

Intelligence had come in that a high-profile dealer was going to be shifting several kilos of cocaine that afternoon. After some discussion, the decision was made not to interrupt the move, but to simply observe and gather what info we could about his operation. This would be a full-surveillance deployment, which meant a convoy of five cars, out for six hours, with an outrider on a motorbike to cover any emergency gaps in visibility.

Covert surveillance is a fine art, and these guys were masters. We acquired our target, and with complex, split-second coordination, one car flawlessly made way for another in convoy, so as not to alert him he was being followed.

'Alpha 3 with the visual on West Green Avenue. We'll pursue till next set of lights, then hand over. Can we get someone in position please?'

'Roger that. Alpha 1 in position, ready for takeover at lights.'

'Alpha 2 here. We've got the eyeball. Target indicating left, we're going to have to overshoot. Backup from Alpha Bike please.'

'Alpha Bike ready.'

These guys would speed to 140mph just to be able to take their next position, all while planning several steps ahead like chess masters. I was in awe. This wasn't locking up drunken idiots on the street; this was dynamic, highly targeted, intelligence-led police work.

Then we ran into trouble.

Our target pulled over, ditched his car and walked into a council estate. There was no way in by road, and we had lost our line of sight.

'Shit!' exclaimed Rob, one of the experienced detectives up front. 'There could be any number of exits from that bloody estate, and we've got no idea what he's even doing in there.'

'I'll go in.' I didn't hesitate for a second.

Rob snapped his head round sharply.

'What?'

'I'll go in on foot, see where he goes and where the exits are...don't worry, I can do it.'

The two detectives exchanged a glance, then Rob just shrugged. 'Well, go on then, what are you waiting for?'

I leapt out of the car, then slowed my walk and hunched my shoulders as if trying to keep off the cold. I turned the corner into the estate just in time to see our target entering a house on the right. I walked by slowly, keeping my eyes fixed on the ground, but making a note of the house number. I radioed the team under my breath: 'This is Alpha Foot. Suspect has entered house number 47. The only exits are Alpha 2's current position, and directly opposite. Move one car there and we'll have him pinned. I'll maintain current position in case he leaves on foot.'

'Roger that, Alpha Foot,' came the reply in my earpiece, 'good work.'

The rest of the operation went smoothly. We picked him up as he left the estate, now carrying two large sports bags, and followed him to his drop-off point. That deployment yielded a lot of valuable intelligence, especially about house number 47, which turned out to be the hub of a significant local cocaine network.

It also won me some grudging respect from the DS team, and over my month-long attachment they used me as their foot guy several more times. I was young and fresh-faced enough that no dealer would ever take me for an experienced DS detective. I also had an eye for detail and an ability to blend into my surroundings. I was slowly discovering a talent for surveillance work.

But what most fascinated me was how the Drugs Squad would use informants to build a picture of how the narco trade operated in a particular area. They would pick someone up on a minor possession charge, then offer to 'not write it up' if they became a regular source of usable intelligence. Occasionally they would even throw in a bit of money. It was amazing how quickly they were able to compile and analyse their data in order to map how the supply networks operated.

This was where I found my place – the same instincts that made me effective in interviewing suspects also helped me in recruiting informants. A lot of these guys were types who were more into music than football, and I was sometimes able to talk to them on more of a level than even the other DS detectives.

It was a point of pride for the Drugs Squad that they only went after high-level gangsters and organised crime groups – or OCGs as they called them. Each of these guys was a veteran copper, with stories of major busts, gunfights and taking down heavy gangsters.

Rob, in particular was an amazing guy. Officers are usually limited to five years in any specialist team. The bosses say this is to deal with stress and fatigue, but it has as much to do with preventing corruption. Rob was so talented, however, they'd given him a second tour of duty.

Soon enough my attachment ended and I was rotated back into regular uniformed police work; it was a major comedown. But a couple of months later, Rob popped in and sat across my desk.

'Listen, Neil, do you fancy coming back and doing some more work with the DS?'

I tried to contain my excitement. 'Well yeah, certainly. But it'll be difficult to square with the bosses. I've done an attachment already.'

'All right, look – apply again, but do it through Sergeant Kotchie, not Hanford. I'll have a word and fix the paperwork so it goes through.' I didn't need to be asked twice.

What I didn't know was that the DS already had a plan for me. A few days into my new deployment Rob turned and very casually dropped a question that would change the entire course of my life. 'So, Neil, don't suppose you fancy trying your hand at doing some buying, do you?'

Undercover operations were still very new, and rarely employed, in British narcotics enforcement. The Derbyshire DS had only used the tactic once or twice, but had scored a major success the previous year when an officer named Webby had made a splash in the local paper after busting a high-level crack dealer.

There was increasing political pressure at the time on all forces to stamp down on crack in particular. Not a week went by without some story in the press about the horrors of the drug, often with more than a hint of racial bias. The politicians needed to be seen to be 'doing something', and they spun that pressure onto the police.

For whatever reason, I was the guy they turned to. I agreed without a second thought. My experiences with the Drugs Squad were the best I'd had so far on the force and I wanted in.

The target was a known local hard-man named Danny Anderson. He had a constant stream of sketchy people coming and going from his house, so we set up an observation point with a video recorder across the street and off I went. That was it. There was no training, or even advice. It was just, 'All right Neil, here's twenty quid, go buy some crack…Don't let on you're a copper, and find out what you can.'

Adrenaline makes me calm. It slows everything down. When I walked up to the shabby red-brick house I felt in absolute control. I was also young and stupid, and had no idea how dangerous what I was doing really was. Sometimes ignorance can be a powerful weapon.

I rang the bell and a young guy answered, wearing torn jeans and a wife-beater vest.

'Uhh hi,' I began sheepishly, 'is Danny about?'

'What you want? Who are you?' the guy snapped aggressively.

This threw me. I was so unprepared I hadn't even worked out a cover story. I just froze. For a moment I was in real trouble. The young guy just peered at me curiously. 'You a student or something?'

'Yeah. I'm a student, yeah.' I shuffled and looked at the ground self-consciously, relief flooding through me.

I managed to steal a glance into the house. There was a woman glowering at me from the darkness. She must have been about thirty years old, wearing a stained tracksuit, with a wild-eyed expression and missing half her teeth.

The young guy looked me up and down once more, then said, 'Wait here,' and slammed the door. I kicked my heels for a few seconds, not really knowing what to do with myself. Then the door swung open again. There was Danny Anderson, a big West Indian guy with long dreadlocks, also wearing a wife-beater. The toothless woman was still hovering in the hallway, glaring out. 'You dis student, den? You wantin' a ting, bwah?' Danny asked in a thick Jamaican patois.

'Yeah . . . a "ting", yeah,' I repeated, almost under my breath.

He paused and gave me the once-over. 'Right, come over 'ere den.'

Danny led me across the street into an alley. Then he turned towards me and opened his hand to reveal eight small paper twists. 'Go on, den.'

I took one of the twists, and on instinct began to unwrap it to have a look. 'Oi there's nowt wrong wi' dat,' Anderson snapped, as if genuinely offended that I would doubt his product. I hurriedly stuffed it in my pocket, handed him the twenty quid and turned to go.

Following the plan, I walked straight back to the police station to get the evidence to our drugs lab. That's how naïve and amateurish those early operations were. There is no way an undercover operation should be run from an actual police station – in fact, it's completely insane. All it takes is the wrong person to walk by and spot you coming or going, and you're a dead man.

But on that day, I strolled back quite pleased with myself. Rick 'Johnno' Johnson, who had been manning the observation point, was out of breath, having sprinted to get back before me to show off the video. Seeing how nonchalant I was, Johnno gave me a slap on the back. 'Look at this guy – it's like he's just been out to get the fucking papers.' The entire squad crowded around to congratulate me. It was a big moment.

The next time out though, things got a little more complicated...

The door swung open to reveal the woman with the missing teeth. She glared out at me with a twitchy, wired expression in her bloodshot eyes.

'Is Danny about?' I muttered, trying not to stare at her gums as she slobbered and gurned.

'Not in!' she shouted, and violently slammed the door in my face.

I suppose at that point I could have wandered back to the station and tried again another day. But I had come out to score some crack, and that's what I was going to do. So, I just sort of wandered around the neighbourhood asking anyone who looked a bit *crackhead chic* if they knew where Danny was.

Looking back, I can't believe I pulled this off. Within two years such an obvious stunt would get an undercover operator beaten or killed. But in those early days the addicts and dealers were as naïve as we were. Eventually though, some guy with gaunt cheeks and a complexion like overcooked meat went, 'Yeah, try the bookies, he's always hanging about in there.'

I walked into the little council estate bookie joint, and straight into a cloud of ganja smoke so thick it made my eyes water. The place was rammed with dreadlocked West Indian guys getting stoned and watching football on the wall-mounted TVs. I stood out like a very skinny, very white, sore thumb. Within thirty seconds I was surrounded.

'What you doing here, bruv?'

'Uhh…I'm just looking for Danny.'

'What you wantin' Danny for? Danny not here, man.'

'I just want to buy a ting, Y'know…a stone?' I shuffled in place awkwardly, keeping my eyes fixed on the floor.

One of the bigger guys stepped forward and jabbed his finger aggressively into my shoulder.

'What you doin' just comin' in 'ere for asking for tings? Who are you, bruv? Where you from?'

'I dunno,' I stammered, 'I'm a student, I'm not really from around here. I just want a stone y'know…I've got money.'

The fact that I felt seriously intimidated, and that my eyes were streaming from the choking weed smoke, probably helped me look more convincing as an addict on the rattle.

The big guy gave a contemptuous snort. 'Boy, you wan' a stone, I'll sell you a fuckin' stone – you don't need no Danny.' With that he reached into his pocket and offered me up a plastic wrap.

'Cheers,' I blurted as I grabbed the package and handed over the money.

'Yeah boy. I'm Freaky Man…you wan' stones, you come see, boy.'

By the time I got back to the station, Johnno was actually shaking. I hadn't even thought of it, but of course when I had wandered off to the bookies, I'd gone out of observation.

He'd had no eyes on me, and had immediately assumed I was in a derelict garage somewhere with a gun to the back of my head.

'Don't worry, mate, I bought the stuff off another guy down the bookies.' I flourished my wrap of crack.

'No Neil – you don't understand!' he thundered. 'We're not fucking playing here...last time Danny Anderson thought he had an informant, he stabbed the guy eleven times through the chest...And that's just the one we know about – these people don't fuck around, Neil.'

That was a wake-up call. I knew we were chasing bad guys but I hadn't quite registered just how brutal the drugs game really was.

Later that night I looked over Danny Anderson's record. He had a string of attacks to his name. He'd been sent down for GBH with Intent, but in my book he was lucky not to have been charged with attempted murder. I felt a strange sense of pride. These guys were nasty and I had to watch my step – but I also somehow knew that I could outsmart them.

After my encounter at the bookies, my face was known. I scored at Danny Anderson's house a few more times, then hung around outside the bookies until I just happened to run into Freaky Man again – but this time with Johnno around to catch it on video.

Finally, the entire Drugs Squad was called in for a briefing, and we planned out the arrest phase.

The morning of the bust I took a few banknotes, copied down their serial numbers, ran them through the photocopier and logged it all in my evidence book. I then went and scored a rock of crack off Freaky Man and Danny Anderson in turn. As I left Anderson's place and turned the corner, I passed a crew of twelve uniformed officers in body armour. I didn't even turn round as I heard the screech of tyres and the sirens start to wail.

This was the biggest crack bust the Derbyshire force had ever brought home. Fifteen properties were simultaneously raided, with seven separate stashes discovered, along with eight massive cannabis hauls.

At Freaky Man's place another dealer attempted to escape by jumping out of a second-floor window, and ended up being bailed to hospital with smashed-up ankles. Freaky Man himself also turned out to have prior GBH convictions, and both he and Danny Anderson got significant prison sentences. The woman I had encountered at Anderson's house turned out to be his girlfriend; she apparently just sat on the sofa, smoking crack all day as Danny cut it up.

The bust made it to the front pages of the local papers, and overnight I became a bit of a star on the Drugs Squad. It was a new and strange feeling to suddenly have elite detectives walking up and randomly slapping me on the back. What I didn't know then, amidst the backslapping and celebratory pints, was that it would never be this easy again – or that I could never celebrate my achievement with anyone else.

The evening we wrapped the investigation, the Drugs Squad Detective Sergeant, Jim Horner, gave me a lift home. Just as we pulled up outside my house, he grabbed my arm.

'You did well with this Neil. Are you interested in any more of these jobs?'

'Definitely sir, of course,' I replied eagerly.

'Right. Well in that case you can't tell anyone what we've done here. And I mean anyone. Not your family; not your girlfriend; not your mates at the station. The only thing an undercover has is their anonymity. If your name becomes known, there's no way you can ever do another job with us.'

'Well, I can tell other cops, can't I?' I asked in disbelief. I had been rather looking forward to bragging about my exploits.

Jim gave a derisory snort.

'Neil, uniformed coppers leak like fucking sieves – and the bloody CID as well. You tell one guy, he'll tell his mate – and the next thing you know, we send you out undercover, but now some gangster knows your name or your face – and you end up discovered in a car boot somewhere in the Pennines. Do I make myself clear? You tell no one.'

'Yes sir, I get it.'

I walked to my front door, took a deep breath, and got ready to pretend that I had just had a completely normal day at work.

As satisfying as it was bringing those convictions in, before I could even think about taking on another undercover job I had issues to deal with at home.

It was now 1991, I'd finished probation a few months earlier and Sam had moved up to Glossop with me. We'd found a beautiful old cottage in the old town, covered in lush green creeping ferns, a real romantic little hideaway. For a while I felt giddily happy.

Sam found a job with a chemicals company and also started a one-day-a-week degree in Manchester, where she was doing well. The fresh start seemed to be good for both of us. As my own communication skills improved at work, so did my ability to play my protector-role, talking her round when I thought she was feeling down and reassuring her that everything would be OK.

We had been in Glossop several months before I noticed the change in atmosphere.

Derbyshire cops like a drink, and I would often go out for an after-work beer with the rest of my team at the end of shift. But when I opened the cottage door I would often find Sam standing in the hallway holding a glass of wine, looking unimpressed and demanding to know where I'd been – particularly if I had gone out with any female officers.

I could sense a hard edge in Sam's voice, and always tried to keep my tone as calm as possible and explain that I was just out for a drink with the guys, and there was nothing at all suspicious going on. And it was the absolute truth. I was still completely in love with Sam and, at this point at least, totally uninterested in chasing other women. I'd even been planning to ask Sam to marry me – though I found this new tension developing between us profoundly troubling.

But I tried to push my concerns aside. We were just adjusting to our new way of life. And whatever happened, I was a cop who had just cracked his first undercover case – even if I could never tell the ones I loved, I felt I could take on the world.

CHAPTER 4

DERBY II

J im Horner sauntered up, sat on the corner of my desk and leaned in conspiratorially.

'All right Neil? The Derby DS have a little situation going on...we've basically figured out who's running crack and heroin for all of South Derby, but we haven't been able to get anything on him with surveillance. We thought it might be an idea for you to have a whirl?'

'Yeah, absolutely.'

Having been rotated back to uniformed PC work for a few months, I felt an immediate surge of adrenaline at the thought of another undercover operation.

'Only thing is, Neil,' Jim continued, 'I don't think we can get you another formal secondment – you'd have to do this one on your rest days.'

I gave a pointed glance at the pile of paperwork on my desk.

'Fuck it. I'm in.'

'Good lad. Come in Thursday for a briefing.' Jim gave me an approving slap on the back, and he was off.

The target was Bigga Williams. Looking over the surveillance photographs it was easy to see how he earned the name. This guy wasn't just fat; he was planetary. Almost as important a target was his main lieutenant, a seriously nasty character named Meshawn, connected to a string of stabbings and other assaults.

As we were going through the briefing, Johnno piped up, 'Chief, don't you think it's a bit risky sending Neil out in Derby? He was a uniformed copper here a year ago, people will know his face.'

Jim gave it some thought. 'Well, anyone who would recognise him is probably in prison now, anyway. I'm sure it'll be fine.'

Still, at least for this job, the team had set up an autonomous headquarters in a disused office space at the edge of town, so I wouldn't have to report directly back to the police station.

Another thing I insisted on was that I wouldn't work under observation.

This was a very different scenario than the Danny Anderson job. There was no Intel on how Bigga ran his operation, and no known address. I'd have to figure everything out from the ground up. I needed to be able to move around at will, to get to know people and work my way in. It would be far too restrictive to always be worrying about maintaining visual contact and not sending Johnno into a panic. Video evidence was the endgame. We could get these guys on tape only after I had got my face known and established trust.

Almost to my surprise, the whole team nodded and agreed to work my way. In those days there were no protocols to follow, but a lot of what we improvised back then eventually became the standard that the force still follows – or at least is meant to follow – to this day.

So, the hunt began. I spent days trudging through the grey Midlands drizzle, beating a circuit around the dingy, blighted South Derby council estates where Bigga was known to operate.

It took about a week before I caught a glimpse.

Bigga liked to play the big-time dealer, tooling around in a flash Mercedes with an air of untouchable swagger. At first I just watched, hanging out on street corners and in shop doorways, a baseball cap pulled low over my forehead. I'd thrown together a junkie outfit from a local charity shop, and made myself indistinguishable from every other skinny, pasty addict haunting the streets.

With some careful observation, though, I was able to put together a basic picture of Bigga's movements. It wasn't until my sixth time out that I even attempted to score. I waited outside one of Bigga's safe houses until he arrived and disappeared inside with one of his lieutenants. This wasn't Meshawn, but an almost equally unpleasant character named Carlo who I recognised from the Intel photos.

Taking a deep breath, I steeled myself and knocked. The door swung open and Carlo stood there, fixing me with an aggressive glare.

'What you want, bruv?'

'Uhh... Is Bigga about?'

'Yeah, what you after?' he spat back.

'I just need a stone, yeah.' I played the addict on a rattle, making myself as humble and non-threatening as possible in the face of his hostility.

'Hang on,' he hissed, slamming the door in my face.

I stood there for two minutes before the door swung open again, and he held out the now familiar little twist of plastic torn off a supermarket carrier bag. I handed over £20 and took off.

I booked it back to HQ to find I had indeed been sold a stone – a stone from the bottom of the guy's bloody garden! The entire Drugs Squad roared with laughter, but I was furious. All those hours hanging around the dismal streets of Derby to get sold a stone? Bigga had made this personal now.

So, I hit the streets again, biding my time for another two days. Finally I spied Bigga's Mercedes parked on a corner. This time he was sitting on the passenger side, with Meshawn behind the wheel.

I kept my eyes to the ground as I approached and tapped cautiously on the window.

'What?' Bigga demanded.

'Mate, could you do me a ting?' I asked, once again assuming a humble, begging addict tone.

'Yeah whatever,' sneered Bigga contemptuously, 'give us the cash and wait over there.' He gestured towards an alley across the road.

I passed the money through the window and shuffled across the street to wait.

Three hours later he still hadn't shown up. By now, the drizzle had turned into a downpour, so when I finally gave up and trudged back to the base I was soaked through, freezing cold and very pissed off.

But, it was also a moment of realisation. This was a junkie's life. Addicts get ripped off all the time. They might beg and steal all day to scrape together their £20, only to be sold a stone or have a dealer disappear, leaving them to suffer through their rattle. Inhabiting this role meant more than throwing on a charity shop tracksuit. I needed to understand that every moment of every day meant a constant, desperate search for a score. This was a world of incessant, grinding need and uncertainty, and I had to adapt to its rhythms.

The Drugs Squad guys were completely understanding about my setbacks, but I could feel my hard-won reputation crumbling in front of me. I needed to fix this. It was time to get dramatic.

I lay in wait on Normanton Road, a quiet residential street where I knew cars would have to stay below 20mph. It was five hours before Bigga's Merc finally trundled into view through the sickly, ash-grey mist.

I waited till the absolute last second, then leapt out in front of the car, forcing it to a screeching halt. I immediately started banging on the bonnet, shouting, 'Oi, you never gave me my stone!'

Meshawn was out of the car like a shot. 'What the fuck you think you're doing bruv?' He shoved me hard in the chest.

I immediately dropped my voice, speaking very fast in a pleading, apologetic hush. 'Look – I'm not bothered, yeah – but you never gave me my ting the other day. But just serve me up now, yeah. Go on, just do me one now, yeah.'

I guess I must have got his attention. He took a furtive glance around, then reached in his pocket and held out the magical little plastic wrap.

This time, it was no stone. I carried the rock of crack triumphantly back to base and sent it down to the lab for testing. It came back over 60% pure, which was very impressive for Derby and indicated that these guys were connected to a significant supply chain.

The stunt worked. Now they definitely knew my face, and I was able to score off both Bigga and Meshawn several more times. Meshawn in particular was a nasty, aggressive character. He would hold the gear in his mouth and spit it on the ground, making me scrabble around in the dirt to pick it up.

Many dealers back then would 'mouth-carry', as we called it, so they could swallow the bag if they were stopped by police. Most stopped when they realised all they were doing was coating the wrap with their own DNA. But with Meshawn there was something extra vicious. He enjoyed the power trip of making me crawl.

Then things stepped up a gear.

Ten days later I was waiting on a corner to pick up a bag of crack, and one of heroin. Meshawn pulled up in his car and I jogged over to lean into the driver's side window.

'Drop the money. Drop it on the floor,' he hissed. Some dealers back then laboured under the misapprehension that if they weren't filmed physically taking the money, then somehow they couldn't be charged.

But in order to drop the cash where he was pointing I had to lean further in through the window.

That's when I saw it. Nestled in his lap was a large, chrome semi-automatic pistol. My breath caught sharply, but I kept my cool and dropped the money exactly where I was told. Meshawn gave me a pointed stare, handed over the gear and sped off without a word.

My mind was racing. Meshawn had obviously meant for me to see that gun. Was it a warning? Had I let something slip? Or was he just throwing his weight around, showing off like any other common street bully? Eventually I came to the conclusion that if Meshawn and Bigga had any suspicions that I was a cop, then I'd likely be dead already.

I made it back to HQ, wrote up my evidence in a hurry and presented it to the DC collecting evidence that day. His reaction taught me more in a few seconds about how policing really works than all my previous training combined.

'You sure you want to write it up just like this?'

'How do you mean?' I asked, genuinely not following.

'Well, you could write up that this guy had a gun, but if you do the higher-ups will probably pull the job. It'll be deemed too much of a risk. It's your call, I'm just thinking about all the work you've put in so far, and . . . '

He didn't have to finish the sentence. 'Understood.'

I grabbed the paper out of his hand and went back to my desk to rewrite my statement, leaving out the most serious piece of criminality I had seen on the job so far.

Sometimes fighting the good fight meant having to lie to your own commanders. I was learning.

When we took Bigga and Meshawn down, we took them down hard and fast.

This was to be my first buy-bust: we would take Bigga red-handed as he and I did the deal.

I waited on the corner for Bigga to roll up in his car. I handed over the money, he handed over the gear. Then, just as he was pulling away, three squad cars screeched out of nowhere, boxing him in. Simultaneously a foot squad sprinted up from round the corner.

In desperation, Bigga revved his engine and tried to ram one of the squad cars. He managed to dent its bumper, but ended up smashing up the entire front of his Merc.

At first Bigga seemed most upset about the damage to his motor. As they were snapping on the handcuffs, he kept moaning, 'Oh...my fucking car,' like a child who's broken his favourite toy. But then, as Johnno was guiding Bigga towards the back of the squad car, he suddenly jumped back and screamed, 'Oh God, no!'

The entire team snapped to attention, assuming some emergency, before Johnno continued, 'Oh Christ, he's only gone and shit himself!'

Apparently in the heat of the moment Bigga had let himself go. This was a guy who weighed in at around 250lbs, and lived almost exclusively on chicken shop junk food. By the time we arrived back at the nick, Johnno, who had had to ride in the back of the car with him, looked sick as a pig.

Bodily functions notwithstanding, Bigga ended up getting five years and Meshawn three and a half. Though of course, the most serious crime I had actually seen Meshawn commit – possession of a firearm – had never even been written up.

For me though, the real pay-off from the case came the evening after the bust. We were at the pub for a celebratory pint and Rob slapped me on the back. 'Great bloody work, Woodsy, great bloody work.' It wasn't the compliment that stuck with me though, it was the *Woodsy*.

Most of the guys on the Drugs Squad went by a nickname. Rick Johnson was Johnno; Andy Maclean was Mac; and Jim Horner was always *the Chief*. It was only from the moment I became Woodsy that I felt I had really earned my place on the team.

This feeling was made official when later that evening Jim Horner pulled me aside. 'Just so you know, you'll be getting a Divisional Commendation for this operation.'

My eyes lit up, 'Bloody hell! When do you think the ceremony will be?' In my mind I was already inviting Sam and my parents, letting them see that maybe joining the police hadn't been such a mad idealistic quest after all.

Jim gave me one of the raised-eyebrow looks that only he could pull off.

Of course – I was an undercover. There would be no ceremony. I'd get the handshake from Divisional Command, but it would be in a closed room with no camera flashes from the local press. I would never be able to tell a soul.

I may have earned a nickname – I may have even received a Divisional Commendation – but I would never really be accepted by the guys on the Drugs Squad until I had gone through my initiation.

It was an honour for any non-DS cop to get an invite to the notorious Drugs Squad Christmas party, and the guys told me to get to the bar early. This was meant to be a combined bash for the entire Chesterfield and Derby teams, with some detectives from other regional units down as well, but when I walked in all I could see was Bomb Damage.

His real name was Paul, but Bomb Damage seemed to fit. He was 6'4" and built like a tank with a beer belly. He was a hard-drinking, skirt-chasing local legend with a huge ginger beard and a booming Brian Blessed-type voice. He was originally from Doncaster and spoke exclusively in broad South Yorkshire slang. Beer was *larrup*, a woman was a *gert*, and to have a look was to *ay a gleg*.

Bomb Damage bought us a pint each, sank his in fifteen minutes, and burped, 'Your round, lad.' I got a couple more in. Fifteen minutes later Bomb Damage was back at the bar...and fifteen minutes after that his glass was empty again. 'Your round, isn't it?' he demanded.

I had been there for less than an hour and was already four pints in. It was only then I realised this was a stitch-up. When Bomb Damage went out, he drank a pint every fifteen minutes, four per hour, all night long. That's just how he was. I'd obviously been sent in early to see if I could hold my own.

'Fuck off Bomb Damage, I need to last past nine o'clock tonight.'

Bomb Damage roared with laughter, knowing he'd been rumbled. 'Well you can bloody buy me another one before you stop, lad.'

About an hour later the rest of the gang piled in. I got a slap on the back, 'Still standing then, Neil?'

'Yeah, I know what you're up to, you bastards.' The sniggers turned to guffaws and the night was on.

There were several women on the Drugs Squad, and many were excellent officers, but it was a lads' culture. These guys drank, and drank hard. They would pull thirteen-hour shifts all week, then get smashed on beer all weekend. The nights usually started at the police station itself. In those days most stations had a subsidised bar, so the pints were cheap. The irony of a bunch of detectives busting drug dealers all day, then getting pissed out of their heads on government subsidised booze, didn't sink in for me till years later.

That Christmas party was no different. The drink was flowing and the guys got raucous. One of the out-of-town detectives, obviously a hard-nut, got bevvied up enough to think it would be a good idea to take on Bomb Damage. Suddenly the whole room went quiet, as this guy bounced back and forth, throwing jabs at Bomb Damage's shoulder. I assumed it was all a joke... until I saw Rob begin to move away.

'They are just messing about, right?' I whispered to Johnno, who just shrugged. It was well-known that Bomb Damage liked a fight. There was an infamous story of him going up to Glasgow to give evidence at a trial, but ending up getting arrested himself for battering some Scottish hard-man. He'd used his phone call from the cells to ring Jim Horner to get him off the hook.

In the end though, Bomb Damage just reached out his enormous bear-like hand, put it right over this guy's face and pushed him down onto a chair. The whole place roared with laughter and the atmosphere relaxed again.

But later that night, when I was about fourteen pints in and we had inevitably ended up at the worst nightclub in town, I staggered up to Bomb Damage and clapped a hand on his shoulder. 'All right mate, how you holding up?'

'Fuck off,' he hissed out of the corner of his mouth.

'What?' I asked, taken aback.

'I'm eyeballing the bouncer. I'm gonna do the cunt. Fuck off.'

At that point Mac took me by the arm. 'Come on mate – when he says to fuck off, it's best to fuck off.'

We fucked off.

I don't know if Bomb Damage ended up fighting that bouncer, but I didn't see him for the rest of the night. What I do know is that this was considered completely normal behaviour. At the time, though, it was a serious eye-opener. I'd scraped up the wreckage from people being drunken idiots on the street; I hadn't expected a bunch of veteran detectives to be those idiots. But, once again, this was just my own naïveté coming up against reality.

And, as much as I may have been a little shocked, I laughed as loud as anyone. These guys were fun. I was a young man like any other, and it was actually pretty liberating to learn that just because you were fighting the good fight, it didn't mean you had to be a saint.

The tone of the whole outfit was set by the DI, Jim Horner, one of the last of the old-school rogues, but an amazing police officer with an encyclopaedic knowledge of drugs and criminal structures.

The guys on the Drugs Squad were wild, but they knew the job. Every one of them put their lives on the line, and they watched each other's backs in a way I truly admired. It was a great feeling to actually be winning some respect from this gang. The fact that for a skinny lad I could hold my booze certainly helped. If you want to run with the pack you have to become a dog.

And I was soon to get the chance for some police-sponsored hedonism of my own.

I was about to get paid to go clubbing.

*

'OK Woodsy, here's the job. We need you to infiltrate Progress.'

As strange as it may sound now, there was a period in the 1990s when Derby was considered the underground nightclub capital of northern England. And Progress was the night that put it there. Rated as the top dance club in Britain for two years running by *Mixmag*, every weekend Progress brought coachloads of people piling in from all over the country, and hosted every top DJ, from Pete Tong and Paul Oakenfold on down.

That meant pills. There were hundreds of thousands of pounds of ecstasy, speed and coke being traded in the clubs of Derby every night. There was no way the police could just stand by. But without a heavy-handed strategy of constant mass raids, it was impossible to gather usable evidence as to who was supplying the scene. So, someone had to get inside the clubs and make some buys.

This presented me with a real dilemma. I loved dance music. After my joyous, life-changing nights in Manchester, I had got heavily into all the jazz-driven, progressive drum and bass by people like LTJ Bukem, Adam F and Earl Grey. I would still occasionally drive up to see big acts like Orbital or Underworld at the Hacienda, and when Goldie released his *Timeless* album it blew my mind along with the rest of the country.

I didn't take ecstasy, though I couldn't pretend not to know that folk around me were wolfing it down. But somehow I couldn't think of these people as criminals. I'd chased down career gangsters and violent street thugs. The hippy guy from my local record shop, and the girls with the

Björk-style bobbles in their hair, flyering for the local clubs, just weren't it.

As much as the idea of getting paid to go clubbing did appeal to me, if it meant busting a load of kids holding a couple of pills on a night out, I wanted no part in it. Regular police could sweep up enough unlucky students on meaningless possession charges. There was no call for an intense undercover operation.

Jim understood my point and took pains to reassure me that this was a serious, targeted investigation, not just an easy option to bump up the department's statistics. He slid a photograph across his desk.

'Neil, this chap's name is Chaz – on the street he's known as "Shotgun". He's called that because two years ago some security firm crossed him... so he found the boss, stuck a shotgun in his face and pulled the trigger. He got off on a technicality in court. This guy has a network of bouncers and dealers working for him, but no one will testify. All we know is that he works mainly out of Progress. Either we nail him, or we'll have to shut the whole club down.'

I had a look over Shotgun's record sheet, an impressively grim litany of assault and weapons charges, none of which had been made to stick. This definitely wasn't one of my raver mates out for a dance on a Saturday night. Jim's words also put things in a new perspective. While the ravers themselves may have been idealistic party kids, the gangsters supplying the drugs were hard-nosed, ruthless criminals. If anything, it was the criminals who threatened the dance scene more than the cops.

There was no question about who ran the scene in those days. Regardless of the club owner's wishes, every major club had its own gang of dealers who had either taken over or paid off the security. Any rival caught dealing on their territory would be taken round the back for a beating or worse. The idealistic musicians, promoters and ravers never stood a chance – the sums of money involved were just too great. Even the Hacienda had been forced to close for a period in 1991 before reopening with massive new security restrictions. If this guy Shotgun was allowed to keep using Derby as his base, the same thing would happen not just to Progress, but to every decent club in the city. In the end, I agreed to infiltrate the dance scene in order to protect it from its own worst elements.

Everyone knew this deployment would be a bit different. There was no way we could get a camera in there, so I had to choose a partner to act as a verifying witness.

I picked a fellow cop called Jenny because not only was she sharp and professional, but she also knew quite a bit about dance music. I do also have to admit to thinking that when working a nightclub, it might be helpful to have a stunningly attractive woman onside. Even the roughest dealers can fall for a pretty face.

The only other condition I set was that we got to choose the nights we went in. Not even my idealistic notions about fighting the good fight were enough to get me to go to some awful handbag house night. So, Jenny and I started poring over club listings to check when the really good DJs were on.

We started with Danny Rampling, the founder of UK acid house himself. We booked our tickets courtesy of the Derbyshire Constabulary, and got ourselves ready for action.

Things didn't get off to a great start.

At Manchester raves everyone wore trainers. It was common sense – this was acid house, not lounge jazz. But this Derby club was apparently making some half-arsed attempt to 'smarten the place up a bit' and had instituted a shirts and shoes policy. We got turned away at the door for being too scruffy. I had to jog round the corner to where Jim Horner and two other cops were waiting as a support team, and swap shoes with Jim. The whole gang roared with laughter. Even then I knew I would spend the next ten years having the piss taken out of me over this.

On our second attempt we actually made it in. And it was fantastic. The music was thumping soulful house, and the lighting rig was shooting a crazy neon rainbow across the room. The place was almost full, and the crowd of around 800 were bouncing around like jackrabbits.

I surveyed the scene from the dance floor, and fairly quickly worked out who was selling. They didn't even make an effort to hide it. Shotgun himself was nowhere to be seen, but Jenny and I scored some pills off two of his runners with no fuss whatsoever. I did the exchange and palmed the baggie to Jenny, who immediately stuck it in her bra. This was totally unnecessary – you get searched on the way into a club, not on the way out – but she made sure to give the dealers a flirty bit of eye contact. It was a nice touch.

Then we went and had a dance to Danny Rampling. We eventually emerged from the club at 3 a.m., buzzing with excitement and covered in sweat.

'Where the hell have you two been? We've been waiting here for hours!' Jim Horner exploded.

'Well Chief, it would have looked pretty suspect if we had just bought some pills then immediately buggered off. We've got to stay realistic, haven't we?'

Jenny and I shared a smile over their shoulders. This had been our plan all along. There was no way we were going to a Danny Rampling night and not having a bit of fun. In fact, the only downside was that Jim wore a size nine shoe, and I was a ten and a half. After all that dancing in his boots, my feet were aching for days.

Our next time in, I spotted Shotgun in seconds. He was swaggering his way through the club as if he owned the place – which in a way he did. I motioned to Jenny and we followed him out to the club's chill-out room, which ironically also served as his office.

It was surprisingly easy to get in with him. I just shuffled over like any other buzzed-up raver, and asked if he could do us some pills and whizz. He snatched my money, and I was told to wait in a corner. I kept my eye on him, actually managing to make a note of exactly which henchman he went to pick the gear up from. He then strode over and handed me the baggie. Instinctively, I glanced down at it.

His right hand immediately shot out, seizing my throat and violently pulling my face to within millimetres of his own. 'Don't you fucking look at that in here...You fuckin' watch what you're doing.' His grip was like iron. I barely managed to nod my head as I frantically gasped for breath. He pushed me away roughly, spun on his heels and strode off.

My eye caught Jenny's as we walked back out to the dance floor. In that moment we both realised that this operation wasn't just an excuse to go out dancing; we were hunting a genuinely nasty character.

Over the next few months, I scored off Shotgun and his cronies several more times, and got to know just what a vicious little bully he was. I remember watching him giving orders to one of his runners. The guy obviously couldn't hear him amidst the noise of the club and kept leaning in. Without the slightest warning, Shotgun lashed out and split the guy's ear wide open. Two bouncers, obviously working for Shotgun, were on the scene in seconds to scoop the guy up and drag him out through the back. The more I observed the arrogance and violence of Shotgun's whole demeanour, the more positive I was that I had made absolutely the right choice in taking on this job.

But, as much as I was looking forward to busting him, the night we did our raid was actually a massive disappointment. Jenny and I knew the investigation was coming to an end and scoured the listings to get in one last good gig. When we saw the legendary techno DJ Tony De Vit on a flyer we decided there was no way we were missing that. I even briefed the team that absolutely no action was to be taken until at least halfway through de Vit's set.

We went in and I scored a bag of pills off Shotgun, as planned. Then Jenny and I raced to the dance floor for one last whirl.

Tony De Vit stepped up to the decks and the entire crowd let out a roar. Then the lights slammed on, and the music cut out in a screech of feedback. Forty cops in hi-vis jackets stormed through both the front and back doors. The bastards had come in too early!

They went through the club like terriers, immediately picking out Shotgun and the other high-priority targets, then making everyone else line up for searches. Of course, to maintain our cover, we also had to go through the process of being searched and arrested so we were shunted out into the covered smoking area and lined up with everyone else.

I watched Henry from the Drugs Squad walk up to a group of eight young guys next to us and shout, 'Oi you lot, hands in the air!' He then had to do a few other searches, and it was at least fifteen minutes till he made it back to them. Each was found to be holding a couple of pills. Henry was incredulous, and actually asked them, 'I've had my back turned for ages, why didn't you just throw the drugs on the floor and pretend they weren't yours?' One of the guys looked up at him, and with absolute naïve sincerity replied, 'Because you told us to keep our hands in the air.'

Henry laughed and shook his head in disbelief, but he was now obligated to arrest the whole crew and stuff them in the back of the van. None of this lot were dealers. They were just students on a night out, without even the street smarts to chuck their stash when a cop wasn't looking. Now all eight of them would have possession convictions on their permanent records.

But the real shame of it is that, though I had him red-handed, we didn't even put Shotgun away.

This was the first case in which I had to undertake a proper line-up identification parade. Shotgun's solicitors insisted that because he was unusually tall, all eight potential suspects had to be sat on ridiculous little wooden school chairs, wearing identical blue boiler suits and hats. It made no difference whatsoever. I picked Shotgun out in seconds.

Then Jenny went in. She emerged wearing the most sheepish expression I've ever seen. 'I don't know which one he is,' she muttered.

'What are you talking about? Shotgun was sitting right there—'

'No you don't understand,' she cut in, 'I've never seen him before with my glasses on. In the club he was just kind of a big blurry mess.'

I was stupefied. Jenny hadn't worn her glasses to the club, or even contact lenses. But there was nothing any of us could do. Failure to identify gave the CPS grounds to rule that a successful prosecution would not be likely, and they decided to drop all charges.

I knew that Shotgun was a truly dangerous character who needed to be taken off the streets. But he was able to go right back to dealing, only this time with a good deal of knowledge about how police undercover operations worked. Chances are he got even more vicious in response.

I ended up getting another Divisional Commendation for my role, but this was an infuriating end to the operation and no amount of backslapping from Command, or nights out clubbing on the police dime, could make up for it.

It also certainly wouldn't be the last time I'd see a painstakingly planned and executed deployment come to absolutely nothing.

I was starting to adapt to the pressure of not being able to tell a soul about my undercover escapades. And one thing I was very careful not to do was mention to Sam that my new deployment largely revolved around dancing in clubs with a gorgeous blonde.

To me, things still didn't seem right between us, but I tried to focus on the positives. Our little cottage had thick walls that allowed me to play music as loud as I liked, and Sam was doing well both in both her job and her degree. We often had friends over to open a few bottles of wine, and laugh into the wee hours.

As teenagers we had had naïve, romantic talks about one day getting married, but this time I asked her for real. A few months later, on 1 May 1993, we tied the knot at a lovely old church in Derbyshire.

So, newly married, we set about creating our family and finding a new house for us all to fill and grow into. It was an exciting time, but also a confusing one. I was wildly in love with Sam, but I could still feel a tension between us. Tempers would flare up, and it seemed like tiny incidents could spark days of trouble. When I was undercover, it was my instinct that kept me alive – I had to absolutely trust myself in every decision, move and thought. Yet in my personal life I found myself putting my intuition on mute. It's horrible to feel that you can't trust your own inner voice, particularly in your own home. But, once again, I tried to keep my head down and maintain my focus on the job at hand.

CHAPTER 5

CHESTERFIELD

Between undercover jobs I would be rotated back to 'regular' work as a uniformed police officer in Glossop – manning the response car, making arrests and wrestling with mountains of paperwork.

It created a very weird atmosphere around the station that I kept getting mysteriously called away, but was unable to tell anyone what I was doing. Other cops started looking at me strangely and I knew people were starting to whisper.

But it was the undercover operations that really excited me. It was obvious to me that this was where my talents lay.

It was also obvious to Jim Horner. He knew that when he sidled over and hopped up on the corner of my desk, I'd jump straight into whatever he had in mind, even if I had to do it on my rest days. Jim knew how to read people – it's something you learn from decades as a cop. He could tell that I had that impulse – almost a compulsion – that I could never walk away from a job, never let a challenge go unanswered.

This time when Jim sauntered up with his mischievous grin, it was for a different type of operation. It was an under-cover drugs sting like the others, but this time we weren't even chasing drug dealers.

For months Chesterfield had been plagued by a string of domestic burglaries. The cops there knew who the culprit was, but despite a massive surveillance-led investigation they just couldn't catch him. Most burglars work during the day when people are out, but this character, Billy Scheres, was burgling properties at night, with people asleep in their beds. It was only a matter of time before someone got hurt.

The Chesterfield guys had picked up intelligence that Billy was also heavily into amphetamine, and dealt a bit on the side to fund his own habit. If they couldn't catch him for the burglaries, maybe I could go in undercover and bust him as an amphetamine dealer? One way or another, this guy needed to be taken off the street.

Once again, I began the operation by just observing. I was getting good at staying anonymous; becoming just another one of those invisibles you pass on the street every day but never notice. Shabby tracksuit, baseball cap pulled low over the eyes – you forget us the second you pass by.

Billy's patterns were erratic, but there were people constantly in and out of his grotty low-rise council house. It was obvious he was running some kind of clandestine operation.

One of his customers in particular caught my eye. This guy would always stop on a park bench to drink a can of cider and smoke a cigarette before heading in to score. He was skinny like me, and seemed to combine the nervous twitchy disposition of the speed-head with an awkward sort of shyness. This was obviously no career criminal, just a loner who had partied too much, and got more into the powder than he ever intended.

I rocked up as he was glugging his way through his customary black tin of rotgut K Cider. 'Sorry mate, got a light?'

He instinctively reached in his pocket, and I took the opportunity to sit down next to him.

'Want one?' I offered him a fag from my pack of Benson & Hedges. He gave me a look of gratitude, as if offering a tab was the sublime peak of human generosity. I knew I had him.

We smoked and chatted, and I casually asked him where he was off to. 'Just goin' round my mate Billy's for a bit of whizz,' he replied innocently.

'Ah, mate – is that Brimington Billy from Ringwood Road? I've heard he does some wicked powder. I can only get shite where I am. Maybe I'll pop down with you and get some myself.'

He nodded absent-mindedly, suspecting nothing.

'Who the fuck is this?' Billy was immediately on the defensive.

'Ah mate,' I stammered. 'I just heard you did some really good powder, and I keep getting ripped off – I can only get shite.'

'He's all right Billy, he's a good bloke,' piped up my new friend from the park bench.

With that assurance Billy seemed to relax. We trooped through into his living room, and he quite happily chopped me out an eighth of speed then and there.

I made it back to HQ and we sent the gear down to the lab. It came back as 8.5% pure, which was right at the top end for the street-level retail market. But even an eighth – meaning 3.5 grams, or an eighth of an ounce – wasn't nearly enough to put Billy away for any real time. Had it been crack or heroin then perhaps those small deals would have been sufficient, but with amphetamine we would need to get Billy to trade in far larger quantities.

So, I came up with a plan.

The first thing I needed to do was win Billy's trust. I bought off him a few more times, hanging around his living room as he paced up and down, speeding his nut off and bragging about the various hustles he pulled. He was a hard house and techno freak, and seemed impressed that I knew a fair bit about dance music and had been to some big nights at Progress and the Hacienda.

I still had to bluff my way through most of the drugs talk. At this stage I just mimicked stuff I'd picked up on the club scene. I'd heard someone say they liked a 'candyflip' – a mix of ecstasy and LSD – so I'd say, 'Ah man, I did such a hardcore candyflip on the weekend, I was higher than the fucking sun, mate.'

I think Billy actually just liked having me around to smoke my cigarettes. I'd started smoking as an undercover prop – *Want a fag, mate?* is too good a conversation starter not to use. Gradually though, I'd become addicted, and was now only too happy to charge packs to the Drugs Squad account.

It very quickly became clear that Billy was an intensely unpleasant person, who would switch in an instant from hyperactively talkative to explosively threatening. Injecting amphetamine probably didn't help.

By now I'd seen plenty of people swallow pills and snort powders. But the first time you sit in a cramped room watching someone cook a shot on a spoon and slide the needle into their vein – the powder fizzing into that weird bubbly goo, the little red flower of blood sucked back into the syringe before being slammed home – it's a completely different order of intensity. Particularly when you're an undercover cop, and the guy has a tendency to wave combat knives around, screaming about how he hates the pigs.

One of Billy's habits was that as soon as he had shot his speed, he would load up a giant gravity bong, built from a bucket and a cut-in-half Evian bottle, and smoke a giant bowl of hash – 'just to take the edge off the powder'. It was one thing for me to turn down the offer of sharing his needle – that was generally accepted among druggies – but refusing to smoke a bong with him would have blown my cover straight away. In the drugs world, weed is the universal solvent. To skip my turn on the bong would have immediately exposed me as a narc, or at best marked me out as a weirdo and aroused suspicion.

So, I took my turn. And I got absurdly high.

Gravity bongs are heavy artillery. You get a huge load of water-chilled smoke straight to your lungs, and you feel it immediately. No one on the Drugs Squad ever actually asked why I was giggling maniacally while filling out my evidence book, but I think they could have hazarded a guess.

Eventually, I figured I had gained Billy's trust enough to start luring him into my plan. He had just smoked his bowl, and I figured he was in as open a mental space as he was ever going to be.

'Hey Billy…I've got this mate, yeah, who deals at travelling parties, y'know, the raves and all that. He's been let down by his usual guy. You reckon you could sort him out? He's after a fair bit – could be some decent cash in it.'

At the mention of cash, Billy immediately perked up.

'Oh aye, how much is he after then?'

'He says he needs two kilos.'

'Two fucking kilos?' Billy exclaimed, a little too excited.

'Yeah, see they take it to the parties and that's where they cut it up, y'know.'

If Billy did have any suspicions, they were outweighed by greed. For a small-time hustler like him, this could be quite a tidy little deal. 'Aye, I can do that. No bother, mate. I'll sort it for next week.'

So, I had Billy on the hook. Now all I needed was someone to join the operation and pose as my supposed drug dealer mate. The best the Drugs Squad could come up with was Bomb Damage.

At first I was horrified. Bomb Damage had been a Derbyshire cop for fifteen years, and was fairly hard to miss. There was every chance his face was already known on the underworld drugs scene.

When I raised this point, Bomb Damage just glanced at an intelligence photo of Billy and dismissively growled, 'Well, I don't know him lad, what're thou worried about?'

The rest of the team seemed to accept this, and scanning the room I realised that he probably was our only option. In this game you learn to work with what you've got.

I set the date with Billy, and drove Bomb Damage down to the car park where the arrest team had set up in advance. Billy approached the car and I slid out so he could hop into the front seat to do the deal. Through the open window I could still follow their conversation.

'Listen mate, sorry, I could only get one kilo today, but I can do the other one next week – no bother.' Billy was speaking in an absurdly fast, speed-addled garble.

Bomb Damage just smiled broadly, slapped him on the back and said, 'Don't worry yourself about it lad, we'll sort it out.'

Of course Bomb Damage didn't care about the missing kilo. He knew what was coming next.

Once again, two squad cars screeched up and a foot team pounced out of nowhere. Billy did a fair bit of screaming about how he'd *kill every fucking pig there*, but mercifully managed to control his bowels better than Bigga Williams had.

In the end, Billy got five years and the operation was deemed another significant success. But, while it was nice to get more backslaps and congratulatory pints from the team, this case actually presented me with some troubling questions.

When we sent that kilo of speed down to the lab, it came back as only 1% pure. Billy had obviously tried to run a scam. He'd taken his own usual stuff and cut it enough to make a kilo. He must have thought that trying to get two kilos out of it would be taking the piss, hence him only turning up with the one.

What that meant was that Billy wasn't a real amphetamine dealer. He was just a low-rent burglar trying to turn a quick buck. More importantly, it was me who had lured him into the idea of selling wholesale to Bomb Damage. Had I not set that deal up, he would never have tried to punch above his weight. Truth be told, this was entrapment. I acted as an agent provocateur, tricking Billy into a crime he didn't actually have the capability to commit. In the eyes of the law it made no difference that his gear was only 1% pure – he had sold a kilo. I expected his defence solicitor to tear that case to pieces in court. Billy wasn't that lucky, and was advised to just plead guilty. The case never even went to trial.

On the other hand, the burglaries stopped overnight. Billy was a genuinely dangerous guy, and by taking him down I had protected many others from harm. I told myself that I just had to accept that sometimes fighting this fight meant punching below the belt. I picked up another official commendation and put the operation down as a sharp lesson: to get the job done, I'd occasionally need to colour outside the lines.

However, if this deployment had made me question the ethics of my work, the next mission would call into doubt the very competence of the team I was working with.

CHAPTER 6

CLOWNE

Mike was a slippery fish.

The DS had been chasing him for years, but he had evaded countless arrests and beaten every charge they managed to throw at him. The previous year the squad had launched a major raid on Mike's operation, only to have him execute a well-orchestrated emergency escape, dumping his stash into a mixture of water and Epsom salts, and kicking the contents all over the floor. Despite the obvious drug paraphernalia everywhere, the CPS ruled the evidence contaminated and wouldn't take the case.

The DS lads took this personally. They regrouped and spent painstaking months gathering granite-hard, irrefutable evidence. Then, two days before the meticulously planned bust was set to go down, Mike was shot four times in an orchestrated gangland hit.

So, instead of arresting him, the Derbyshire Constabulary found themselves on twenty-four-hour guard duty as Mike lay in hospital, just in case the shooters decided to have another go. It was incredibly frustrating and a major drain on resources, not to mention all the boring night shifts guarding a hospital corridor.

The shooting made the news, leading to pressure from the regional higher-ups to solve the attempted murder and crack down on the criminal networks involved. A major intelligence operation ensued, linking the shooting to a mob war Mike's crew had been fighting with a Sheffield gangster known on the street as Hal.

Hal was another league of criminal altogether. This wasn't some thug slinging crack on a council estate. He was a high-level operator, plugged into international narcotic supply networks, who knew how to keep his hands clean and evade police surveillance. The Sheffield cops had nothing on him.

They did know one thing, though – Hal had family in Clowne, a small town neighbouring Sheffield, and he sometimes used these people as assistants and runners.

So, it fell to me to avenge a drug dealer's shooting. My mission was simply to go into Clowne and see if I could pick up any scraps of Intel that might form the basis of a proper investigation.

Clowne, like so many towns in the north, was an old coal village still reeling from the annihilation of the mining industry. And where coal had gone, alcohol and smack flooded in. An oppressive cloud of poverty and dereliction hung heavy in the air. I walked down street after street on which every business had long since been shuttered; the listless stupefied deadness ran deep. There were only three pubs left in town – and only one where even a low-level gangster would let himself be seen. So, I started hanging around, quietly nursing pints and letting myself get drawn into conversations.

For this operation I wasn't posing as a street-level junkie. We were hunting serious gangsters. For these guys to even talk to me, I had to play a mid-level hustler, someone who might offer an opportunity. So, I threw together a slightly smarter set of charity shop clothes, and a whole new persona.

It's easy enough to tell if someone is connected. I could scan the bar with a pint and a pack of B&H in front of me and decide in seconds who was worth watching. Getting a conversation started, however, was a different story. You can't just barge into town and start asking about drug deals. Above all else, these operations required patience.

But even I started getting a bit bored, so instead of just sitting there with my pint, I walked up to the pool table, laid my 50p next to the coins already there and hung back to watch the game. Both guys were pretty handy players, particularly a big lad in a white roll-neck jumper.

He won, so I stood up for my crack at the winner-stays-on rotation. I racked and roll-neck jumper broke. He could definitely play, but I had been hanging around snooker clubs since my teens, and had sharpened my skills on the table at the police station bar. One game turned into four, and he introduced himself as Terry. I let him win two games in a row before gently and unobtrusively asking what he did for a living.

'Oh, I work here and there with my cousins over in Sheffield,' he replied, just a little too quickly.

I said nothing, letting the silence hang.

'What about you?' he shot back, testing me.

'Me? Oh I do a bit of driving for some fellas around Stoke and Manchester and that.'

Now it was his turn to let the silence sit. He had given me a criminal's evasive answer, and I had given him another straight back. We stood across the pool table eyeing each other up. He broke eye contact first and bent down to take his shot. Some sort of understanding had been established.

For the next hour I could see the wheels spinning in his head as he tried to figure me out. I started dropping more subtle hints that my business might not be entirely legitimate, that I might just make my money doing drug runs up and down the country.

At the very hint of drug chat Terry seemed to come alive. We had each gone through a few pints by now and he was beginning to loosen up. He obviously liked to show off: 'Oh yeah, I can get pills, coke, whizz. Whatever you want mate. My lads in town got it all.'

'Actually mate, I could do with a bit of powder. I've got a long run to do – all the way up to bloody Glasgow – could do with a bit of rocket fuel, know what I mean?'

'Mate, I can do that for you right now, just come back to mine, I'll sort you out.'

We threw on our coats and trudged down to his place, where he promptly produced a massive bag of speed and weighed me out an eighth. Finally my patience was paying off. Even if Terry had nothing to do with the shooting, he was obviously a hustler and could be my lead into something else.

When I reported back to the Drugs Squad the whole team was intrigued. No one had any idea who Terry was, but I had obviously unearthed something interesting.

After the success of our last operation, Jim and the higher-ranking officers were keen to repeat the trick of using Bomb Damage to pose as another dealer. So, I put together a plan to manoeuvre Terry into leading us further up the food chain.

My way in was flattery.

The next time I saw Terry I immediately launched into a little rant about how wicked his gear was, and how even my mate in Glasgow had been impressed. Terry beamed like a schoolboy. He enjoyed playing the big man with the heavy connections.

I did a few more scores, each time giving him a little ego boost and making him feel like he was really doing me a favour by sorting me out. Then, when I thought he was well primed, I hit him with the proposal.

We were round at his place and he'd just chopped me out another bag of speed when I leaned in and lowered my voice.

'Actually mate, there was something else I wanted to talk to you about. I work with these bouncers down in Stoke, yeah. One of them has just been fucked about, and he needs to buy some coke. I'm talking some weight here, like half a bar or something...you reckon your guys in Sheffield could sort that out? There'd be some cash in it for you.'

At the mention of half a bar of cocaine, Terry's eyes widened a little. A nine bar is a nine-ounce block, one of the standard units in wholesale drug supply. A half-bar of charlie would come in at a few thousand pounds, quite a decent little score. It also meant another chance for him to show off. He nodded, and without a word picked up his phone and dialled.

'All right mate, it's Terry...yeah I'm all right...I've got this bloke here, says he needs a half a thing...yeah, I know him, he's all right...*yeah, I'm saying I know him*, it's fine.'

He held the phone out with a self-satisfied expression.

'Uh, hello,' I muttered into it.

'Who's this then?'

'I'm Danny,' I stammered, giving my cover name for the operation.

'All right Danny, I'm Hal. Terry says you want a bit of the great white shark.'

I was speaking to the primary suspect in our entire case.

My gut gave a lurch. This was now moving too fast. If this really was Hal, then preparations needed to be made – warrants filed, and a case put together. I had to buy my team some time.

'Yeah well, I know a guy who might take a weight. But I'll need a bit of your product to show him what's what. Let's say I take an eight-ball now, then we can talk things through.'

I was just improvising and playing for time, but actually this was exactly the right move. No real player would ever just go in for half a bar from an unknown source without at least testing the gear. Entirely by accident, I had just made Hal take me seriously.

He paused for a moment. 'Yeah all right. I'll meet you Sunday, one o'clock. Tell Terry to bring you to the usual place.'

'You'll never guess who I was just speaking to today,' I said breezily as I walked back into headquarters.

The entire team hit the roof. I had a potential line on a suspect who the entire regional force had been chasing for years. Everyone suddenly seemed full of advice, trying to tell me how to play it at the meeting. I ignored them all. Hal was an extremely dangerous man, but this was my investigation. By now I trusted my own instincts.

When the day rolled around I met up with Terry and he drove me out to *the usual place* – which turned out to be under the rugby goalposts of some isolated playing fields outside town. Hal was no fool. He knew he was under surveillance. If he was meeting someone new, then it was going to be in an open space with no high windows nearby to snap photos.

Terry and I waited, smoking cigarettes and shuffling around nervously, until Hal finally showed up. He was very quiet, ultra-polite and obviously didn't trust me.

He stood a few feet away and started asking questions. Who was I? Where was I from? What was this 'driving business' I supposedly ran? Who were 'my guys from Stoke'?

He never raised his voice or made a threat. He didn't need to. Sometimes he would throw the same question in a different way, laying little traps for me – a classic technique we used in police interviews. I mirrored him, staying absolutely calm and matching the intelligence of his questions with my answers. I had to make him believe this was one serious operator talking to another. There was no need for street-level macho posturing. Eventually I seemed to have passed the test, and we exchanged £150 of police money for an eighth of coke as a tester pack.

As I turned to leave, Hal grabbed my shoulder. 'Look, I sorted you out because Terry said you were all right. But your man from Stoke? I'll have to meet him and see the cash before I do any sort of deal.'

'Fair enough. We'll arrange a meet,' I replied. And it was fair enough. A half-bar deal meant several thousand pounds, and serious prison time if caught. It was only sensible that Hal would take precautions.

Back at the station the team were beside themselves. This was a guy who had evaded all their surveillance for years, and now I had his home phone number scribbled on a bit of paper. Undercover operations were so new in those days, they could achieve spectacular results where traditional methods failed.

I laid out my plan for the squad. 'We'll go with Bomb Damage again. If anyone can pass as a bouncer, he can...But look, Hal won't have any drugs on him for the first meeting. He needs to meet "my guy", see the money, and make sure everything is legit. So the first meeting we'll just observe. We'll make the bust next time, when the deal actually goes down.'

'Yeah all right,' Henry butted in, 'but we should have a contingency in place in case he does have the drugs on him.'

'Mate, he's not going to have anything at the first meet,' I repeated. 'He told me straight – he wants a meet before any product is exchanged. This isn't some street-level idiot. Forget about busting him the first time round.'

'Yeah, but we still should have a contingency *just in case* he does bring the drugs on the first meeting,' Henry replied as if I hadn't said anything at all.

There was a general muttering of assent around the room. I looked around in astonishment. Everyone seemed to be agreeing with Henry, even though I was the one who had actually met Hal and set the whole deal in motion. 'All right then,' I sighed in resignation, 'what's your contingency plan going to be then?'

Here Bomb Damage cut in. 'OK lads, if he's got the stuff on him, I'll stick my arm out the car window and rest it on the roof all casual, then give the roof a couple of taps.'

I wasn't worried. I knew nothing would happen until drugs actually exchanged hands, so I put in calls to Terry and Hal, and set everything up for a car park in town a few days later.

This time Hal wasn't worried about surveillance – he knew he wasn't going to be carrying any dope.

The day itself was very casual and relaxed. Terry turned up with his three-year-old niece as if it was a day out in the park, and asked me to look after her while Hal and Bomb Damage were introduced. So, I took this three-year-old girl for a little stroll around the car park while Bomb Damage squeezed himself into the passenger seat of Terry's car, carrying £4,000 of flash money the DS had signed off from a very nervous Regional Crime Squad DCI.

Then everything went to shit.

What nobody on the Drugs Squad had calculated was that Terry drove a tiny Ford Escort, and Bomb Damage was 6'4". Holding his arm out the window was his natural position. As soon as the conversation got going and he started to relax, of course his arm went out and rested on top of the car.

The first I knew about it was seeing Rob, Johnno and Henry sprint past me as I wheeled the little kid around in her buggy. I immediately spun round, just in time to see Terry burst out of the car and try and do a runner.

I just stood there as the DS surrounded the car, and hauled everyone out. Bomb Damage and I had to pretend to be arrested along with Terry and Hal, so as not to break our cover. We were all shoved into the back of the van and taken to separate cells. Bomb Damage and I were released later and ushered out the back of the station.

But, of course, there were no drugs in the car. Hal was never going to be carrying anything that day. So, he walked away scot-free – but knowing the police were actively after him again, and having learned about our tactics.

It was a total, unmitigated disaster.

The squad wrote it up so it didn't sound quite as bad, but we all knew the truth. It gnawed at me in particular. This screw-up had undone weeks of difficult and dangerous work. That a dangerous gangster could get away because of such a stupid mistake was completely infuriating.

Most maddening was that the operation had failed because the team had refused to listen to me. I was the guy on the ground. When I told them there would be no drugs in that car, they should have listened.

But the *I told you so* didn't need to be said. Everyone already knew. I just let it hang silent in the air, the crashing zeppelin in the room at our next few briefings.

Sam and I had moved from our little cottage into a newer house with more space, but considerably less charm. She was coming to the end of her degree and I wondered if the pressure was taking its toll. I began picking up signs in her body language, a tightness around the jaw, a shortness of breath and tension in the shoulders. It felt like she was snapping at me continually and there was nothing I could say or do to stop it. After only six months, it had got so bad that it felt like our marriage had hit a spiralling breakdown. This was more than just a married couple getting annoyed with each other – it felt like there was something else at work.

It was terrifying. I couldn't understand what was happening, and everything I tried just seemed to make things worse.

But before I could even think about finding a way through this, something even more momentous happened – Sam said the words that change everything for anyone who ever hears them: 'I think I'm pregnant.'

The next nine months were a whirl of hospital appointments and DIY to get the house ready for a child – interspersed with the odd undercover crack deal.

But when I first held our daughter, Tanith, it was an emotional rush like nothing I had ever felt. Just to have this perfect little thing cradled in my arms made me instantly rededicate myself not only to my relationship with Sam, but also to my work with the police. If I could make the world one tiny bit safer for my little daughter, if I could put away one bad guy who might hurt her, then any danger or sacrifice was worth it.

I would need to call on that resolve sooner than I could know. After a brief paternity leave, I was about to be sent on my most dangerous and complex mission yet.

CHAPTER 7
WHITWICK

I had to admit the intelligence was impressive.

The photos and files spread out in front of me painted a lurid picture of just about every species of criminality in the rainbow. Dealers, gangsters, pimps, thieves and street-level thugs – the Intel boys had done well. Even more importantly, they had discovered the golden thread that linked all these seemingly unconnected villains together. But this link wasn't a drug-supply chain, money-laundering ring or even a crooked lawyer. It was a pub.

The Lord Stanley was a pleasant, old-fashioned boozer just off the main road of the otherwise sleepy town of Whitwick, almost exactly halfway between Leicester and Derby. What made this pub unique was that it had been completely taken over by criminals. The Intel unit had set up an observation point, and apparently just about every single regular drinker there was connected to the underworld in one way or another. Villains were coming in from all over the Midlands. The Lord Stanley was where their deals were struck, and their schemes hatched.

The mastermind who ran the place, keeping the peace among all these volatile types, was a notorious gangster named Alec. This guy was involved in everything, from drug dealing and extortion to running gangs of antiques thieves that operated all over the country. My mission was to hang out at the pub, gain the trust of the crooks and gangsters and gather whatever evidence I could, while maintaining the focus on Alec as the primary target.

This wasn't a job I could do alone. The partner I chose was Phil Foster, who was originally from a tough neighbourhood in Sheffield and not only could pull off the accent, but had real grit and could handle himself under pressure. This was also not an operation we could busk our way through. We needed a solid backstory and we had to know it back to front.

So, we rehearsed. We drilled lines, practised scenarios and anticipated trick questions and ambushes. We'd grown up in Sheffield, and come up together through petty crime and burglary. Then Phil had moved down here with his missus, and I was stopping with them for a while, having had woman troubles of my own. We gave the story some Technicolor by digging into the department's archives and adopting some of the more eye-catching scams out of the case files. After long hours honing our patter over pints at the station bar, we could play off one another like any couple of low-rent street hustlers.

The Intel team hadn't been exaggerating – the place was intense. From the second we walked in, it was obvious every single person there was on some sort of shady business.

Phil and I sat down and sank two pints just to get our bearings. Alec was nowhere to be seen, but it would be impossible to approach a guy like that directly anyway. We would have to work our way up. I spotted one of his lieutenants from his Intel photo right away though. This guy's name was Deano, instantly recognisable because of the 'half-smile' scar running all the way from the corner of his mouth to his right ear.

Deano was standing at the pool table with a couple of other shady-looking guys.

We gave it another half an hour or so, just to have our faces seen; then I made my approach. Their conversation hushed warily as I strolled up.

'Sorry mate – you seen Pricey?'

'Have I seen who?' demanded Deano.

'Pricey,' I responded, 'big bloke, Irish traveller type, y'know. He told us to meet him in here, said people would know him.'

'Well, I don't know who the fuck you're on about mate and I know the people in this bar,' Deano shot back testily.

'All right mate, didn't mean to hassle. Just I'm meant to get something off him and thought you lot might know him.'

'Wait a minute,' cut in one of Deano's pals, 'Pricey, yeah...Irish gypsy, right? I know who you're on about. That bloke's not been round here for ages mate.'

There's no way that this guy knew Pricey. Pricey didn't exist. I'd just invented him to start a conversation. But some people will always want to make out they know everyone.

'Bollocks – fucking Irish prick's done me over.' I made out I was seriously annoyed.

'Why, what were you meant to get off this bloke anyway?'

'Ah nothing mate – just a bit of business, y'know.'

Deano stepped forward.

'Don't *nothing mate* me. If you're doing business in this pub, it's my fucking business.'

This was perfect. Criminals never volunteer information, but now Deano was dragging the story out of me I could reel him right in.

'Actually mate', I said, leaning in conspiratorially, 'I was meant to buy 500 pills to shift to some students I know up Derby way.'

'Well why didn't you just fucking say so.' Deano broke into a sly grin. 'But why are you buying pills off some gypsy cunt. I'll sort you out right now. 500 pills? I'll do that in two fucking minutes, mate.'

'You serious?' I acted taken aback.

'500 pills? No bother.' Deano smirked, clearly enjoying playing the big man.

'Well look…' I played it cool. 'Let's do ten now, and if my people like 'em then we can do a bit more in a few days, yeah?' I didn't want to come on too strong. Why not make him feel like he had to prove himself to me?

I sipped my pint as Deano disappeared, returning with a little baggie. I slid him thirty quid and Phil and I made our exit.

Even if we had wanted to bust Deano right there, he probably wouldn't have gone to jail.

We sent his pills down to the lab and it turned out they contained zero per cent MDMA, but were actually just a mixture of ephedrine and ketamine. At the time both of these were controlled substances, but not actually illegal.

As it happened though, this gave me the perfect way in.

'All right mate. Those pills you gave us weren't bad. I like 'em with a nice speedy edge.'

Of course I hadn't taken any of Deano's pills, but I did know they were exactly 68% ephedrine, so of course they'd be a bit speedy. I was marking myself out not just as a buyer, but as a connoisseur.

'Oh you like a bit of the old amphets, d'ya?' Deano gave a nod of acknowledgement.

'Mate, I love a decent bit of powder. But there's fuck all around here – it's all shite. I'll take 250 more of those pills if you can get 'em, though.'

'Yeah, 250's no bother mate. Give us two ticks.' Once again he disappeared to a room upstairs, returning a few minutes later with a big bag of his little blue tablets.

From there on in Phil and I became regulars at the Lord Stanley. We were probably the handiest pool players on the Derbyshire force, and were soon playing the Lord Stanley boys for twenty-pound pots, using pool table banter to work our way in.

Then, a few weeks in when we'd all had a few beers, Phil jokingly asked Deano how he'd got the scar on his face.

'Well,' Deano replied breezily, 'some bloke beat me at pool so I smashed the cue over his head. I just didn't realise he had a couple of mates there who took me out the back and done this.'

Phil and I shared a quick glance, and promptly let Deano win the next couple of games.

Intimations of horrific physical violence aside, though, Deano and his mates were actually quite a good laugh. They could all tell a story, and their rough humour wasn't actually a million miles from that of Bomb Damage and the Drugs Squad lads – it just happened to be told from the opposite perspective.

We kept buying pills and started moving into coke as well, picking up plenty of Intel as we went along. But we hadn't yet made any progress towards Alec. He was always around, holding court in his little corner, but there was no way we could approach him directly. We needed to bide our time and wait to be invited in.

Deano was pissed.

He and his mates were sat round a table heaving with empty glasses, all three sheets to the wind. We walked in in the middle of a story.

'...So this cunt that owes us two grand, yeah,' Deano slurred drunkenly, 'his thing is robbing phone boxes, yeah...but now everyone's starting to get mobiles, he can't make what he owes. Something may have to be done.'

The whole table roared with laughter.

'Ah yeah,' I cut in, 'I used to do a bit of the old phone boxes but the cunts figured out the security too well. It's not even worth the effort these days...but you know what is?' I leaned in and hushed my voice. 'Pay and display parking machines.'

'You what?' asked Deano incredulously.

'Seriously – you know those machines at pay and display car parks? They work the same as phone boxes did five years ago. The companies barely even send anyone to empty them – so if you get 'em at the right time, you can make a few hundred quid off each one.'

This scam came straight out of the Derbyshire CID case files. It was a real crime they'd busted someone for the previous year. I'd just appropriated it for our own cover story. Through his pissed haze, Deano gave an approving nod and took a thoughtful sip on his pint.

Three days later, while Phil was playing one of the other guys at pool Deano waved me over.

'Keith, this is Alec. Tell him again about that car park thing you were on about.'

There he was, staring me down through thick Elvis Costello-style glasses with an expression of total blank inscrutability. I launched into another description of the pay and display scam, raking my memory to get the facts right while also keeping the delivery casual and off-the-cuff.

I had studied the case like a true geek, and was able to fill in authenticating technical detail on how the car park machines worked. A cover story lives or dies on its detail. The more specific, the better the lie holds.

I finished up and Alec just looked at me. One second passed. Then several more. His face was completely unreadable. Alec let the silence sit for significantly longer than was comfortable. Then he leaned forward and quietly asked, 'Who did you say you were again?'

'Ah, he's all right Alec, he's bought about a thousand pills off me already,' cut in Deano.

Alec's head snapped round. Deano immediately fell silent under his gaze.

I defused the situation, mumbling about being from up Sheffield way and down here because of trouble with the missus. Alec nodded slowly and motioned me to sit down. Then the questions started. Who was I selling the pills to? In which prisons had I done time? What other scams was I involved in?

By now Phil had come over to join us, and we bounced off each other like an experienced double-act. As with Hal in Sheffield, I could sense Alec testing us, going back over the same question in a slightly different way each time to see if we changed our story.

Throughout the interrogation, Alec would frequently disappear to 'his office', returning a minute later rubbing his nose and getting a little more excited each time. This guy was obviously very into his coke.

We must have passed the test – or perhaps he was just getting very high – but two hours later Alan had not only tried to recruit us to run pay-and-display knock-over scams, he'd also offered to sell us two stolen antique tables, a vanload of wide-screen TVs and a MAC-10 automatic pistol.

Alec was hard to keep up with. He had a manic intensity, jumping from one subject to the next at lightning speed, but simultaneously keeping every tiny detail present in his mind. But it was drugs we were after.

'Actually mate, what we need is an ounce of charlie... and a little bit of rock if you can get it.'

'Oh that's no bother,' he replied, 'I can grab all that next time I'm up north. Say – you lads after a motor? I've got a BMW 3 series, a red Mitsubishi Shogun and a sweet little Mazda all going. I'll do you a deal 'n all.'

'Actually mate, I might be interested in the Shogun,' Phil chipped in, 'let's chat next time, yeah.' It would have looked odd if we were just after drugs and nothing else.

'Yeah, no bother. Just come back Thursday.'

We were in.

So, that Thursday, Phil and I found ourselves chain-smoking out in the Lord Stanley's car park, until Alec finally screeched up in a flash green Audi. He leapt out of the car and grabbed my arm, even more manic than before, talking a thousand miles a minute.

'Mate, mate, mate...sorry yeah, sorry...I smoked your rock on the way down. I've got your charlie yeah, and I had the rock, yeah...but I just smoked it. I smoked it, yeah. I'll get more, yeah but I smoked that bit.'

Through this torrent we managed to work out that Alec had gone off to pick up a big package, including our coke and crack, but had got so excited on the way back down that he'd smoked it all himself.

What can one say? The man liked his rock.

'Mate, mate – I'm going back on Saturday, so no bother – I can get your crack then. Tell you what though? You still interested in that Mitsubishi? I've got another two BMWs on the go and a fucking Jag too. Any motor you're after I can get it – no bother.' Alec was seriously wired. We held off on the cars, but set a plan to meet the following Saturday for the crack.

But, when Saturday rolled around, exactly the same thing happened. Alec jumped out of the car, high as a kite, manically apologising for smoking all the rock and trying to sell us more stolen cars. The guy just couldn't help himself: if there was crack in his car, he was smoking it.

This happened again and again. He would sell us pills, coke and smack by the ounce, but every time we wanted crack, he'd have smoked it by the time we met. It became a running joke for the other guys on the Drugs Squad.

Aside from his taste for crack, though, Alec was quite an extraordinary guy. He had an intense, manic charisma that was at once captivating and terrifying. It was easy to see why Alec had become the kingpin at the Lord Stanley. When he spoke, you listened. He dealt in stolen antiques, and had teams of break-in artists recruited from the Irish traveller clans working all over the country. Through this he had become a real expert, and would deliver long lectures on the precise craftsmanship of a Chippendale cabinet or Wedgwood vase. Being a bit of a history geek, I was able to win his favour and trust by filling in bits of knowledge on the Industrial Revolution around Yorkshire and the Midlands.

Over time we actually became quite good mates. We'd spend hours over pints at the Stanley, as I tried to keep up with his coke-fuelled boozing. I kept up my role as a mid-level hustler, adapting the more interesting scams from the police archives to my needs. One of the key character tics I continued developing from my first encounter with Deano was that I was a serious speed fan, and a connoisseur of all things amphetamine.

Alec was also obsessed with cars. Every time Phil or I hung out with him he would have a new set of vehicles on offer – a Mercedes here, a couple of Saabs or Toyotas there. It got to the point where one day, when I felt loose enough after a few pints, I turned and asked, 'Alec, how the fuck do you have all these motors coming through all the time? What've you got going on?'

The change was instant and shocking. His head snapped round with a hyper-aggressive glare, 'Why the fuck do you want to know what I'm up to? What the fuck is that to you?'

'All right, mate – I was only asking, like.' I immediately adopted a tone of total subservience and surrender.

A few days later though, he got high and told me his system without me even asking. That's the thing about cocaine – it doesn't half make people talkative.

Car manufacturers in that era had been making huge strides in automobile security. But, there were still cracks in the system. If you got hold of a car's petrol cap, and had some very serious technological savvy, you could produce an exact replica of the ignition key. So Alec had teams of guys out stealing petrol caps all over northern England.

He'd always leave it exactly three months between nicking the petrol cap and taking the car, so his system could never be traced. He even had a way to get hold of licence plates matching the make and model of each motor. That meant he either had a contact inside the DVLA, or his own high-end factory. Either would have been impressive. As he put it, 'These are my cars. They might be parked on someone else's drive for now, but they're my fucking cars.'

At any one time Alec was keeping track of up to 200 cars, all at various points in their three-month waiting period. Each week a new batch would become available. He never wrote anything down, just kept the numbers in his head with unfailingly exact detail. Alec was a genuinely brilliant mind, perhaps some sort of genius. I have no doubt that if he had gone into legit business he could have made millions.

But, for all his intelligence, Alec was also a brutal, vicious gangster. He kept order the same way as every other mobster: through violence, fear and intimidation.

He'd give one of his henchmen a nod, and some poor sod would be dragged out the back of the pub for a kicking. His conversation was shot through with references to having people 'done'. Alec may have had good scams going with the cars and antiques, but as ever, the most profitable business was drugs. And that business only ever works one way.

Every one of these beatings I witnessed was a direct reminder of what would happen if I let my character break for even a second, but all I could do was note every instance of violence, or mention of firearms, and log them as evidence.

But, at the Lord Stanley, it was all just accepted as how the game worked. Often the victims would be back in the pub a few weeks later, still bruised, but having paid off whatever debt was owed.

A few instances though, disturbed me profoundly.

One of the local geezers had brought down his young girl-friend and a gaggle of her mates. They all got a bit drunk and flirty, and one very pretty brunette sidled up to Alec, batted her eyes and asked for some pills. Her charms must have worked some kind of magic, as Alec sorted them all out right there.

One of her friends obviously reacted badly to the ephedrine in the pill, and went into a little panic attack, hyperventi-lating in the corner. The brunette completely lost it and rushed up to Alec shouting, 'You've killed her, you've fucking killed her. I'll get the fucking pigs down here!'

Alec turned icy cold. 'Oi Deano, make this cunt under-stand I'm not someone to be spoken to like that.'

Deano sprang into action, grabbing the girl's arm and dragging her through a door leading to the pub's back room.

This threw me into an instant crisis. I'd seen people dragged into that room before. But those were gangsters. There was obviously no way I could break character to help her, but my concept of 'fighting the good fight' didn't include letting teenage girls get beaten by thugs. I was frozen on the spot, not knowing what to do.

Thankfully the door swung open and Deano emerged, still with an iron grip on the girl's upper arm. She appeared unhurt, but her face was white as ash. Whatever Deano had said, the message had got through.

As much as I sighed with relief that she was all right, the cold ruthlessness with which Alec had delivered his order made my skin crawl. As charismatic and intelligent as this guy could be, I had to remember he was a genuinely dangerous criminal.

And soon Alec's sociopathic side was to impact me much more directly.

I was sitting in the Stanley with Phil, quietly nursing a pint, when Alec burst in, obviously high and very excited about something. He rushed straight over.

'I've got something for you, mate.' He sat and waved to the bartender for a drink. 'Here have a look at this—'

He was cut off as another figure bounded up from across the room. 'Alec, mate, Alec... I've got it, yeah – I've got the cash.'

It was Will Skipton, a low-rent hustler and Stanley regular who everyone called Skips. Alec's face twisted into an irate grimace at the interruption.

'See, it's all here – it's just a tenner short,' Skips babbled, holding out a handful of crumpled notes. 'I'll get that to you tomorrow – promise. Really mate, tomorrow.'

Alec broke into a broad smile. 'Mate, don't worry, tomorrow is absolutely fine. Not a bother,' he intoned with the exaggerated friendliness of an American politician.

Skips visibly deflated in relief. 'Ah Alec, you're the best mate. Tomorrow, yeah – promise.'

As Skips sat back down, Alec turned and made eye contact with Dom, another of his lieutenants. Alec gave the minutest flick of his head, and I watched as Dom stood up and walked over to where Skips was sitting with his back turned.

The first blow caught him on the side of the face, the meaty crunch echoing around the pub.

Skips went sprawling to the floor, and Dom went straight after him.

Smack. Smack. Smack. Dom drove his fist again and again into Skips' face, which exploded in a gush of blood. He didn't even scream, just made a sort of croaky gurgle through his caved-in jaw. It was one of the most disturbing sounds I've ever heard. Without a word, Dom grabbed the back of Skips' coat and dragged him out the door.

At which point Alec turned back to me, all smiles as if nothing had happened, and picked up right where he had left off. 'Yeah, as I was saying, I've got something for you.'

He reached into his inside pocket and pulled out a plastic baggie.

'You know how you were saying you like decent speed, but everything around here is shit...well I fucking guarantee you've never had anything like this before.'

He chucked the baggie on the table with the self-satisfaction of the parent who knows they've got their kid just the right Christmas present.

It was a toxic pink sludge that looked like it was actually starting to dissolve its way through the plastic wrapping. 'Oh...uhh...yeah, thanks Alec, cheers,' I stuttered, still trying to process the beating I had just witnessed.

'Nah mate – go on, do a bit.' Alec laughed, slapping me on the back. 'I wanna see your reaction. This is proper good stuff man, I got it just for you.'

What the fuck was I meant to do? I had built myself up as this big amphetamine connoisseur – it was an essential thread of my cover story. And here I was with a bag of what looked like Chernobyl waste in front of me, and a guy who had just had someone's face smashed in telling me to take a dab. I locked eyes with Phil. No help there. He was as lost as I was.

'Go on mate,' cried Alec, pushing the bag towards me.

There was nothing else for it. I picked up the bag, took a tiny bit of the pink goo on my finger and knocked it back with a slug of beer. The gag was instant. This stuff tasted like chemical warfare. It was all I could do not to throw up all over the table.

'No no no – take a fucking proper hit mate. Go on – it's on me.' Alec was really enjoying this. He was genuinely proud of his product and wanted to see me enjoy it.

I could already feel my heart starting to race. But what could I do? I'd just watched Alec have someone beaten over a ten-pound debt. There was no option. I took a massive lump of the stuff, and slammed it down.

The effect was instant. An awful chemical heat rising up from my kidneys; an unbearable dryness of the eyeballs; my heart starting to pound in my ears like a pneumatic drill. I couldn't seem to fill my lungs with air and I felt a band of sweat beading around my forehead.

Alec burst into laughter as my face turned red. 'Yeah, you love a bit of it, don't you mate! Tell you what, give us £20 and you can have the rest of the bag.'

I tried to reply, but my mouth didn't open. On sheer instinct I ripped a note from my pocket and gasped, 'Yeah, thanks mate – top geezer.' And with that Alec just walked off, giggling to himself.

Phil got me the hell out of there as fast as he could without drawing too much attention, and slung me in the back of the car. By now the initial white-light-white-heat rush had settled into a steady, soaring amphetamine high. Everything was too clear, too bright, too real. My hands beat a twitchy, compulsive rhythm on the dashboard.

We got to the station and Phil wrote up our evidence as fast as possible – leaving out the fact that I had boshed a load of amphetamine. Then he put me back in the car and took me home.

Sam and the baby were asleep. I went straight to the fridge and found eight cans of Stella Artois. Thank God. I necked them all down in under two hours, just hoping for something, anything, to take the edge off.

Nothing worked.

I didn't sleep for three days. That was the Friday night. I had the weekend off and was due back in uniform on the Monday morning. By 4 a.m. on Sunday I had to admit I couldn't face it, and left a message for my uniformed shift Sergeant that I was going off sick.

That weekend was a stage-managed hell. I couldn't let on to Sam what was happening, so I just kept things as under control as possible and stayed out of her way. But I felt unutterably vile. I've tried a few drugs in my time but speed is just not for me. That chemical rush feels like being dragged out to sea by an undertow.

On the upside, though, our house had never been cleaner, and I was able to let Sam sleep through a few nights without having to get up to feed Tanith.

When I next checked in with the Drugs Squad, Phil pulled me aside. The chemical analysis on Alec's speed had come back 40% pure. The best street-level stuff in Britain is usually around 5–7%. With zero tolerance, no wonder that pink ooze had sent me arse over tit.

Thankfully though, Alec never had the opportunity to put me in that position again. The Lord Stanley bust was about to go down.

Our plans were made, our positions set, our teams in place.

This bust was always going to be messy. With the regulars at the Lord Stanley being who they were, we knew we were going to be dealing with a chaotic scene and multiple arrests. But Alec was always the primary target.

The plan was that Phil and I would go in and take our usual places at the bar. The team would have spotters outside the pub – the second they saw Alec enter, they would give the signal and our armed response teams could rush in.

It all started so well.

Phil and I sat at our usual table, keeping our eyes on the door. I scoped Alec as he walked in. The spotters must have seen him too, and given their signal.

The door flew open and thirty hard-as-nails Leicestershire task force cops, in full body armour, burst in. It was pandemonium. Pretty much everyone in there was either carrying gear or on an outstanding warrant. The main drug stash in the back room was thrown open, and many arrests made.

But there was no Alec. The team tore the place apart, but he simply wasn't there.

We knew he had entered the pub. I saw him come through the door with my own eyes. He must have walked in, triggering our signal, then immediately slipped right out the back.

Something felt very wrong about this. After months of dangerous work, I was fuming – our main suspect had just slipped away. It didn't make any sense.

When I burst into his office later that evening, Jim Horner looked completely defeated, smoking a cigarette and staring into space.

'What the fuck happened today?'

'Well, he went in one door and out the other,' Jim replied in a stoic leaden monotone.

'What are you on about? How could this fucking happen?'

'Well, there's two options, aren't there?' Jim looked me in the eye. 'Either someone was working for him, or he was working for someone else.'

'Jim, what are you bloody talking about?'

'He got tipped off, Neil – it's fucking obvious. He knew he had to be seen entering the pub, and he knew he had to get the fuck out again.'

My eyes widened in horror as Jim continued.

'Our operations are secret, right? So, either he's got someone in this department – but I doubt that, or you'd would have been dead months ago – or he's working for another agency.'

This stopped me in my tracks. 'Another agency? Christ, you mean Alec is a...'

'Yes Neil – he's a fucking informant. Could be Regional Crime Squad, could be National, could be fucking MI5. I don't know … and we'll never know.'

I walked out of Jim's office completely stunned. Could it be? It seemed completely impossible, totally absurd. But as I sank into a chair at the police bar and turned it all over in my mind, the more it seemed like the only explanation.

Even most of our own squad didn't know about my operations. We kept information tightly controlled to protect against leaks. Guys like Bomb Damage were brought in only as the deployment moved into the arrest phase.

But other agencies were also running their own covert ops. When we had set up the bust, our tight ring of secrecy had been broken – and someone, somewhere, had moved to protect their own intelligence asset. But, if violent, borderline-sociopath gangsters like Alec were now our allies, what did that mean for my sense of purpose, for fighting the good fight?

Perhaps for the first time I began to gain an understanding that I wasn't involved in some simple battle of good versus evil. This was a labyrinthine complex of worlds upon worlds. There were forces at work that I could not comprehend, and decisions being made over which I had no control. Actions had consequences, outcomes and reverberations that no one could foresee, let alone claim to have intended.

I needed to set aside what I thought I understood, and make myself willing to begin learning everything anew.

The first thing I needed to learn about was drugs themselves.

I could still taste the toxic alkaline horror of that 40% amphetamine – I could still feel the panic shooting up my torso. I had put myself in that situation out of sheer ignorance. I was hunting down drug dealers, yet I knew next to nothing about the commodities on which their empires were built. Most worrying of all, even in my ignorance, I probably already knew considerably more than most of my colleagues on the force.

Obviously I wasn't about to start smoking crack or slamming needles into my arm. But what I could do was dive into the police archives and hit the library.

Once again, the geeky side of my character came out, and I was soon spending hours poring over everything from university pharmacology textbooks to William Burroughs novels. It wasn't long before I became a walking narcotics encyclopaedia, and other cops started coming to fact-check with me about their own casework.

Over the course of my research I noticed an ad somewhere that Narcotics Anonymous were doing their first European-wide conference in Manchester. I decided to take one of my rest days to go along and see what knowledge I could pick up.

It blew my mind.

I heard story after story of struggle, hope, relapse and redemption. These were no woolly, self-pitying, New Age confessionals – they were hard-headed, ultra-realist analyses of the processes and cycles of addiction.

There were people from all walks of life, from coddled privilege to the most desperate grinding poverty. But they all had this one thing in common – they were locked in a life and death struggle against the disease of addiction.

As I was scanning the programme I noticed a keynote seminar on 'Addiction and Criminal Justice'. Obviously, I made a point of sitting in.

The thrust of the argument was that addicts would be better off being released to recovery programmes rather than sent to prison, where their addictions tended to get worse and their life chances narrowed yet further.

The second they opened the floor for questions I raised my hand. I was a cop; I wrestled with these issues every day, and was sure I could see the fundamental flaw in their argument.

'Don't you think it's a bit pointless sending people to recovery when they aren't ready? Don't they have to make the first move? If someone doesn't want to address their own addiction, can they really be forced into it?'

I suppose I had expected people to be impressed with my hard-hitting insight. I was caught off guard as a deathly silence fell over the room. People looked around at me with thinly disguised contempt, as if to say *who let this this ignorant schmuck in the room?*

The chair of the panel gave a patient sigh and turned to his fellow speakers. 'Is there anyone on this panel – in fact, is there anyone in this room – who first came here out of choice? Is there anyone here who was not dragged in kicking and screaming? This isn't a simple question of *making a decision to quit drugs.* That has to be earned over time through serious work and self-questioning... ultimately we each only save our own lives, but that's no reason not to throw a drowning man a rope.'

I collapsed back in my chair. In that one moment I recognised that I needed to fundamentally reassess everything I knew, or thought I knew, about what addiction meant.

I realised that deep down I still had that Ronald Reagan news clip I had seen as a child playing in my head. Like most of my police colleagues, I thought addiction was fundamentally just a question of willpower. People simply needed to make a decision to stop – and if they couldn't then it was down to their own moral failings. This was the standard police mentality. It was certainly the prevailing attitude on the Drugs Squad.

What I now understood was that I didn't know what the fuck I was talking about. And neither did my fellow cops. I didn't have any answers. But I emerged from that conference at least knowing that I hadn't even been asking the right questions.

Even my previous revelation after the speed incident with Alec had been misguided. I thought my job meant I needed to learn about drugs, but what I really needed to learn about was people.

Law enforcement agencies could follow drug-supply lines from the mountains of Colombia and poppy fields of Afghanistan to the council estates of British cities, but to what end? If you don't understand people – how they operate, what they need, why they do what they do – how can you hope to protect them, or even investigate them?

Don't get me wrong – I hadn't suddenly turned into a utopian pacifist hippy. I had enough experience of gangsters and thugs to know that fighting the good fight meant getting some bloody knuckles. I was prepared for that. I just realised now that the assumptions I had been working under were totally skewed.

Fighting tough meant fighting smart. I needed to start asking better questions.

Looking after a newborn baby is never easy. Sam and I were as strung out as all new parents have been since the dawn of time. But with tiredness came the shouting. Once again, it felt like I was under attack – throughout the day and night – it was utterly, excruciatingly exhausting. Even if Sam and Tanith were asleep, after each episode I would find myself unable to shut off – lying in bed, twitching and turning for hours, my eyes screwed shut, but my heart racing. It got to the point where I was almost convinced that Sam was keeping me awake purposefully. I'd lie there, doing my best to ignore her, trying not to respond – but then the alarm would blast, and once again it was time for work.

The constant exhaustion got to the point of physical pain. Maybe this helped with my pose as a smack addict on the streets, but as a uniformed officer you need to be ultra-alert. The safety of fellow officers and the public relies on you having your wits about you.

But, in those moments that things were good, I still loved being around Sam. We were childhood sweethearts and that kind of bond doesn't break easily. It was in one of our moments of reconciliation that our second child was conceived.

And once again, the moment I held our son Gareth in my arms I felt a surge of love and pride that obliterated every negative emotion I had ever known. Whatever issues Sam and I might have, I swore to myself I would give my children the best life I could, and do everything to hold our family together.

Somehow we would piece our relationship back together. We had to try to make this family work.

CHAPTER 8

STOKE

I have to warn you Neil, this bloke sounds like a stone-cold psychopath.'

The call had come in from Staffordshire police. They were tracking a heroin dealer named Kyle who had seized control of the smack trade in Fenton, one of the six towns that make up the city of Stoke-on-Trent.

Kyle had established himself by repeatedly stabbing anyone who failed on a payment or got in his way. He was leaving a bloody trail in his wake, but the Staffordshire force couldn't seem to catch him. So now here I was receiving my briefing from Jim Horner and Ronny Braddock, the Staffordshire Detective Sergeant who would act as my handler for the case.

Of all the places I worked as a cop, Fenton was probably the most run-down, hopeless and desolate. Row after row of terraced houses stared out at you like empty skulls. About half were already abandoned and boarded up, the rest may as well have been. This place had never recovered from the collapse of manufacturing, and seemed like it never would. There was simply nothing there – no activity, no hope, no life. It was a ghost town, and the only thing that kept the ghosts from rattling their chains was heroin.

I had no direct way in with Kyle. He was by far the biggest dealer in Fenton, and operated between three different addresses to store and cut his product. A guy like that would never sell to someone he hadn't met. Once again, I needed to find an introduction.

That meant making connections among the town's junkies and addicts. I had to become one of the ghosts.

I put together my roughest charity shop outfit yet, and spent hours pacing the dead streets to get my face seen. Eventually I started approaching down-and-out smackheads, posing as a fellow addict and offering to kick in a few quid for their own wrap if they knew where we could score. These people were desperate. For them a couple of pounds meant the difference between their next fix or their next rattle. Of course they agreed to help.

I did one score after another in filthy abandoned houses – most with the electricity shut off and the copper piping ripped out of the walls to pay for skag.

The people were as broken as the homes they squatted. Each had their own story of poverty, domestic violence, sexual abuse, parental abandonment, and beatings at the hands of dealers or pimps.

No one can encounter that sort of misery day after day without taking some of it on oneself. After that NA meeting in Manchester I had vowed to make people the focus of my investigations. Only now did I begin to realise just what kind of commitment that entailed.

And yet I was no closer to Kyle. The junkies I was dealing with scored from other addicts or small-time local dealers. I would occasionally hear the odd terrified whisper about 'the boss', but nothing that would ever give me an entry to ask who that was.

These people lived in fear. Any mention of the boss and they immediately fell quiet, their eyes locked on the floor. There was an obvious code of silence in place. The weeks slipped by. I did deal after small-time deal, and heard countless stories of misery and horror, but Kyle was still out there beating and stabbing the people of Fenton into submission.

What first marked Stan out was that he tooled around in an ancient, beaten-up Ford Cortina. A career junkie who actually manages to keep hold of his car is pretty unique. He was a long-term addict with filthy clothes and missing teeth, but somehow he managed to hold his life a little more together than the other skagheads. I figured that if a connection to Kyle was going to come from anywhere, this was it.

But obviously I couldn't just ask him. I had to engineer it so he would lead me in without even knowing what was happening.

'Mate, mate, you won't believe what happened.' I pounded on the door of Stan's freezing bedsit. 'This woman left her bag on the bus, right in front of me. I got sixty fucking quid mate.'

Stan's eyes widened. In the street junkie netherworld, a 'left handbag' is like striking Texas oil. I knew I had his attention and leaned in close. 'Listen, I was thinking... since I've got this cash, maybe we could buy a proper bit of gear, a weight y'know – maybe like a-half T or something. You know anyone that could sort that out? I'll give you a shot off my bag.'

Stan's eyes narrowed. 'Give us a tenner too, and I'll do it.'

Of course. A free shot was fine, but I had told Stan I had £60, and he'd calculated exactly how much he could get out of me. In the drugs world there is always a better deal to be had, always a better scam to be pulled.

Of course what he didn't know was that unlike every other junkie in town, I didn't care about the money. The calculation in my head was that the only dealer in Fenton slinging half-T's was Kyle.

To explain – in those days heroin was usually sold at £10 for a 0.2-gram bag. If you were really flush you could buy a teenth or T – which was 1.75 grams – for around £60. Between that, there was the half-T of 0.8 grams, which would generally go for about £30.

Obviously, from the addict's point of view it's better to spend £30 and get 0.8 grams, rather than buying four separate £10 bags. But, most smackheads usually can't put £30 together for a single score. A half-T is for special occasions like a stolen handbag or successful house burglary.

If that all sounds a bit confusing, imagine trying to figure it out on the street, knowing the smallest mistake will expose you as an undercover cop and put you in either the hospital or the morgue.

We drove over in Stan's Cortina. The door swung open and I instantly recognised Kyle from the surveillance photos. He was the archetypal northern scally: tough and wiry, wearing a Kappa tracksuit and Nike trainers, hair cropped short and an expression of pure malevolent aggression.

'Who the fuck's this?' he demanded, glowering at me.

'It's Jimmy, he's a mate,' Stan replied for me.

Kyle sullenly stood aside and we filed past. His living room was a dusty mess, strewn with empty cans and drug paraphernalia, much like every other flat in town I'd seen. The only difference was that Kyle still had hot water and a TV. In Fenton, that was the line between user and dealer.

I handed over £30 in marked bills. The Staffordshire cops marked their notes by colouring in the Queen's left eye with a biro, joking that it made her look like someone had given her a smack. Once again, just a few years later a technique this shockingly obvious would get you killed. But Kyle just stuffed them in his tracksuit pocket and handed over the gear.

I left it five days. Long enough that Kyle could assume I had finished my half-T, but recent enough that he'd still remember my face.

It was a miserable grey afternoon as I trudged up to his door through the Staffordshire rain. I knocked, and waited as it creaked open.

'Uh mate...Hi...I was wondering if I could get another half-T off you.'

The door flew open and Kyle sprang forward, pinning me against the wall. There was a flash of silver and I felt cold metal on my skin. He was holding a sword to my throat.

'You're fucking DS, you cunt. You're fucking Drugs Squad. I know what the fuck you are,' he hissed into my face.

I froze.

Keeping my head absolutely still, I flicked my eyes from the blade to Kyle's face, then to his hallway, where I could just make out his girlfriend standing and watching.

'Uh...no mate...' was all I could manage. I tried to project total humility, subservience and abasement.

Kyle leaned even closer, locking eyes with me. I could feel his breath on my face. For one moment the entire universe shrank to the razor edge of the curved samurai-style blade.

Then I felt the metal come away from my neck.

He turned and walked down the hall. As he passed, the girlfriend piped up, 'Christ – I thought he was gonna say he was fuckin' DS for a minute there.' They both gave abrasive laughs, very much at my expense. I kept my head down and followed Kyle into the living room.

'So, what you want?' asked Kyle, now more bored than aggressive.

'Well mate, I was wondering if I could get another half-T, like the other week?'

'I haven't got anywhere near that weight – what the fuck are you playing at?' All the threat and malice flooded back into his tone. My heart jumped and I instinctively glanced towards at the sword, now lying propped in a corner.

Then he continued. 'I can do you four bags, but I don't have a half-T chopped out.'

Now it made sense. He just wanted to sell me four bags for £40, rather than a half-T for £30. Same amount of gear – more money for him.

I handed over the cash, grabbed the four little foil twists, and left the house thankful that I'd never have to go back there again.

A few feet away from Kyle's gate I paused to stash the wraps in my cigarette pack. Then I felt something pressing into my chest. I looked down. There was a large hunting knife hovering at my solar plexus.

'Gie'us the gear,' demanded a strong Stoke accent. 'Gie'us it fucking now.'

I was being robbed.

This is a standard of the drugs game – one junkie watches another leave a dealer's house, then mugs him for his score on the way out.

But I wasn't having this. Not after the afternoon I'd had. This smack was my evidence. If I lost it, it meant having to score off Kyle again and go another round with his samurai sword. I just wasn't doing it.

'Fucking gie'us the gear now!' shouted the robber.

I backed away slowly. The guy looked at me in confusion – he hadn't expected this.

'Fucking gie'us the gear,' he tried again. I kept backing up, keeping my eye fixed on the serrated blade.

Then, with three feet between us, I ran.

He may have had the knife, but if there's one thing I was fairly sure of it was that I could outrun a heroin addict. He tried to keep up for about half a block, but I wasn't taking any chances. I sprinted off and didn't stop till he was a dot on the horizon.

Of course, when I got back to HQ, the response was, 'Hmmm, yeah probably shouldn't write it up like that, yeah.' They didn't have to say it. By now I knew how things worked.

Kyle liked to flash that sword around, though. On the day of the bust, our observation team spotted him carrying the weapon as he moved between his safe houses.

So, we had to have an emergency tactical briefing to decide whether a fully armed response team was necessary. My opinion was that whenever possible we should avoid bringing guns onto the street, and in the end it was decided that fifteen hard Staffordshire cops could get the job done – sword or no sword.

That afternoon I did one more buy with marked money, then the team went banging in. Along with his blade, Kyle was holding three ounces of heroin. He got five and a half years.

After my disappointment with the outcome of the Whitwick case, this success did something to reaffirm my faith in the system. Kyle needed to be taken off the streets, and we had all worked hard to get the job done well.

I got another commendation, but for years afterwards there were moments when I could still feel the edge of that sword pressing against my throat. It could be a stressful moment at work, or arguing with Sam in our own kitchen, but suddenly there it would be, a phantom blade just at the base of my neck.

The next time Jim Horner sauntered over to my desk, it was regarding a very different kind of deployment.

'All right Woodsy, you've been doing so well that the bosses are starting a nationwide training course. Fancy coming along to help teach it?'

I was a bit taken aback. I knew I had got some decent results, and I was aware that other undercover operations were beginning to be deployed around the country, but I had no special training. I had always just gone on instinct. I had no idea how I would even start teaching this to other recruits.

'Come on Woodsy, it'll be a laugh. Some Level 1's will be there. It'll be good for you to get to know the big fish.' Jim slapped me on the back, taking my agreement as a given.

Undercover work in British policing is divided into two sections: Level 1 and Level 2. The Level 1 operatives are the guys you see in films. They perform deep infiltration on ultra high-level criminal organisations. They receive massive logistical support, with forged documents at the ready to corroborate their cover identities, and the most state-of-the-art espionage equipment available. These guys will spend months working in an area, just so their faces have been seen and their backstory carries more weight.

Then there are the Level 2 guys. Guys who are dropped on a corner and told to go and buy some crack. Guys like me.

Level 1 work had been well established for decades, with a centralised training programme in London. Level 2-style work was only just emerging as a practice, based on operations by myself and a few others around the country.

Now that we had done well as their guinea pigs, the bosses were rolling out Level 2 training on a regional basis across Britain. So, Jim and I signed out a squad car and drove to a massive police station in Wakefield to spend a few weeks imparting what knowledge we could.

It was incredible. The Level 1 guys brought a depth of knowledge and experience that I had never encountered before. They were experts in conducting strategic, intelligence-led operations, targeting only the most senior criminals. Each one had astonishing stories of bringing down major international crime gangs.

I spent as much time learning as I did teaching. They ran intensive courses on the legal issues of undercover work, picking apart the exact limits of what constituted admissible evidence and ethical action.

But, the Level 1s had spent so much time among the high-end dons and godfathers that they actually didn't know much about the dirty streetcraft of chasing crackheads and amphetamine-addled council estate thugs. That's where I came in.

'Yeah, but how do you, y'know...actually cook a heroin shot?'

I found myself grabbing a sample from the confiscated drugs locker, a needle from the infirmary and a spoon from the canteen, then demonstrating to a rapt audience how to mix the powder with citric acid on the spoon, cook it to a sizzling goo, then suck it through a cigarette filter into the needle.

'Yeah, but what if you're there, and you actually need to shoot it up?' one of the recruits challenged.

'Well look – going undercover is about improvising...find somewhere soft, like a couch or a car seat, then pull down your pants like you're shooting into the femoral vein in your groin. You'll probably be able to block their view long enough to shoot it straight into the cushion you're sitting on.'

Without even realising it, I seemed to have picked up a wealth of knowledge and streetcraft. I ended up giving long seminars, to both wide-eyed recruits and super-experienced Level 1s, in the complex codes and etiquettes of junkies and street dealers.

Occasionally I'd glance up and catch Jim Horner watching me with a proud, almost paternal eye. I had to give him credit. He had recognised how far I'd come, even when I hadn't.

The Level 1s and I worked together to develop a programme to test our recruits' observation skills and ability to stay cool under pressure.

We'd send some newbie to confront a more experienced officer, with no instructions other than to 'try and make a deal'. They'd get halfway through their first sentence, then the 'target' would start shouting and getting in their face. The newbie might be able to handle the screaming, but when they emerged from the room we'd ask them how many packs of cigarettes had been sitting on the desk.

You'd be amazed what people can miss. The ability to keep your eyes open under pressure takes real mental discipline. It got to the point where we would leave a decommissioned pistol on a table, and some students would come back reporting their target was unarmed.

We also tested our recruits' 'bullshitting skills'. How good were they at developing and maintaining a cover story? Could they improvise and adapt in the heat of the moment?

It's harder than you think. Everyone rushes it. It's amazing how many people walk in and immediately go, 'Hi, I'm Jim from Birmingham, I deal the odd bit of smack here and there.'

This is exactly wrong. Real criminals keep their mouths shut. The rule is to only give information when it is extracted from you. The best cover story is the one you never use. Any of our students who couldn't check their human urge to give away their story failed the course very quickly.

It was an uncanny feeling watching these students systematically learn all this stuff that I had just made up as I went along. But it was fascinating to see how some recruits seemed to have a natural instinct for these skills, and some very much did not. I never worked out what the *thing* is, but some people have it and some just don't.

The best part, though, was hanging out with the Level 1 guys at the bar after the day's teaching was done. One in particular, Steve, became a good friend, and we spent long hours chatting as he slammed back glass after glass of Talisker whisky.

Steve had been an undercover operative for over thirteen years, and had been personally responsible for taking down some extremely significant international criminal networks. Obviously, he was a tough guy – one couldn't do that job otherwise – but there was absolutely no macho posturing, no showing off, no arrogance.

One evening we were talking about a year-long investigation he had done, infiltrating a cartel shipping drugs between Holland and Britain. I was wondering how he kept his head, staying in character for that kind of prolonged deployment. Steve looked at me and said, 'The thing is, Neil, with undercover work you're never playing a role. You're only ever a slightly different version of yourself.'

That was it. In one sentence Steve had encapsulated everything I had been struggling with in trying to understand the work I did. I paused for a moment to process this.

'Fucking hell man, I don't know how you do it. Keeping that focus for months on end? I don't know if I'd have it in me.'

'You're joking aren't you?' Steve laughed. 'You're the one doing the crazy shit. I wouldn't do what you Level 2 lot do in a million years.'

'What do you mean?' I was genuinely perplexed. Steve was a Level 1. He spent years in deep cover chasing down top-level criminals. To me he was basically a cross between Batman and God.

'Neil, the people I deal with are civilised, they're predictable – they wear fucking suits. The guys you're chasing are lunatics – they're fucking drug-addled maniacs. They're actually stupid enough to think that killing you might be a good tactic.'

Steve paused and took a sip of his whisky before continuing.

'When I take on a case I have more backup than James Bond – yeah, it's dangerous, but I always know there are systems in place if things go wrong. What you do? Just rocking up, scoring some gear and working your way in with some crackhead in a tracksuit – not a chance mate, too wild for me.'

I sipped my beer reflectively. Steve had just spun all my prejudices on their head. And I have to admit that having a guy like Steve say that he admired my work made me feel a little surge of pride. I had never actually thought of myself as courageous before. I knew my work was dangerous, but it was just *what I did*.

But Steve was right. I hadn't even yet scratched the surface of just how vicious and unpredictable the street-level War on Drugs could become.

CHAPTER 9
NEW MILLS

I n 1999 I was transferred to the New Mills station for my uniformed police work. This was a whole new form of culture shock.

The uniformed Inspector at New Mills was a stern, humourless company man named Andrew McAllister, who starched his shirt and wore his moustache primly waxed like a First World War pilot. McAllister liked order and discipline. There wasn't an atom of the maverick daring of Jim Horner and the Drugs Squad.

But his problem with me began at the theatre.

I had only been at New Mills for a couple of weeks, and on a night off I booked tickets to see the Reduced Shakespeare Company do their *The Bible: The Complete Word of God (Abridged)*. The show was a silly, Monty Python-esque riff on the Bible story, and a big hit at the time. At the interval I went to grab a drink at the bar, and whom should I see but McAllister.

I walked straight up. 'Hello sir, didn't expect to see you here. You enjoying the show?'

'Not really,' he barked, giving me a withering look then grumpily stalking off. I thought this was a bit of an unfriendly response, but didn't pay it too much mind as I went in for the second act.

After the performance, however, we were confronted outside the theatre by a loud group of evangelical Christians protesting the production's supposed blasphemy. Right at the front was McAllister, bellowing about the sin of taking the word of God in vain. I managed to avoid him, but grabbed a leaflet to try and work out what all the fuss was about.

It turned out McAllister was a hardcore fundamentalist Christian who had previously taken a year off the force to do missionary work in Africa. From that night on he decided he didn't like me.

It started with spot inspections of my locker. He was perfectly entitled to do these, but it escalated to the point of absurdity. My locker was getting turned over a couple of times a week. McAllister would find some file of surveillance photos and brandish them as if he'd uncovered a grand conspiracy. Of course I'd always explain that they were just part of an investigation, but it didn't stop him hounding me.

McAllister was a chain of command fetishist. He couldn't stand that I would get calls, and have to disappear without telling him where. For him, police work was about maintaining a neat shift rota and hitting the criminals hard. He found the entire concept of covert operations sneaky and deceitful. Much better to just knock heads together and make sure your uniform was freshly pressed in the morning.

McAllister found every obscure disciplinary loophole he could to cause trouble and block my career. I think these days his vendetta would probably fall into the category of 'workplace bullying'. But this was a different era – and I was a cop. On the force you're taught to just get on with it, so that's what I did.

Eventually though, the harassment had a positive outcome. Ever since joining the force I had wanted to join CID. I always knew my talents lay in those kinds of strategic, intelligence-led investigations. Now, with McAllister on my back, I finally put myself forward, just to get out from under him.

In the meantime, there were always the undercover operations to keep me out of the office. There was nothing McAllister could do to stop me, and I went back to doing what I did best.

Throughout the 1980s police forces across Britain had fought a running battle against the blight of football hooliganism. As distant a memory as it now seems, for decades this was Britain's national embarrassment, sending thousands to hospital and tearing communities apart.

As much as the police like to take the credit, what really ended the hooligan era was the rise of acid house in the early 90s. The generation of kids who might have grown up to take over the football 'firms' discovered they could have a much better time getting loved up and dancing in a field. West Ham fans went to the same raves as Millwall fans, and everyone ended up in the same MDMA-fuelled euphoric mess. Getting your head kicked in on a rainy football terrace just couldn't compete.

This meant that by 1999, the only people left on the hooligan scene were the most incurable monomaniac psychopaths. These were the guys who didn't get their kicks through dancing, drugs, or even girls. What they enjoyed was battering people.

In Derby one of the worst of this crew was a guy named Kevin. He was a main-man in the Derby Lunatic Fringe, the notorious local firm that would still arrange brawls with the Burnley Suicide Squad, Nottingham Forest Executive Crew or anyone else who wanted a go.

When football grounds began searching for knives, this lot started sneaking in sharpened coins and apples stuffed with razor blades to hurl at the opposing side. Their particular trademark, though, was to attach an extra blade to a Stanley knife, so that when they cut someone the two gashes would be too close together to stitch properly, and the scar would end up as a grotesque spiderweb covering half their victim's face.

The Derby force was fed up. Kevin was on bail for two counts of GBH, but he had a long history of intimidating witnesses and beating charges in court. This time they were taking no chances. He was involved in all sorts of criminality, from moving stolen goods to acting as a thug-for-hire for local gangsters. But of course, the most profitable sideline was drugs.

There was no question of a prolonged investigation – this lot were too dangerous.

My mission was to get into the pub where Kevin held court, and make one buy-bust as the final nail in his coffin on top of the other charges.

In our briefing we decided that a woman's presence might take the edge off the testosterone-ridden atmosphere, so I chose one of my brightest, toughest students from Wakefield, Ann Williamson, as a partner.

From the second we walked into that pub I knew this was going to be a grind. Kevin and his gang were hanging out on some benches in a covered smoking area. There were about seven of them, all bruisers kitted out in Ben Sherman and Stone Island, with that swaggering menace of men who reckon they're the hardest squad in the pub.

On this job I didn't have months to get my face known, or random junkies I could bribe into an introduction. We had one shot at this – we had to make it count.

Ann and I skirted the edge of the beer garden, nursing a couple of drinks and waiting for a space. After perhaps an hour, a couple of lads left the little table next to Kevin and his crew. We moved in immediately.

There followed another hour of awkwardly miming a conversation with Ann, while keeping my ears glued to Kevin's conversation. I just needed an in – some line or phrase that could conceivably allow me to jump in and try to set up a deal.

Finally, just as things were beginning to get really quite uncomfortable, I caught Kevin turning to a mate and saying 'Yeah no worries – I've got loads of trips.'

It wasn't much, but it was the only chance we were going to get.

I leaned over and quietly called across, 'Oi mate, did I hear you say you had trips? I'd have a couple of those if you've got some going.'

The entire crew fell silent. Kevin turned to look at me as if I was something he had just scraped off his shoe. 'You talking to me? You fucking come here if you're talking to me.'

I stood up and shuffled over, trying not to meet anyone's eye. The second I was within range Kevin leapt to his feet and slammed me against the wall, his hand tight round my throat.

'If you're a fucking cop,' he hissed into my ear, 'then I've got something sharp here, just for your fucking face.'

'Mate – sorry. Don't worry about it, y'know.'

Kevin stared straight through me, his hand like iron round my throat. I could see the colour drain out of his lip as the adrenaline surged through his body. The grip round my windpipe tightened further.

'If you're a cop, I *will* kill you,' he seethed.

'Mate I'm not—'

'No,' he cut me off. 'I *will* fucking kill you.'

He gave my windpipe a final sharp squeeze, then loosened his grip. 'Now, how many do you fucking want?'

'Umm... maybe four, if it's all right?' I gasped for breath.

'Twenty quid,' Kevin snorted, as if I wasn't even worth his time.

He opened his wallet and tore four tabs of acid off a sheet of around thirty. Then he very deliberately held out his hand and dropped them on the floor so that I had to scrabble around his mates' feet on my hands and knees. The whole crew erupted in raucous laughter.

I shuffled back to my table a little shell-shocked, sat down and raised my eyes at Ann. She gave the signal to the boys outside.

Two teams of cops in full uniform body armour exploded through the front and back doors, tearing through the place like a hurricane.

Kevin was on his feet in a second, squaring up to fight his way out. He never got the chance. A riot squad officer caught him from his blind side, dropping him with a brutal sucker punch.

This is very unusual. Police are trained to take someone down with a grapple to cause minimum damage – but Kevin lived for violence, they weren't going to risk him smashing a bottle or pulling a blade.

The entire Lunatic Fringe crew were pulled through the wreckage of the pub and shoved into the vans outside. There was no way he could intimidate his way out of this charge. He got three and a half years.

That bust felt good. Kevin was probably the most thuggishly aggressive target I'd had to deal with yet.

The next operation was the diametric opposite. They were sending me after the hippies.

The intelligence unit had picked up chatter about an upcoming gathering being thrown by one of the sound systems that set up free parties across the UK. The word was that a few higher-level dealers would be coming through from Nottingham to shift their gear.

I would be working with Cate Doyle, who had joined the force at the same time as me, made CID in three years and was known as something of a prodigy. As with the nightclub job in Derby, I would make the score and Cate would act as corroborating witness.

Usually these gatherings would be set in a field or wood somewhere but, November in the Midlands not being ideal for outdoor parties, this rave was being held in a huge room above a pub in Chesterfield.

We walked into a flood of psychedelic lasers, lava lamps and bouncing dreadlocks. Things were just starting to pick up, and people were whirling away to thumping trance music.

Finding drugs wasn't exactly a challenge. Cate and I just walked up to the first person we saw rolling a spliff and asked if they had any pills.

'Yeah, I've got a few. But you should wait for my mate to come down later on, he's got way better stuff than me.'

Cate and I exchanged a confused glance. Professional drug dealers aren't known for recommending their competition. 'Ummm OK... how much you want for those ones you've got?' I asked.

'Oh, no man, you can just have them.' He smiled, stretching out his palm to offer us a couple each.

Cate immediately jumped in. 'You know what? Maybe we'll wait for your friend to come down – no sense in overdoing it. Thanks though. Have a wicked night, yeah.'

I understood exactly what she was doing. If we accepted those pills, we would have to include them as evidence, and this dreadlocked kid would legally be considered a dealer.

As we continued walking around the party it became more and more obvious that there were no real gangsters here. These folks may all have been high as kites, but they weren't criminals in any meaningful sense of the word. I began to feel very uncomfortable about the entire mission. I had joined the force to fight against hardened gangsters, not a bunch of techno crusties leading their pet dogs around on strings.

Just as I was getting quite concerned about all this, Cate turned to me and simply declared, 'I'm not fucking doing it.'

'What do you mean?'

'Look, there's no bad guys from Nottingham here. It's just a bunch of kids. I'm not gathering evidence on these people.'

I was in complete agreement, but we still had a problem. We couldn't just leave – the brass needed to see that we had been there at least a few hours.

'So, what do you want to do then?'

'Well, let's get stoned and dance a lot.'

I almost dropped my pint. 'You what?'

'Yeah, let's score a bit of grass and a bit of hash, and have a dance. If any gangsters do show up, we can gather evidence, but otherwise...fuck it.'

So that's exactly what we did. I went and got some nice Thai stick and Moroccan resin, and Cate rolled a big hash-on-grass spliff. Then we danced our arses off to Detroit-influenced soulful techno and some banging hard house. I would never have done this on my own, but the fact that it was Cate's idea somehow made it all right to just let go.

And of course no gangsters showed up. This was the friendliest, most unthreatening little gathering one could imagine, and I have absolutely no regrets about the decision we made.

Cate and I stumbled out at about 4 a.m., and found our backup team huddled in their van drinking tea. We wrote up our evidence while giggling like naughty schoolkids, but made it absolutely clear to the Intel unit that hounding this lot of free party hippies was a massive misallocation of resources.

It was Johnno who first saw the danger. 'Umm, Chief, don't you think it's a bit dodgy for Neil to be doing another under-cover job in Derby? He's worked this town already, his face is known.'

Deep down I knew it was a bad idea as well. But, by that point I would have taken on any mission just to get away from DI McAllister. Compared to his constant hounding, chasing a bunch of smack dealers in Derby seemed like a break.

My partner for this operation was Patrick Shaw. I had spotted Pat as a uniformed cop, and personally recommended him for the undercover course. He was ex-military, so it was a fair bet that he could handle himself. But it was more than that. Pat was sharp. He could improvise and bullshit like no one else I've ever seen. There wasn't a line you could fire at him without getting a stinging verbal hand-grenade straight back. In many ways his brash, confrontational style was the opposite of my own, but my instincts told me he was made for undercover work, and I had trained him myself.

Derby had a growing heroin problem. Deaths from overdoses and related crimes were soaring, and the force there was overwhelmed. We had no specific targets, but were just meant to go in and see what we could learn about the town's drug supply.

Pat and I figured we needed a calling card, something to raise us above the other junkies. I had a look through the Seized Property locker at the station and found several huge boxes of stolen rolling tobacco. So, we reinvented ourselves as small-time smugglers with a taste for smack, bringing in tobacco from France and buying heroin.

As it turned out, there was quite a market for cheap tobacco. We hung around dodgy pubs, doing a roaring trade, and quickly made a string of contacts. That's how we met Eddie Glass.

Eddie was a small-time crook with an iron in every fire going. He fancied himself a bit of a Midlands Scarface, buying and selling coke and heroin, and talking a big game about the heavy gangsters he knew. He and Pat hit it off immediately. Pat was a natural at playing the wheeler-dealer smuggler –

which allowed me to be the quiet sidekick, keeping my mouth shut and my eyes open. Through Eddie we got to know a whole range of mid-level heroin dealers, and began doing regular buys to work our way up the food chain.

It was here that Pat's cocky, mischievous side started to show. Like most of the country at the time, Pat was obsessed with the film *Lock, Stock and Two Smoking Barrels*. We used to listen to the soundtrack on the way in to deployments. I'd sing along with the James Brown songs, Pat would do the film quotes from memory in his over-the-top mockney accent.

Then, one morning we were haggling over some smack with a couple of rough Jamaican guys Eddie had put us in touch with. Pat managed to talk them into selling us five bags for the price of four. As we took the gear, he turned to me and, doing his full *Lock, Stock* voice, went, 'It's a steal, it's a deal, it's the sale of the fucking century.' It took every atom of self-control I had not to burst into laughter and completely blow our cover right there.

Not to be outdone though, the next time we were walking away, having just scored a half-T off another dealer, I turned and mugged, 'Mate, can I just say... It's been emotional.' This time it was Pat's turn to almost lose his cool.

That's why I liked Pat. He was completely fearless, and he brought out my own reckless, mischievous side.

Occasionally though, he could get carried away.

Through Eddie Glass we'd arranged a meeting with a serious West Indian cartel. This was a big step up for all of us, and we knew it could lead into some heavy international networks. But as soon as we sat down, Pat launched into some story about how he wanted 2,000 pills because he knew a guy from the army who could smuggle them into Cyprus and sell them around the clubs of Ayia Napa. He'd obviously worked out this line in advance, and was quite pleased with it. But he was breaking the golden rule of undercover work – never volunteer your cover story, always make the other guy drag it out of you.

I could see the guys' faces instantly sour. I frantically tried to catch Pat's eye, but he was off on one, babbling about the club scene in Cyprus and his mates in the forces who could move anything in and out.

After about three minutes, one of the gangsters just turned and said, 'Nah…listen mate, dis ain't for us.' There was no explicit threat, but the tone was severe. He was ending the conversation then and there.

As we walked out to the car, one of them grabbed Eddie Glass by the arm and pulled him aside. Without even bothering to wait till we were out of earshot he leaned in: 'Oi Glassy, see dem two – they're old bill, mate. You don't want to hang around with them.' As we climbed into the car I could just hear Eddie going, 'Nah mate, I know these guys, they're all right, seriously.' Pat and I exchanged a look, and got out of there as fast as possible. There was nothing to say; we all made mistakes in those days.

It made little difference in any case – my part in this mission was about to dramatically unravel.

Pat and I were walking through a dreary, low-rise council estate in Allenton, back where I had lived during my initial training. A few streets ahead a small group of guys was approaching from the opposite direction. As they got closer I began to recognise a certain swagger in the way one of this crew walked, something about the way he cocked his head as he spoke into his mobile. But I just couldn't place him. One second passed, then another. The group got closer. Then it hit me. It was bloody Carlo, Bigga Williams' lieutenant, who had sold me the stone during my second undercover job in Derby.

Carlo hadn't spotted me. He was still a block away and distracted by his phone. If he saw me, I was a dead man. Everyone knew Bigga had been taken down in an undercover sting, and Carlo would remember the guy who busted his boss.

There was no time to walk away or even give Pat a warning. I just spun round and hurled myself over the nearest garden hedge.

I landed with a thud at the feet of a middle-aged housewife hanging up her washing. She gave a start and almost screamed. Quick as lightning, I put my finger to my lips with a pleading expression. She must have read in my eyes that something serious was going on, as she gave me a quick nod and deliberately began fiddling with her washing again. I lay there, hidden by the hedge, until I heard Carlo's voice, still talking into his phone as he passed by. Then I picked myself up, brushed off the mud and leaves, gave the wifey a grateful wink and let myself out the gate.

There was no way I could continue this operation. If Carlo had recognised me, then Pat and I could both have been killed. As much as I would have loved to have seen Eddie Glass and the other crooks we were dealing with get taken down, my face was just too well known. All it would take was the wrong person to catch a glimpse of me and put a whisper in someone's ear.

In any case, I knew Pat had the brass to carry on solo, and eventually he did bring in quite a few busts off the investigation.

The only other positive outcome was that even the higher-ups on the Drugs Squad had to admit we'd pushed things too far. It became a protocol that no undercover should work the same town twice. It's always nice, and all too rare, when common sense and national law enforcement policy actually coincide.

A clique of heavy-hitting Moss Side gangsters had moved into Glossop, turning the town into a way station for drugs flowing into Manchester. This had drawn the interest of rival Mancunian mobs, and suddenly the small town had become the centre of a vicious turf war.

Eventually someone ended up getting shot in a local night-club, the press got hold of the story and the brass were finally forced to take action.

Having learned my lesson in Derby, there was no way I could go back into the field in Glossop. But no one else had the experience, so the Drugs Squad brought me in behind the scenes, to help organise and direct the operation. Jim Horner took me aside to ask my advice on what had gone wrong on previous investigations, and how we might do better.

I jumped at the chance to set a few things right. First off, as we were going to be working in nightclubs again, I insisted on properly manned and well-positioned observation points to monitor entrances and exits.

Most importantly though, I thought it was insane that we never monitored and triangulated our suspects' phone calls.

The technology was available. If an undercover managed to get a dealer's mobile number, surely we should be talking to the phone company to see who they had been calling.

Almost to my surprise, the bosses agreed to everything. I was asking for some expensive stuff here. For them to give the OK, the case must be serious.

I assembled a special unit, including Jenny from my previous nightclub job, Cate Doyle and a couple of guys from the training course, Ron Haines and Dom Green.

The clubs of Glossop had turned into such an open drugs market that the investigation was given the codename Operation Betta, named for the shop Bettabuys on Coronation Street.

The undercover group went in and quickly gathered a wealth of information on who was moving gear through the town. Thanks to the more extensive observation posts, we developed an archive of photographs of the gangsters who controlled the town's underworld. I began using my evenings and rest days to help the team sift through the evidence.

Knowing that I was bit of an encyclopaedia, the guys on the Derbyshire squad liked to quiz me about drugs. Eventually the conversation turned to khat, the stimulant that is chewed all over East Africa, and which at the time was still officially legal in the UK.

I didn't think much of it until the evening of the bust itself, when a DS involved in the operation shouted over to me, "Ey up Woodsy, why don't you drive past Manchester and pick us all up some of that khat stuff you were talking about?'

'You serious, sir?' I gave him a look of complete shock and bemusement.

'Aye! This'll be a long night. Sure we could all do with a pick-me-up.'

Right then, bloody hell. I had been meant to go through to Manchester that morning anyway to interview a suspect. Why shouldn't I pick some khat up on the way back? I knew exactly where to find it. From Kentish Town Road in London to the south end of Princess Street in Manchester, the British khat trade was booming, catering to the market of Somali refugees from the civil war. You could buy bushels of the stuff for a few pounds a pop.

I did my interview, raced across town to buy four big bags of khat and began making my way back to Glossop. Unfortunately, I was running late, and got pulled over for speeding by a Manchester traffic cop.

I apologised profusely, showed my warrant card and explained that I was trying to make it back for the arrest phase of an important operation. He gave me a talking-to, then told me to be on my way, and that 'we'd say no more about it'. I apologised again, thanked him for understanding and drove the rest of the way well under the limit.

By the time I made it back to base, everyone seemed more excited to try khat than for the actual bust. They brewed it up into a foul-tasting tea, then we all went off to do a major drug bust while buzzing our heads off on a legal high.

Luckily the raids went off without major incident. The operation cast a wide net, sweeping up everyone from major gangsters to a local DJ who had tried to impress Cate and Jenny by getting them a few pills. Of course, in the eyes of the Drugs Squad and CPS he was no different from the guys ordering beatings and shootings, and ended up getting six years.

The trials themselves, though, turned into an absolute nightmare – and, in a small way, made British legal history.

The law had recently changed in quite a profound way. In the old days, the police only had to present evidence that was directly admissible for the case at hand. Under the new disclosure laws, we had to show the defence team every single bit of evidence gathered in an investigation, no matter how irrelevant.

Unfortunately, no one told the guys manning all our specially deployed observation points.

These were cops, stuck outside nightclubs for hours at a time. Of course the evidence folders were full of shots of women's cleavages, people throwing up, and an almost artistic series featuring an intoxicated couple stumbling out of a club and proceeding to make prolonged and explicit love on the town hall steps.

The DS lads may have thought this was all hilarious – the defence lawyers certainly didn't. They called the entire prosecution case into question, ordering a massive *voir dire* – a pre-emptive examination of evidence.

It got completely ridiculous. Case officers found themselves getting followed home and having their phone records checked by private detectives hired by the defence solicitors, to make sure we weren't colluding to get our stories in order. To my knowledge, this is still the most extensive *voir dire* in British legal history, and formed the basis for quite a bit of future case law.

We were incredibly lucky that we had a detective named Andrew Cooper on our squad who was an expert in disclosure legislation, and who guided us through the process with incredible diligence and precision. It's really down to his superb, disciplined effort that we were able to shepherd the cases to successful convictions. But it was a close-run thing.

There was, however, one further fallout from Operation Betta.

I walked back into the New Mills station a week after the bust, to find DI McAllister waiting for me with an expression of gleeful malice. 'Woods. My office. Now.'

'What's all this about, then?' He triumphantly threw a document down on his desk.

It turned out that the traffic cop who had stopped me for speeding had not only grassed me up after all, but had written the incident up saying that I had been abusive and threatening. Reading over his notes, I was appalled. He had completely misrepresented the incident to make me sound like some sort of overbearing thug.

I've never used abusive language in anger to anyone in my life. I found the implication genuinely insulting. It also made me wonder – if this was how evidence on another cop could get misreported, think how bad it could get on the street. Maybe all those people who said they didn't trust the police might just have a point?

McAllister, on the other hand, was obviously relishing the moment. He'd hounded me for months trying to find some evidence of inner evil – finally he had his ammunition. He savoured it, giving me an hour-long tirade about discipline and duty, and finally notifying me of an official written warning.

I was annoyed, but I also accepted that I had screwed up, and could take a fair reprimand. But McAllister had saved one last blow.

'And you can forget about your CID application. Not this year, Woods...not this year.' He gave me a look of sheer smug self-satisfaction.

I walked out of that office feeling utterly defeated. CID was so obviously where my talents could be put to best use. The fact that McAllister would actually weaken the force just to spite me, and that he would be so shameless about it, was appalling.

All I could do was to keep repeating to myself, 'Six months...six months till the CID application window opens again.' But it was deeply disheartening to feel so undermined by my own bosses.

Things with Sam had actually been getting better. We had started taking Tanith and Gareth for walks together on the moors, and even taking the odd night off to go to the pictures together – just like young parents are meant to do.

Sam had announced that she wanted to quit her job to become a primary school teacher, and had thrown herself into the training with the energy and focus that I had always admired in her. She seemed the happiest I'd seen her in years. Throughout all my recent undercover jobs, and the harassment from DI McAllister, it was this improvement in our family life that had kept me going.

So the fall was all the more brutal when things once again took a turn for the worse. This time, things spiralled further and faster than ever.

Sleepless night followed sleepless night, amidst endless rounds of shouting and recrimination. Eventually I found myself at 5 a.m. splashing water on my face and looking at myself in the mirror. That's when it hit me. Or at least, that's when I first admitted it to myself.

I had made a terrible mistake in my life by marrying Sam. I needed to face that truth and accept its consequences.

There was a massive rush of exhilaration and release as I was finally able to give up the denial and false hope. We didn't work as a couple. Fine. I would leave. I would simply get a divorce, take the kids and—

The realisation shot through me like a bullet in the gut. The kids.

In any divorce Sam would get the children. I knew the law – courts favour the mother, and there was nothing I could do about it. If I left, I would be abandoning my children to be raised by Sam, with no guarantees of how often I would be able to see them. I sank onto the edge of the bathtub, completely winded.

I was trapped. Until the children were old enough to make their own decisions, I would have to stay in this marriage. Gradually the chaos in my mind resolved into a strange kind of order. Somehow making this decision felt fatalistically liberating. At last I knew my role, and could feel a new sense of purpose. I would stay and pour every ounce of love and care I had into bringing up my children.

I splashed some more water on my face, then crept into bed to lie awake and watch the dawn break as I mentally prepared myself for the battles that lay ahead – both on the streets and in my own home.

CHAPTER 10

WAKEFIELD

I was an undercover cop. I knew when I was being watched.

DI McAllister was crossing the line. After the speeding incident on Operation Betta, his constant observation and harassment switched into a new gear. Almost every day there was something: a demand to present my evidence book; my locker getting turned over; a call into his office for yet another talking-to.

I'm all in favour of professionalism and discipline, but there was something else at work here. I'd catch him watching me, taking sidelong glances and making notes in a little black pocketbook. I'd done criminal surveillance. I knew it wasn't a coincidence that everywhere I went in the station, there he'd be, checking on my every movement.

Or was it? Maybe this was just my own weird psychodrama? Maybe with all the pressure at home I was just getting paranoid and imagining it all? Maybe Sam was right? Maybe I was actually losing it?

It's a terrible feeling to doubt your own intuition. Out on the streets, it was my instincts that kept me alive. But now at home and the office – the very places where I was meant to feel safe – I was beginning to mistrust my own feelings.

The doubt gnawed at me. I had to know what was going on. I had to see what he was writing in that little pocketbook.

So, I launched my own little covert operation. I'd worked undercover – I knew how it was done. I waited for a busy night shift, when everyone else had been called out of the station. I reckoned I had about twenty minutes.

I sprang up and snatched the key to McAllister's office from the hook by the noticeboard. I carefully opened his door, and began rifling through his desk for that pocketbook. I went through drawer after drawer. A minute passed, then another. Finally, I flipped open an unmarked folder and there it was.

It was insane.

The front page was simply marked 'Woods'. What followed was a day-by-day account of my every action, just as if he were collecting evidence for a case. He was noting down how many chocolate bars I ate in a day; how many times I went to the toilet. Sometimes he counted how many times I coughed in an hour.

This was obsessive behaviour.

I didn't know if it was part of some evangelical crusade, or just an underlying personality disorder, but McAllister was operating at a level of neurotic fixation that bordered on the sociopathic.

The important thing was that at least I knew it wasn't just in my head. I wasn't the crazy one. But even so, what was I to do?

I put the pocketbook back exactly as I had found it, hung the office key back on its hook and sat back down at my desk.

What should I even do with this information? I couldn't exactly go to the higher-ups and say that I'd broken into my own DI's office. On the other hand, there was no way I could stay in this department under these conditions.

As I saw it, there was only one way out. I would put in another application for CID, and in the meantime keep my performance so perfectly by the book that even McAllister wouldn't be able to sabotage me.

For the next six months I was like a machine. I was early every shift, with my buttons polished just how the DI liked them. I kept my head down and made my paperwork more of a priority than actual investigations. If that's what McAllister wanted, that's what he would get.

Luckily no undercover assignments came up to distract me, and after six months, and a letter of support from Jim Horner, word finally came through.

For the first time I actually felt that I was taking proactive control of my own career. I was learning to fight the good fight in my own way.

McAllister never did confront whatever demons he was battling with. Ten years later he walked out onto the moors and never returned. When the police combed through his computer they found he had been cruising the Internet for months, researching the best way to kill oneself so that the body is never discovered. Whatever issues the two of us may have had, he was still a cop like me. It's deeply sad that he was never able to resolve the turmoil that obviously made him so unhappy.

Detective training was everything I ever hoped it would be.

Every person on that course had made a conscious decision to be there, and the instructors were the most experienced, knowledgeable cops on the force. These guys wore suits, not uniforms, and specialised in highly complex investigations to catch the most dangerous criminals. They drilled us in the tactical fine points of hunting down elusive suspects and weaving together multiple strands of evidence.

It was also fun as the training centre in Wakefield was next door to a nursing college.

Since my 5 a.m. epiphany, I had come to terms with the idea that I was staying in my relationship with Sam for the sake of the kids. But even so, the thought that I was trapped in a destructive, unhappy marriage was deeply depressing.

But, one Friday on the course, the whole team piled into a local club. We were drinking and dancing when with no warning a girl from the nursing school pulled me into a corner for a snog.

I felt a tidal wave of joy and relief – and not an atom of guilt. We didn't take it any further, but it was a deep moment. Sam was the only woman I'd ever been with, and allowing myself this freedom was important and liberating.

As we had our parting kiss, though, that girl gave my tongue a playful bite. By the next day, it had swollen and looked like a length of rope. I had to rush to A&E, where it turned out I had something called glossitis. I was prescribed antibiotics. As much as it stung though, it was nothing compared to the teasing from a group of cops when you're seen copping off with a girl, then turn up the next day with an infected tongue.

My career as a detective began right at the deep end. Usually for a major operation, the bosses would use people with perhaps ten years' experience in CID. But one woman from the course developed a stress-related issue and had to drop out, and I was thrown into the mix to replace her.

This was a firearms job.

A group in Derbyshire were operating as a legitimate busi-ness, selling decommissioned guns. But, under the counter, these guys were also selling the kit and instructions to turn them back into working shooters.

Their record books linked them to sales all over the country, from Fort William to Dorset, and they were reckoned to be one of the major suppliers of clandestine weapons in the UK. Our job was to prove criminal intent.

We were handed twenty bulging sacks full of receipts and invoices, and told to somehow piece this all together and link these guns with those being used on the streets of Britain.

Detective Constable Harry Dick, who ran the unit, is, to this day, probably the most intuitive, insightful and determined cop I ever met on the job. He was also very Scottish. Now, try saying that name with a Scottish accent. One of the detective sergeants happened to be named Phil Cox. So, whenever Harry was making a call, the entire team would crowd around just to hear him say, 'Aye, we'll come down and see you, it's Harry Dick and Phil Cox...No, this is not a wind-up...Yes, those *are* the real names...Yes, *I know!*' and slam the phone down.

Under these two was a team of five other detectives. We worked this one investigation, as a specialised unit, for eighteen months.

Harry worked out a system of matching the sales in the record book with a database of the receipts, then cross-referencing the results with gun crime records in the relevant areas.

These guys made leaps of logic and intuition that left me in the dust. They could scan a file and spot impossible connec-tions between disparate scraps of evidence, which would eventually lead to criminals behind bars and guns off the street. I soaked up their knowledge like a sponge, and found my own work improving in leaps and bounds.

Once you start following a major firearms ring, there's no telling where you will end up. We raced all over the country chasing those guns, finding ourselves in situations that were downright surreal.

Tracing a couple of rifles, we stumbled on an elderly gay couple, newly retired to an old mining village near Durham. But there was something different about this particular couple – they happened to be ex-loyalist paramilitaries from County Derry in Northern Ireland.

The village itself was made up of about seventy small houses, set among the rolling dales. One couldn't imagine a more quaint, sleepy retirement spot. Why would anyone, even ex-Orangemen, need guns in an idyll like this? With these two, however, the guns were only the start of it.

We kicked in their door, and held the two old fellas in the living room. The rifles turned up easily enough, along with another pair of handguns.

Then I was sent to have a look upstairs. I stepped into the spare room, and swung open the door of a large wardrobe set against the opposite wall. Then I saw it.

Sitting on the shelf were several bunches of brownish paper tubes tied together with string; rivulets of a weird waxy type of sweat streamed off each one.

A bolt of pure panic shot up my spine. Images from old movies, and a half-remembered counterterrorism module, flashed into my mind. Was it? It couldn't be…But it was. It was fucking dynamite. That 'sweat' was bloody nitroglycerine.

My head snapped round to the window. It was a blazing hot August day; the sun was streaming through the glass, turning the room into a greenhouse. With my heart pounding in my chest, I backed out of the room very slowly, retracing my steps one by one.

As I went, there was a tiny voice in my head saying, 'Come on Neil, this isn't a minefield, walking backwards isn't going to help if that stuff blows,' but I just couldn't help it.

I made my way downstairs, pulled my fellow detectives aside and related what I had seen. I was immediately greeted with uproarious laughter and a round of, 'Yeah Neil, dynamite, of course there is, mate...right.'

I have to admit to a certain satisfaction when Phil Cox swung open the wardrobe door and immediately whispered, 'Oh...Oh, right,' under his breath, then retraced his steps backwards, exactly as I had.

Of course, we couldn't dispose of this material. We called the Royal Ordnance, who sent over a red-faced officer with a Lord Kitchener moustache, who didn't speak so much as bark like an indignant walrus. 'Right then,' he huffed patronisingly, 'apparently you lads think you've seen some dynamite. Let's see what it really is, shall we?'

He stamped upstairs and I listened to the clump of his shoes as he crossed the floorboards. There followed a much slower and quieter creaking as he crept back out of the room.

When he came back downstairs his voice was suddenly extremely quiet and very business-like. 'Yes, umm, we're going to have to evacuate.'

'Right,' replied Phil, 'we'll pull the team out now.'

'No,' the officer quietly but firmly responded, 'I mean the whole town.'

It turned out that in addition to the dynamite, this old pair of lovebirds had a significant quantity of plastic explosives up in that wardrobe. Lord knows what they planned to do with it, but their entire little retirement village had to be cordoned off and evacuated.

On another job, we tracked five automatic weapons to a house in Teignmouth, a sleepy fishing town on the south coast of Devon. The whole team drove down, assuming that together we could wrap up the enquiry in a night.

The house was large and tastefully done up. It was owned by a guy who lived there with his wife and teenage son; he was reclusive, but otherwise the set-up seemed completely unremarkable.

We stormed in and found the guns we were looking for. But we also found 357 other firearms, and thousands of rounds of ammunition.

This place was stocked for war. There were Navy chests full of pistols; side panels slid back to reveal racks of shotguns, and a belt-fed Vickers machine gun nestled among the rafters in the attic. Along with this, we found several hundred grand in dollars, Deutschmarks, rubles and francs, bags of diamonds, and twenty-four shrink-wrapped tubes of solid gold South African krugerrands.

The entire team was completely gobsmacked. We may have been a major ops unit, but we had definitely just stumbled on something above our pay-grade. We got the guy locked up – freaking the hell out of the local Exeter cops –

then Harry got straight on to Special Branch, who in turn, called in MI5.

By the time we wrapped up late that night, the entire team was completely strung out. We all needed a drink, so we piled into a cab and told the driver to take us to the nearest open club.

Tensions were running high after the stress of the day. People were getting on each other's nerves. We hadn't got a quarter of the way through our first pint before something was said and Phil and another detective were up and grappling each other by the throat.

We broke the two guys up, but I'd had enough. I just said to myself, Oh fuck this, I'm going on to that dance floor, and throwing myself into the arms of the first beautiful woman I see.

And that's exactly what I did. Her name was Celine and she was wonderful. I ended up stopping at her place that night.

But, once again, there was some karmic payback for the extramarital fun. I'd recently had a vasectomy. I had made the decision to stay in my marriage for the sake of my children, but I wasn't planning on having any more.

The next morning I turned up to help catalogue our evidence. By 10 a.m. I was feeling uncomfortable. By 11:30 I was doubled over with excruciating pain where no man ever wants to feel it.

I was rushed to the hospital, sat on a gurney and told to drop my trousers. 'Oh . . . Oh right. Yes, we'll have to do something about that.'

Apparently the sutures from the vasectomy had been sewn too tight. Due to various exertions the previous evening, something had got twisted and now the blood flow was blocked. My testicles were swollen like cricket balls, and about the same colour.

They had to do the procedure then and there, with no anaesthetic. I have never felt such acute, searing agony – nor such immediate, sweet relief when it was over. By 5:30 I was back with the team, cataloguing evidence with an ice pack on my lap.

We never did find out conclusively why that guy had so many guns in his posh Devon home. Harry's theory was that he was the quartermaster for a far-right, white supremacist group, arming themselves for some sort of 'rivers of blood' doomsday scenario.

But what I do know is that he was only sent down for one year. This chap had an armoury that would make Hezbollah wet the bed, and he got less time than people I'd put away for slinging a few pills. One couldn't help the thought that sometimes the law might function differently for wealthy white men.

But, there were a couple of positive outcomes. Not only had we taken a few hundred guns out of the hands of lunatic neo-Nazis, but also Celine and I stayed in touch. When I went back to give evidence, we were able to meet up again.

Like everyone else, I stared at the television on 11 September 2001 and knew nothing would ever be quite the same. Even up in Derbyshire we all knew these events would have reverberations across the world of law enforcement. But no one had any idea what the implications would be. As it happened, our firearms case was about to force me to brush up against the world of terrorism investigation – with very unexpected results.

Faisal Mostafa was a chemistry professor with a PhD from Manchester Polytechnic. He had been raised among Stockport's large Bengali community, then moved to Birmingham to take up a teaching position.

He was also a constant fixture on the security services' watch list.

Mostafa had first been convicted for possession of a firearm in 1996, in connection with a plot to assassinate the Israeli ambassador. Then in 2000 he had been arrested again, on the suspicion that he was using his chemistry skills as a bomb-maker for British jihadi groups. When I interviewed him he was on remand for those charges at Woodhill Prison, a grim Category A facility in Milton Keynes.

Our interest in Faisal was based on the fact that the gun he had been caught with in the 1996 Israeli ambassador plot was one of our very own Derbyshire specials. Jihadi terror-ists aren't known for voluntarily cooperating with police enquiries, so we were very surprised when he agreed to my interview request.

The first thing he did was to apologise for not being able to offer me tea. This was odd. We were in a maximum security interview suite – he was the prisoner, and I was the cop. But as far Faisal was concerned, I was his guest, so he should have been able to offer me something.

This was emphatically not the psychopathic jihadist I had been expecting. Throughout our interviews Faisal was unas-suming, softly spoken and unfailingly polite and courteous.

He also consistently maintained his innocence. He may have had the tips of both middle fingers missing from explo-sive accidents, but he absolutely insisted that he was just a geeky science nerd who loved making his own fireworks. 'Neil, I understand why the security services are interested in me. I know I've been silly in the past. There's no resentment – but really, they will find that I am not who they are looking for.'

I didn't know what to believe. Faisal genuinely did come across as a gentle, interesting, sympathetic character. On the other hand, in the past he had definitely associated with known jihadists, been found in possession of Hizb ut-Tahrir literature, and had been testing explosives in various Birmingham parks. As much as I respected Faisal's intelligence, I didn't want to be suckered into sympathising with a murderous terrorist by a bit of charm and basic good manners.

Luckily, I didn't have to decide. I was there to chase guns. And in this at least, Faisal was incredibly helpful. He detailed with a scientist's precision how he had bought a deactivated gun from our suspects in Derbyshire, along with the kit to reactivate it – which of course, he had the knowledge to do quite easily.

At Woodhill there were two wings in which high-risk prisoners were kept apart from general population prisoners. One was for terror suspects, the other for sexual offenders and psychopaths.

Faisal had originally been held on 'Jihadi Wing'. But when he had agreed to talk to us the other terrorists had started bullying him, so he had to be transferred onto 'Psycho Wing'. This led directly to our most interesting exchange.

It was coming to the end of our final interview. Faisal leaned in close. 'Listen Neil, there is something else I have to tell you. There's another prisoner here who I think you should know about. He's dangerous.'

'Go on.' I was intrigued.

'This man, he comes to my cell and talks to me because I know about guns. He is completely obsessed with guns. But this man – Wesley Dickens – he is evil.'

At that name, I stiffened instinctively. This was a name I knew.

Wesley Dickens was from my hometown of Buxton, and was familiar to every detective in Derbyshire. He had first been arrested at around twenty years old for having a couple of sub-machine guns. But his father was a wealthy land-owner and he was let off with a conditional discharge. A few years later he was living in Stockport and had gone on a rampage in full combat gear, threatening people with a reactivated AK-47. Due to legal technicalities he ended up only getting two years.

Of course, in prison he had made underworld drug connec-tions. A few years later he was arrested again, with three Ingram MAC-10s and about fifteen nine-bars of hash. This time his psychological profile landed him on the high-risk wing of Woodhill Prison.

Which brings us to Faisal Mostafa. Apparently, Dickens was coming into Faisal's cell, and saying some very scary things.

'He says he dreams of killing someone,' Mostafa whispered to me. 'He says that he will never feel truly complete until he has murdered somebody – Neil, I'm telling you, this man is evil. He is sick...but he's up for early release in a few weeks. If he gets out I am sure he is going to murder someone. Is there anything you can do?'

Here was a suspected jihadist warning me that a Derbyshire lad represented a danger to society. This was something I had to take seriously.

I took the story to Harry Dick, and we wrote a letter to the parole board saying we had information that Wesley Dickens was fantasising about murdering someone, that he was obsessed with guns, and that as this was his third firearms offence he needed a full psychological profile done – and should certainly not be eligible for early release.

We received a letter back saying that our concerns had been noted. Of course, a month after, he was released at the earliest opportunity.

Six weeks later he had murdered someone.

In prison he had made arrangements to set up an amphetamine production lab. Once released, he had sourced PMK, the precursor chemical, and found a farmer willing to let them use his land. The farmer then got cold feet, so Dickens and an accomplice broke into his house, dragged him to the bathroom and fired nine shots into his head.

As gruesome as this was, for me there was a bizarre personal element to the story. When we were teenagers growing up in Buxton, Wesley Dickens had been a key fixture in my, and particularly Sam's, circle of friends.

Over the years I've frequently seen Faisal Mostafa's name in the news. He beat the charges for which he was on remand when I interviewed him. But since then he has been arrested, released and rearrested many times, in both Britain and Bangladesh. I have still never been able to make up my mind whether he was just a misunderstood chemistry teacher, or a cold-blooded terrorist bomb-maker.

We wrapped up the firearms investigation successfully – managing to secure a conviction for the Derbyshire arms dealers, and take thousands of weapons off the streets. It had been immensely rewarding, and a real education, to work with such an experienced and talented set of detectives.

But the War on Drugs still needed to be fought. The bosses knew how to exploit people for their particular skill set, and mine was undercover work. Not long after the Derbyshire investigation ended, I got the call.

It was time to leave behind the detective's suit and tie, and go back to the stained tracksuit and bomber jacket of the homeless street junkie.

CHAPTER 11

LEICESTER

Everything changed with the Leicester job.

From the get-go this operation had a different rhythm from anything I had done before. But although it would prove to be one of the most dangerous assignments I ever took on, Leicester wasn't even strictly 'my' job. Once again, I had been brought in to save a failing operation.

Jim Horner took me for a pint and explained that he had been brought in to run an undercover operation for the Leicestershire Constabulary. Two separate teams had been in place for over a month, but no one had been able to get past the lowest street-level user-dealers. They needed someone with experience of infiltrating gangs and working their way up the criminal hierarchies.

I have to admit I was flattered to get called back in after so long. But the more I heard about how this operation had been organised, the more apprehensive I began to feel.

To me, having two teams deploying the same tactics in one small city seemed not just over the top, but actually reckless. OCGs talk to each other. Word spreads around a city's criminal networks faster than the clap around a brothel. All it takes is *one* slip, by *one* undercover, to blow the whole operation for both teams – and potentially put everyone at risk. Undercover operations should be deployed like a scalpel – this sounded like a pneumatic drill.

I was also used to operating alone or with one trusted partner – and I had always designed my own operational strategy. The thought of coming into a larger team and having to start again, not even knowing what mistakes these guys may have already made, made me very uneasy.

But Jim was persuasive, pouring it on thick about how a major new organisation had been created specifically to run undercover ops, so we would now be supported by multiple agencies and have access to the latest cutting-edge kit.

This got my attention. With my experience in CID I was developing an interest in the larger structures of major investigations. But really, once again I was just unable to walk away from a challenge. Jim and I clinked glasses, and I was in.

What I was to learn was that this was not only a transformative moment in my own career, but also in the entire evolution of undercover tactics in British policing.

Up until now I had been operating completely ad hoc. I had a reputation for undercover work, so Jim Horner would get a call from some regional police force. He'd have a word with my DI, and off I'd go.

Now though, five forces had combined to create the grand-sounding East Midlands Special Operations Unit, or EMSOU (we pronounced it *M-Sue*). Undercover tactics were becoming professionalised.

Under the new system, if any force wanted to initiate an undercover operation they would have to clear it through EMSOU, who would allocate resources and monitor progress. This seemed like a positive step – undercover work is intensely invasive, and should only ever be used as a measure of last resort.

But the EMSOU revolution went far deeper. Thus far my deployments had primarily been short, sharp, in-and-out jobs. The new organisation promised a network of shared intelligence and planning between different agencies, allowing for far more complex and ambitious operations. Deployments would now last for months, instead of days or weeks.

Instead of focusing an operation on one specific target, we would now be given the time, support and equipment to go into an area and build our own picture of how criminal networks operated. This meant that when the bust came down we had the potential to generate hundreds of arrests, rather than just a handful. The EMSOU bosses made wild pronouncements about how we were the elite of British policing, and would receive the best equipment and tech support that money could buy.

But much more significant than any shiny new kit, the formation of EMSOU meant an entirely new operational command structure.

To preserve the anonymity of the undercover agents, and prevent leaks amidst the new sprawl of agencies, the identity of each undercover would now only be known by his DI, his DS and one other experienced cop, known as the Cover Officer. The Cover's job was not only to sort out logistics and act as a conduit between the undercover and the bosses, but also to act as the undercover's advocate, looking out for their interests if the brass started making unreasonable requests or ignoring potential hazards.

I could see the wisdom in all this. It was a good system – when it worked. But, while big organisations might enable ambitious missions, they also allow greater potential for atrophy and error. There would be many moments when I would come to long for the amateurish, making-it-up-as-we-went-along mentality of the early days.

The first briefing was a complete disaster.

Just as I was being officially introduced to Carl, the DI for my new squad, and Rajesh, my Cover Officer, there was a loud knock at the door. Without waiting for a reply, in walked Richard, the DI from the other squad, stationed across town.

'Ah, so this is the new boy then? Woods is it?' he jibed in what sounded like a deliberately affected cocky, laddish tone.

This was a concern. Under the EMSOU rules this guy shouldn't even have known where our squad's HQ was. And he definitely shouldn't have known my name, or seen my face. Wasn't the whole point of EMSOU to protect our identities? The system was still new and there were bound to be some teething problems while it bedded in, but I couldn't shake the feeling that the operation was falling apart before we'd even begun.

Jim shot me a *let's just get on with it* glance, and tried to continue. 'Yes gentlemen, this is Neil Woods. As we've had trouble penetrating the gang organisations in Leicester, Neil is going to take over some of our undercover work and see if he can bring his extensive experience to bear.'

He didn't get another word in before Richard interrupted, 'Well, I would like to point out that street crime in our sector has actually fallen.'

'Yes – thanks to Intel from *our* team on the ground,' Carl immediately snapped back.

I noticed Raj, who had been taking notes, drop his pen and roll his eyes. It only went downhill from there.

Over the course of the briefing it became painfully obvious to me what was going on. The two teams deployed on this operation weren't working together. In fact, it looked more like Carl and Richard had an obvious rivalry, and the two squads were actually working against each other. As far as I could tell, all the macho posturing was actually getting in the way of the investigation. No wonder this lot were making so little progress.

This didn't bode well at all.

Carl's squad had set up in Highfields, a rough part of central Leicester near the railway station, while Richard's team maintained their positions in the equally run-down peripheral estates of Beaumont Leys.

Highfields embodied the classic story of the post-industrial British provincial city. The area was constructed around endless rows of terraced Victorian red-brick houses, built for an urban workforce that no longer existed. As the middle classes had moved out to the suburbs after the Second World War, it had fallen into poverty, squalor and disrepair.

By the time I was deployed, Highfields was in the grip of a profound crisis. The estates were flooded with crack and heroin, and openly run by the gangsters, who enforced order among the largely Afro-Caribbean and South Asian communities through sheer terror and intimidation.

The previous year, the local council had attempted to regenerate the area by blocking off several streets and building shiny new playgrounds for the local kids.

Inevitably, the playgrounds were immediately turned into open-air drug markets, while the pedestrianised streets made it exponentially easier for the gangs to hide their activities from the police.

From my first in character walk-through round the Highfields terraces I could sense the palpable atmosphere of fear and menace. People would just stand outside their doorways, staring at me in my homeless junkie guise with utter contempt – then flit back inside as soon as one of the local gang members swaggered by. No one spoke. No one made eye contact. Very young teenagers, kids really, would sprint past me from playground to playground, obviously carrying messages or product for the older dealers. Highfields wasn't just a rough estate – it was occupied territory, completely controlled by the drug gangs.

One of the brighter sparks on our squad was a guy named Sammy. He could play guitar, and had had the initiative to start busking in the city centre to establish his cover identity. I started building my own cover story by playing a fellow beggar/busker and harmonising with him on Beatles songs outside the shopping centre where the local homeless guys congregated.

This was the perfect cover. It got our faces seen, and identified us as 'of the street', without us even having to volunteer any information. Besides, undercover narcs are hardly likely to be hanging around street corners doing 'Lucy in the Sky with Diamonds' in perfect two-part harmony. I was amazed at how much money people actually threw down. If only all that cash wasn't considered evidence for the investigation, Sammy and I could have been on to a decent little side-earner.

The busking gave me the perfect opportunity to make first contact with the local scene. As soon as we had £20 in the hat, I would snatch it up and shuffle over to the homeless guys to ask where we could score. People were only too happy to make a call in return for a scrape of gear from my bag.

But it was always them who made the score. I supplied the cash, but I was never allowed anywhere near a dealer. Any time I tried to get an introduction to an actual gangster I just hit a wall. All my techniques for working myself in towards dealers that had worked so well before now just met total refusal. Something had changed on the drug scene.

So, I worked on building a relationship with one homeless guy named Tommy. After we'd scored together quite a few times, I casually asked, 'Hey man, you reckon I could get your guy's number? You weren't about the other day when I needed something – and you know what it's like.'

Tommy gave a look of scathing disgust. 'Nah mate, we don't give no numbers.'

'All right mate, sorry. Was just asking, like.' I backed off, surprised at the anger in his response.

'Oi, you see Shakey over there?' Tommy cocked his head at one of the other beggars. 'You know how he lost his eye? He gave someone his dealer's number . . . the fucker took a screwdriver to his face.'

Shakey had a massive scar covering the entire right side of his face. He wore an eyepatch, and had earned his nickname because he was always trembling somewhere between heroin withdrawal and delirium tremens from the booze.

'You fucking serious?' I gave a horrified gasp.

'Yeah well there's fucking cops everywhere isn't there. They're all fucking plain-clothes now – you go giving someone's number out, next thing they're selling to some cop, and they're fucking busted. There's fucking rules now, innit?'

Then Tommy paused, his eyes narrowed. 'How long you been round here for anyway?'

I had fucked up. By asking for a dealer's number I had revealed I didn't know the rules. 'Ahh mate,' I stuttered, 'I'm just down from Matlock. Different vibe up there, innit – the countryside's a bit more chilled, y'know.'

Tommy just sniffed and nodded, but from that moment on there was an air of suspicion around him. Suddenly I was being kept at arm's length. This was a dead end. Tommy and his gang obviously operated by a new code. It would take a radically different approach to make contact with a dealer on my own.

It was about ten days in that I first spotted Digsy.

Sammy and I were busking our way towards £20, belting out 'I Shot The Sheriff' by Bob Marley – which I thought a good bit of gallows humour for a couple of undercover cops – when this new figure loped across the square.

He was wearing box-fresh Nike trainers and a dazzling silver tracksuit with one leg rolled up, as if he was in some LA gang movie. The look was completed by cropped hair, big gold rings and two studs in his left ear. He immediately set himself apart from the scruffy homeless dropouts lolling on the shopping centre steps. But it was more than just the clothes. He moved with swagger, a *fuck-you* scally confidence that lent him an edge of real danger.

One look at this guy and I could tell he was the real deal – a career dealer, not just some smackhead trying to finance his own habit. The way he dressed, the way he walked; everything about this guy screamed *gangster.*

But I hesitated before making an approach. Tommy's story about Shakey and the screwdriver was fresh in my mind. Gangsters weren't just letting strangers walk up to them and ask to buy drugs any more. This was a new era – the old tactics wouldn't cut it.

But I also knew that if I didn't start making progress, then this operation was dead on the ground. I needed to take a risk.

'All right mate, haven't seen you in ages.' I walked straight up to him with a big smile on my face.

Before he even had time to register that we had never met, I had lined myself up beside him as though we'd known each other for ever. 'How've you been, mate?'

For a split-second he threw me a skewed look – some deep centre in his brain must have registered that he had never laid eyes on me. But just as I was getting ready to be told to fuck off, or worse, he just sort of grinned and went, 'Yeah mate, all right?'

It's amazing what a big smile and just enough confidence can do. Even gangsters have the same social reactions as anyone else, if approached in the right way. You just have to be fast enough with your patter and not give them enough time to think.

'So…you still down with the Bs?' I pressed my advantage, using the Leicester slang I'd picked up (*B* for brown).

'Yeah – What you after? Just the one?'

I felt relief wash over me. He'd bought it. I suppose for drug dealers, after a while all homeless smackheads must start to look the same. But I still needed to know if this was just a scally with an attitude, or a real gangster who walked around with individually weighed and wrapped product.

'Actually mate, have you a got couple of point fours?'

Now it was his turn to pause. He looked me up and down, obviously doubting whether anyone as scruffy and downbeat as I looked could afford that sort of weight.

'That's fifty quid, yeah. You got it?'

'Yeah – no worries,' I shot back, patting my pocket, 'been a good day.'

He jerked his head for me to follow, and led me towards a phone box. He placed two cellophane wraps onto the little metal shelf next to the receiver, then came out and stood in the door, waiting for the money before allowing me in.

Before he split I managed to get his mobile number and arranged to call him a few days later. This was the key. One unrecorded buy would have been useless. I needed to score a few more times to establish trust before moving on to recorded deals. I even managed to wheedle a name out of him. His street nickname, Digsy, wasn't much to go on, but it was a start.

Digsy's wraps came back from the lab 80% pure. This was no street-level dope – it was gangster product.

Carl and the EMSOU brass were completely thrilled. I'd achieved more in a few days than the entire operation had in over a month. But not everyone seemed excited – Richard from the Beaumont Leys team wasn't happy that the Highfields squad was getting all the glory. I made a mental note to stay out of his way.

The next day, Jim and Carl briefed us that from my description of Digsy, along with his street name, Intel had identified him as a genuinely nasty gangster, suspected of a string of violent incidents and connected to mobs in Birmingham and Moss Side. He instantly became our number one target, and the entire team's highest priority.

I managed to score off Digsy a few more times over the next couple of weeks. But just as I was getting ready to try out one of EMSOU's new body cameras, he went cold. Suddenly all I got from him was, 'I'm lying low for a bit, mate. Call in a few days, yeah.'

I didn't know what he meant by 'lying low', and I didn't like it. Had I let something slip? Had he caught a rumour of undercover teams operating in Leicester? Was this just another example of dealers getting more and more paranoid? On the other hand, trouble had been kicking off between rival gangs in Leicester, and he could just as easily be genuinely keeping his head down out of fear of attack.

The EMSOU brass were furious. There was considerable pressure on me to keep calling him day after day. I had to patiently explain that after three or four rebuffs it would have looked unrealistic. Any real junkie would have found a new dealer within a day or two. I didn't forget Digsy though. It wouldn't be till the very end of the operation that our paths would cross again and I would finally bring him down.

I found these new developments deeply troubling. This operation just didn't feel right. There was a gnawing feeling of uncertainty that I couldn't put my finger on. In particular, the story Tommy had told me about Shakey getting mutilated by his dealer just for giving out a number kept playing and replaying in my mind.

It was just so extreme. I always went into undercover operations in the full knowledge that if I blew my cover, I could end up dead or in hospital. But I was a cop and they were gangsters – it was all in the game. To take out one of your own customer's eyes with a screwdriver just for handing out a phone number was an entirely different level of savagery. Over the eighteen months I'd been off chasing firearms as a detective, the rules of the undercover game had changed.

Something felt fundamentally wrong about the whole Leicester operation, but no matter how much I turned things over in my mind, I couldn't say what it was. From the moment I had set out on those streets there had been an unnameable sense of angst, which only intensified when Digsy suddenly went cold on me.

The day I officially told Carl and Raj that I wasn't calling Digsy again, I drove home in a deep funk. That evening I was on autopilot as I cooked the kids' dinner, put them to bed and did my utmost to avoid anything that could set Sam off on a rampage. Right now I just didn't think I could deal with that.

After everyone had gone to bed, I needed a little time on my own, so I slumped on the couch with a can of Heineken. Just wanting to switch my brain off, I started absent-mindedly flipping through the channels on the TV.

On Channel 4 there was some documentary on about the Cuban Missile Crisis and the Bay of Pigs disaster in the early 1960s. I sipped my beer vacantly as I watched black and white footage of Kennedy, Kissinger and Khrushchev pompously blabbing on about the potential nuclear annihilation of the human race.

That's when it hit me.

In one moment, I made a realisation that would force me to reconsider every basic principle on which I had based my life thus far. In one flash, my entire perception of my work, and what it meant, was completely transformed. After this, nothing would be the same.

People talk about the War on Drugs as if it was like the Second World War; one army against another – the dealers and the cops, the good guys and the bad guys, the defenders of society and the criminals. But that was bullshit. If the War on Drugs was a war at all, it was the Cold War. And, like the Cold War, it was a fucking arms race.

Suddenly I understood why EMSOU had been put together. It wasn't because our early undercover operations needed to do better; it was because we had done too well.

We had used undercover tactics to send a whole generation of criminals to prison. But for gangsters, prison is just graduate school. It's where they trade knowledge, streetcraft and intelligence. They'd figured our tactics out, and they were now responding in the only way available to them – by becoming more vicious and brutal.

Even in my last few undercover ops before CID, chasing down Alec and Kyle, I had noticed things getting tougher. But I had put that down to us going after higher-level crooks. Now I realised, our targets hadn't really changed; the criminals had just been learning.

There was no other way this dynamic could play out. The police could become smarter and develop new tactics, and the only response for the gangsters was to get ever more savage – to instil more fear in potential witnesses, to stab out the eyes of customers who gave out their number. People were getting mutilated not for being informants, but just on the off chance they may have given a phone number to the wrong person.

Just like the arms race between the Cold War superpowers, there was an inevitable, inexorable logic to this madness. There could only ever be more firepower, more missiles – or in this case, more police tactics, more brutality from the gangsters. But unlike the Cold War, we couldn't sign treaties with our enemies. There was no potential whatsoever for de-escalation. Things could only ever spiral in one direction, towards violence and mayhem.

I sipped my beer in horror as the black and white footage continued to flicker on the screen, and these thoughts chased each other pell-mell around my mind.

These revelations shook me in a profound, seismic way. But sitting there on my sofa I didn't know quite what to *do* with them. Perhaps I lacked the moral courage at that point to follow them through to their inevitable conclusion. Or perhaps I still defined myself through being a cop. I was still Neil who fought the good fight. I still had my mission, and I was going to complete it.

I got up quietly, so as not to wake Sam and the kids, drained the rest of my beer, and crept my way upstairs in the half-light to rest for the fight ahead.

With Digsy's trail gone cold, there was nothing left to do but hit the streets once more and see what scraps I could pick up.

This was how I met Ali.

I first spotted him while busking with Sammy. He was a *Big Issue* seller who walked on crutches and set his main pitch directly across from where we did our Beatles numbers. He had addict written all over him, but I could see something more there as well. He was of Asian origin, but had grown up in Glasgow and spoke with a lilting west coast Scottish accent that instantly put a smile on your face. But it was more than that. Ali had a real energy. He would engage with passers-by, calling them by name, remembering little details about their lives and even teasing and flirting a little. He had that uniquely Glaswegian gift of the gab, and the charm of a true salesman. Needless to say, he did a roaring trade in *Big Issues*.

I observed him for a few days, watching how other homeless people seemed to come to him for advice and help. In communities as harsh and intense as that of the inner-city homeless, there are often these characters, who are just that little bit smarter and more together, who come to act as elders for an entire street network. In Leicester, Ali was that guy. Of course, my first thought was that someone this plugged in could be just the link I needed to tap in to Leicester's criminal gangs.

I made my usual approach, shambling up and offering a bit of my score if he knew where to make the connection. Ali had obviously already scoped me busking. He recognised me as a fellow street hustler – a step above the other broken-down junkies on the street.

I waited as Ali hobbled down a side street on his crutches to do the buy, making sure not to ask for his dealer's number just yet. This was still a trust-building phase. I had a feeling Ali was the type who would introduce me carefully when the time was right.

He returned and invited me back to his squat to cook up. I was led through the back alleys of Highfields to the abandoned industrial park where he squatted.

I was struck by how clean and cosy Ali had managed to make the bleak, derelict factory space. He had the standard junkie mattress and sleeping bag set-up, but he also had his toothbrush and toothpaste neatly laid out by an old industrial sink, along with a kettle for tea and even a few pictures of his family Blu-tacked to the wall.

In the opposite corner another homeless man was passed out on a sleeping bag. I recognised this guy as one of the beggars I had spotted around town. Later I would learn that this was Billy, a long-term junkie who Ali had taken under his wing. Billy was a hopeless case. He didn't have Ali's patter, charm or organisation to sell the *Big Issue*, so he just begged and shoplifted. The way Ali looked out for this broken-down character was a really touching display of care and camaraderie.

Ali cooked up his shot. I spun a story that I was still cruising from my morning dose, and was going to save my part of the score for that evening when I'd be rattling. Ali accepted this as perfectly normal junkie logic. He slid the needle into his arm, pumped in the gear and leaned back in a warm junk haze.

After his initial rush had faded, I made us some tea and soon he was spilling his guts, telling me his whole story.

Ali had got involved in heroin in his late teens. In that era Glasgow was a city virtually synonymous with hard drugs, poverty and extreme violence. He had followed the depressingly standard path from casual use to addiction to minor dealing. Eventually his family kicked him out, and he had tried to get clean by moving down to London to escape his old life.

All things considered, it was probably the worst place he could have chosen. The mid to late 90s were a heroin boom-time in London, with Russian and Turkish mobs using the opening of the Eastern Bloc to rush in and flood the capitals of Europe with Afghan brown.

Within months Ali had fallen into debt to a nasty gang, and tried to work off what he owed as a mule and runner. But he wasn't any kind of career criminal, and didn't know the tricks of the trade. Before long he was busted holding £2,000 worth of smack.

The police offered Ali every opportunity to walk away from serious prison time in exchange for grassing up his criminal bosses. He didn't take any deal. He kept his mouth shut and did his three years like a soldier.

The moment he was released, he was scooped up by his old OCG. He assumed that having kept his silence, and done a stretch inside to protect them, they would help him find his feet on the outside.

No such luck.

The OCG explained to Ali that not only did he owe them for the £2,000 of heroin he'd been busted with, but the time inside counted as interest. The total was now £4,000.

When they realised that Ali really was penniless and couldn't pay, they took him to an old warehouse, tied him to a chair and poured acid over his knees.

Ali described how they'd stood in a semicircle watching him writhe as the acid burned its way through his kneecaps and tendons. Eventually they drove off, untying one of his hands so he could call an ambulance. But they made sure they waited long enough that he would never walk properly again.

That's how Ali ended up on his crutches. Even through the fug and glow of his opiate nod, I could see the pain flickering just below the surface as he spoke.

My mind immediately flashed back to my realisation on the sofa a few nights before. Once again, here was the arms race dynamic of the War on Drugs playing out. A few years earlier Ali would have been right to assume that keeping quiet would have earned him loyalty from his dealers. But the inexorable logic of the drugs war only leads one way: the police get smarter, so the criminals get nastier. Things can only ever go from bad to worse, from savagery to savagery.

Of course there was always the suspicion that Ali might be tweaking his story to gain sympathy. But working under-cover you learn to spot when someone is bending the truth, and I believed Ali was telling it straight. His voice started to crack and falter as he told me how he had tried to return to Scotland but had only got as far as Leicester, where he was now stuck.

'When I first got here – when I was at my lowest...before I found the *Big Issue*...I had nothing. I was rattling for a fix so bad that I snatched a woman's handbag. I–I–I tried to just grab it and run but I was on my crutches...I was trying to limp away, but she ran after me and started hitting me, so I just threw the bag at her and went as fast as I could.'

Ali paused before continuing, 'I never thought when I was a kid that I'd be the one who ended up snatching women's bags on the street...That was never meant to be me.'

This was devastating. Ali was so obviously a decent guy – a good soul trapped in a system that wouldn't offer the help he needed. Instead, he was injecting street heroin in a squat in Leicester, getting used by me for introductions to drug dealers.

I often think back to Ali. Over the months I knew him I was amazed at the way he chatted to people to make his *Big Issue* sales. It still depresses and enrages me that this guy, who had such brains, charm and sensitivity, ended up in the situation he did. If he had just been given a bit of support, instead of being turned into a criminal, there is no telling what a person like that might have achieved.

I left Ali's squat that day shaken, rubbing my temples and wondering how to find any sense or logic in what I was doing.

But I was still in Leicester with a job to do. I told myself it was exactly the people who had burned Ali's knees that I was trying to bring to justice. And over the next few months, Ali became an invaluable resource as I began to penetrate the criminal gangs that ran Highfields.

One of the perks of the new EMSOU long-deployment system was that I usually got the weekends off, so I was able to spend more time with the kids.

As a family, we entered a phase of relative calm and I almost began to feel like we were getting back on track. It had been so long since I had felt safe and confident at home that I was almost shocked at how unfamiliar these feelings had become. But, encouraged by this new sense of security, I decided to try and sort myself out and get healthy.

I had been smoking cigarettes since early on in my under-cover career. It was too good a prop for the job not to use. But now I was sick of it. I had a hacking cough and I hated being so reliant on this psychological crutch.

So, I quit. I threw away my last pack, suffered for a week, but willed myself through.

It was a pleasant surprise that I was able to stick to the decision, so I decided to see if I could improve my whole life-style. In my work I was constantly surrounded by addiction, toxicity and physical degradation. Few things focus the mind on one's health quite like a hepatitis-infected heroin addict offering you his needle to share.

So, I started running. The first day out I got about half a mile before collapsing in a phlegmy, spluttering heap, but I persisted, and it turns out that one actually does improve quickly with regular training. Before long I was going out for several miles at a stretch. One of Sam's friends from her teacher training course had a boyfriend who was into fell-running. He heard I was trying to get fit and invited me out onto the fells with him.

Within minutes of hitting the hills for the first time I knew I had found my new personal addiction. There was something about being able to disappear into the mountains that just hooked me. Off-road running demands a constant awareness of potential obstacles and changes in terrain; the steep climbs pushed the body and mind to their absolute limits. This was not only an escape from the feral underworld I worked in, but also from the situation at home. I could come back for the weekend, take the kids swimming in the morning, then head into the mountains to be on my own and run off the stress of the week.

This new feeling of strength and fitness was hugely liberating and empowering. But there was a catch. I began to get the sense that Sam didn't appreciate my newfound enthusiasm for healthy living. I started to notice how her expression would change as I laced up my shoes for a run. Things really went downhill when I tried to complement the exercise by cooking us healthier food. It seemed that every time I went out of my way to pick up really good ingredients or experiment with a new recipe the tension between us would return.

Sometimes I almost had to laugh – this all seemed like the exact reversal of every cliché of the grumpy husband berating his wife for not having his tea ready just how he liked it when he got home. But any possible humour in the situation evaporated very quickly. Once again we spiralled into a period of stress and hostility and it felt like our marriage was falling apart all over again.

A simple disagreement over a plate of pasta would find me once again at 6 a.m. splashing water on my face and staring at myself in the bathroom mirror as I once again prepared to go back out and face the Leicester gangs.

It was only once I was behind the wheel, heading back out to the streets that I felt the weight begin to slip away. When I was heading towards the job I could feel a sense of purpose, a sense of fighting for something meaningful and important.

I had been making progress. Carefully establishing trust with Ali over several weeks, I had slowly managed to make contact with a number of dealers, and eventually to start buying directly from them on my own. I was beginning to piece together an idea of how the gangs in the area were structured.

As the weeks turned into months it became all too easy to lose track of time. Addicts don't differentiate between days; their only measure of time is from one score to the next. I began to slip into what I called 'junkie time', each day blending into the next in a seemingly unending round of tense scores, grimy squats and furtive evidence drops.

But then, one evening at our HQ, I remember looking around and being amazed at the amount of information I had gathered. With EMSOU our operations had become much more slick and professional. There were huge whiteboards plastered with individual target photos, connected by coloured bits of string in a tangled web. It was like an FBI staging post in some Hollywood movie, if Hollywood detectives paused every twenty minutes to brew cups of Yorkshire Tea.

EMSOU streamlined and codified every aspect of the investigation. We were all handed official new evidence books to replace the haphazard note-taking of the old days. Setting down my every interaction on the street, recording the serial numbers of every banknote I used, and all the rest, was a slow and painstaking process.

The most genuinely irritating part of the new procedures was that printed on the first two pages of our EMSOU evidence books were the new rules of engagement for undercover officers. 'You will not wilfully endanger yourself or fellow officers; You will not act as an agent provocateur, etc'. Our commanding officer had to read these rules aloud to us before every single deployment; every day I had to listen to Carl or Raj drone through the procedure, despite the fact that I could recite every clause by heart. But with EMSOU, rules were rules.

But despite its kinks, the new system was paying off. We had gathered a genuinely impressive amount of info and intelligence on the Leicester drugs scene.

There were two competing, but somewhat interconnected mobs that seemed to rule the chaotic world of the Highfields estates. The first was a gang of Montserratians – definitely some of the strangest gangsters I ever encountered.

When the Montserrat volcano obliterated almost half the island in 1995, the UK, as the former colonial power, ended up taking in several thousand refugees. Many ended up in Highfields. A few were plugged into international drug smuggling in the Caribbean, and quickly realised the vast earning potential of their connections on the streets of Britain.

I was under no illusion: these were ruthless, exploitative, brutal criminals who ruled the estates through intimidation and violence. But they were also lively, charismatic and very charming. The gang spent most days sitting around one of the new council-built playgrounds, singing along to a guitar that they passed around, and all seemed able to play very well. It was extremely disconcerting. One minute they'd be singing this upbeat samba-influenced music, then in an instant the mood would change and they would viciously lash out. Music aside, the estates lived in terror of this gang and their reprisals.

The Montserratian patois was also outlandishly unique. They called heroin 'boom ting', but pronounced it 'boom tang'. So, heroin was *boom tang*, and crack was *zing tang*. After spending months cosying up to these guys, getting to know each member of the gang, I even started using that slang in police briefings, and got some very odd looks from the brass.

The rival mob was a more traditional local black British set-up, running crack and heroin into the estates, along with guns, gambling and protection rackets.

This lot were truly malignant. And they were shockingly young. Most drug gangs use young teenagers as messengers and runners, but with these guys some of the soldiers themselves were barely out of school. One of the ringleaders went by the street name JB. He couldn't have been much older than seventeen or eighteen, but there was already a deep, hardened violence in him.

Every time I managed to score off JB he would eyeball me in the nastiest, most unnecessarily threatening way, sometimes giving me a shove or slap, just to let me know who was the boss and who the low-down junkie.

I made good headway into both gangs, making buys, establishing familiarity and identifying the main dealers in each crew. More and more photos started going up on the EMSOU whiteboards. From tracing the serial numbers of the banknotes I painstakingly copied into my evidence book, we knew there was some level of trade between these gangs. But from our lab reports we worked out that they must be hooked into different drug-supply chains.

The next step was to get past the street-level dealers and discover where they were getting their product. But these crews were guarded. They had cottoned on to police tactics, and were ultra-careful not to let anyone they didn't absolutely trust get a glimpse higher up the food chain. It was the arms race at work.

So, I decided to strengthen my cover by bringing in Cate as a girlfriend character. Even the most ruthless criminals will read a human element into someone's relationship, a bit of personal drama they can relate to. If you can chat to them about trouble with your girl, they start seeing you as a human being rather than just another junkie.

Also, women are much less likely to be searched for recording equipment. Many gangsters have a latent chauvinism, assuming that a woman couldn't possibly be a real threat. We could use this to our advantage.

We turned ourselves into just another junkie couple trapped in a classic, mutually destructive addict relationship that neither one of us could leave. This is something every dealer has seen countless times, and it immediately established familiarity. Cate played the role perfectly, developing a wonderful twitchy eye, and erratic movements that perfectly captured the spasmodic, chicken-like motions of the smack and crack addict with a shot nervous system. Several weeks in, we were starting to build a rapport with the Montserratians. But we still needed something extra to win their trust.

Cate had the brainwave. We would stage me getting arrested. If a bunch of gangsters see you getting roughly bundled into a police van, not only do they not believe you could ever be a copper yourself, but it might even establish some empathy. It's something every dealer has gone through at some point.

So, on the appointed day Cate and I made our score in one of the playgrounds the Montserratians had taken over. Then, just as we had got far enough away that the gang wouldn't have to run, but close enough that they could definitely still see us, a police van screeched up. Out jumped four uniformed coppers from our squad. I was shoved roughly to the ground, then slammed up against the wall. The officers made a great show of finding the wrap of skag in my shoe and slapping on the handcuffs.

This is where Cate's talent for drama kicked in. Perfectly playing the part of the distraught junkie moll, she started wailing and screaming at the police officers.

'Just leave 'im alone. That's my man, you fuckin' bastards.'

I was totally flabbergasted. She was properly going for it, in floods of tears, with a real desperate screech in her voice. I already knew Cate was a good undercover, but this was Oscar-winning material.

'I love you Zack. I fucking love you,' she wailed as if this were a particularly dramatic moment on *EastEnders*.

Then she did something really unexpected. Pushing through the uniformed cops, she grabbed me and started snogging me right there.

Now, this was quite strange. Here I was wearing handcuffs, getting passionately kissed by a beautiful woman. I guess even busting crack dealers has its perks. The other cops, though, were completely agog, just watching as their two colleagues made out in front of the van. Eventually I had to give one of them a subtle kick – *come on, bloody arrest me, then*.

The arrest gambit worked like a charm. I left it about three days, then shuffled back to the playground, acting as sheepish and dejected as possible. The Montserratian guys even asked how things had gone with the cops, and showed some sympathy when I told them I'd been bailed, but had to check into the police station every two weeks.

It was about ten days later that I caught the big break.

I was dropped off at the usual point about a thirty-minute walk out of Highfields. That solitary walk in was always the time I used to clear my head and really *become* my down-and-out, vulnerable addict persona.

I wandered into the playground, but instead of the usual crowd there was just one guy, Jacko, slouching on a bench with a sullen expression.

'All right Jacko,' I said, sidling up, 'you got the whites?'

'Nah Zack,' he sighed back, 'ain't got nuttin' on me, man.'

Then he paused for a second, looking me up and down. I did my best to look as pathetic and unthreatening as possible, and for a split-second I almost thought I could see a grain of pity in his gaze. For that one moment, maybe I became a human being desperate for help, rather than just another grasping junkie rattling for a fix.

'Come on man – me tek you upstairs n' we get de zing tang. We go to Darren.'

This was it. My weeks of painstaking trust-building were paying off. I was finally clawing myself above the street and moving up the food chain.

Jacko led me out of the playground, down two streets and into the entrance of a run-down high-rise. I followed, ignoring the flickering of the broken strip-lights and the ammonia stink of urine as he buzzed the lift.

As we ascended, I saw Jacko's foot start to tap compulsively. His hands began to clench and unclench and he looked around nervously. Something was up.

He turned to me and started to say something, but then stopped and looked away. He tried again.

'You are all right, yeah?' he stuttered.

I realised in an instant what was going on. He was taking me up to see a high-ranking gangster, and had just started panicking that he didn't really know who I was.

'What d'you mean mate, I'm fine.' I assumed a tone of slight mystification.

'Yeah...all right. So, you're...you're good, yeah?'

The poor guy was really sweating it. I could see his mind turning somersaults as he raced through all our previous interactions, searching for evidence that I was anything other than a poor, but generally good-natured smack and crack addict. I almost felt bad for old Jacko; he was in a terrible position. But my overriding concern was making sure he didn't panic and back out of our mission.

'Yeah man, I'm fine. Just need a ting, mate. What are you on about?' I laughed, as if I genuinely assumed he was enquiring after my health. It's the game of misdirection and double-bluff that all undercover work is based on.

The elevator came to a halt and the doors slid open. Jacko was committed.

I followed him down another piss-stained walkway, then hung back as he knocked on a door, noting the flat number and scoping the hall for escape routes in case things got out of control.

The door opened a crack, and Jacko immediately launched into a flurry of the thickest West Indian patois I have ever heard. I had by now developed a decent ear for Caribbean dialects, but this exchange was so fast and convoluted I couldn't pick up a single word.

The meaning, however, was crystal-clear. Jacko was frantically trying to 'sell' me to this Darren character, to convince him that he knew me and I could be trusted. There was a tense, high-volume exchange before I was motioned forward.

I walked up to the door and locked eyes with Darren. He was a tall West Indian guy with long dreadlocks and a stare that went straight through you. One look at him and you knew this was not a man to cross. I played it as submissive and non-threatening as I could, casting my eyes down furtively – letting him know that he was in charge of the situation.

Darren said nothing. We just stood there looking at each other for about 15–20 seconds, which, when you're an undercover cop getting a death stare from a Yardie gangster, feels like an eternity.

Then, without a word, Darren thrust out his hand and handed me a rock of crack in a cellophane wrap. The second it was in my palm, the door slammed violently shut.

The moment I was out of Jacko's sight I rushed to a phone box and called in an evidence drop. We needed lab results on this, and we needed them fast.

That one rock of crack proved to be the key piece of evidence in breaking open one of the major drug rings in the Midlands. It's incredible how much we were able to figure out just by tying the lab analysis of that single £20 rock to one flat in a tower block.

It all came down to the chemical signature. The mid to late 1990s were a revolutionary time for crack production. Up until then producers had had to refine pure cocaine to make the stronger, smokable product. Then benzocaine hit the scene. Benzocaine is a local anaesthetic widely used by dentists. If you've ever had a filling and felt a disconcerting kind of numbness in your gums, chances are the dentist was using benzo.

What the drug cartels realised in the 90s was that not only does benzocaine produce a similar numbing effect to cocaine, making it the perfect cutting agent, but, crucially, it freebases at exactly the same temperature as pure coke. This meant that instead of producing crack with pure powder cocaine, then cutting it, dealers could now freebase already-adulterated coke, exponentially multiplying their profits.

The real masters of this process were always the South American and Caribbean OCGs. The European gangsters were way behind in the crack market.

When we got our lab results back on Darren's rock, they showed a unique chemical make-up with an extremely high density of benzocaine. This was far purer than anything I was getting from JB's crew, which was full of lidocaine, a far inferior and very carcinogenic cutting agent.

Using these results, we were able to separate out the Montserratian supply chain from where JB was getting his stuff. Through EMSOU we triangulated our results with intelligence from Interpol, who in turn contacted the American Drug Enforcement Administration.

The DEA results were stunning. The unique chemical signature of the rock I scored tied Darren to a major Jamaican drugs cartel that was running crack through the Caribbean and supplying a large section of the British market.

I scored off Darren several more times, just to make sure my first encounter hadn't been a fluke. All further lab tests confirmed our conjectures. Darren and the people he worked with were tied to a massive international smuggling operation.

Obviously, in my guise as a street junkie, I couldn't get any higher in the organisation than Darren himself. But after I identified the flat, another squad was able to undertake surveillance and put together a picture of how his crew operated. When the bust finally came down months later, it wasn't just Darren who had his door kicked in. Our lab results matched his product with a crack network stretching all over the country and even back to Jamaica and the US. It was a major operation involving multiple teams across the country, and resulting in hundreds of arrests. But it all came down to that one little £20 rock that I had managed to score.

The brass were overjoyed with our breakthrough and so was I. It felt good to finally be making leaps forward. But our elation was cut brutally short.

We were sitting waiting for our morning briefing when Jim Horner entered the room with a grim, stony look. He paused gravely, before saying the words that every undercover operative most dreads. 'It's my duty to inform you that one of our operations in Leeds has been compromised.'

He paused to steady himself before continuing.

'Our officer was identified by a powerful OCG, but was unaware that he had been discovered and went out on a routine drug buy. He was told to go to a certain payphone, then to another. They moved him from phone box to phone box until he was in an isolated industrial park. It was only then that he twigged there was something wrong. He panicked and tried to run. The targets chased him down some alleys, then they...there's no other way to say this – they beat the fuck out of him with baseball bats and left him for dead.'

There was an appalled silence in the room as we took in the mental image of one of our own being herded to a remote industrial estate, then chased down and battered. Once again, it was the drugs war arms race playing itself out: for every new police tactic like advanced undercover work, the gangsters needed to send a more savage message.

The Leeds officer spent months in hospital fitted into a wire brace. It was a stark reminder that the guys we were hunting weren't charming playground guitarists, but calculating, brutal gangsters who would maim or kill anyone who got in their way.

It also had implications for our own operation. Leeds wasn't exactly close by, but it was close enough to assume that OCGs from there had some contact with the crews we were tracking.

And things were now beginning to spin out of control on our own turf as well. We had two independent teams in place, each led by competing DIs pushing for higher numbers. There were simply too many undercovers, making too many buys, from too many different dealers. Inevitably, the gangsters were starting to catch on.

It was a matter of criminal psychology and basic arithmetic. A junkie's only concern is maintaining a steady supply of dope. If they have a reliable dealer, they will keep going to that one guy until he gets arrested or killed. Our squads were being pushed to score off one dealer in the morning, then another that same evening. This generated more evidence for their DS, but it was totally inconsistent with realistic addict behaviour. The dealers in Leicester weren't stupid. They observed our patterns, and shared info the same way EMSOU did between enforcement agencies. Things were starting to get frightening.

I noticed it most with JB and his crew. I remember once walking down a narrow alley between two council blocks when JB skidded around to block my way with his bike. 'Why you ain't been to see me, man? Why you buying off those other twats?'

I froze on the spot. I could tell he was suspicious, and for a kid who still did his heroin deals on a pedal-bike, JB was a mean, hyper-aggressive little bastard. He'd kick your head in as soon as look at you. I had to be careful how to play this.

'Well mate...that last rock you gave me was all right but, y'know, I've got to go where the really good stuff is, man.'

It was a gamble. By insulting the quality of his gear, I risked getting a smack. But I did have one advantage. I had seen the lab results. When I said his product wasn't anywhere near as good as what the West Indian guys were pushing, I was right. And I knew that he knew I was right.

JB just kissed his teeth in contempt, then moved his bike a fraction of an inch so I had to squeeze by while he stared me down and spat on the ground.

Back at HQ I worried that we were rushing things – building trust with ruthless career criminals takes time and patience. I talked to Carl and he responded with some platitudes about the need to move the whole operation forward, but I couldn't help feeling that he was more concerned with the idea of the Beaumont Leys squad achieving better results.

I appealed to my Cover Officer, Rajesh, for some backup. This was the guy whose sole job it was to protect my interests. But despite the fact he was a skilful Level 1 undercover himself, he seemed reluctant to step out of line.

The Beaumont Leys team seemed to be operating in a similar way. There appeared to be an urgency to do more and more, instead of better and better. It was always going to end badly.

In a way, I'm glad it was me who ended up bearing the brunt of the resulting crisis. If it had been one of the less experienced members of the team, it all could have ended so much worse.

Cate and I were making our usual walk into Highfields to buy a twenty-bag of smack off one of JB's crew. We had a place and time set, but as we approached, he was nowhere to be seen. In fact, the whole area was weirdly empty. None of the usual faces were about. Street after vacant street seemed beset by an eerie calm.

The silence was broken by the tinny ring of my cheap, early-model mobile phone. I recognised our dealer's number and picked up.

'Yeah mate. Come down Abney Street.' The phone went dead.

Cate and I reversed our direction and headed towards Abney Street. Just as we got there the phone rang again.

'Mate – had to move. Come up Dore Road, yeah.'

Once again we changed course and followed the instructions. And once again the phone pinged to life.

'Nah bruv. Walk up Hazelwood Road – nah nah, not that, I mean, come up Rowsley Avenue, yeah Rowsley Avenue.'

This was not right. Something was very off. Visions of that undercover cop in Leeds getting herded and battered flashed through my mind. But if we cut and run now, our entire cover would be blown. There was only one thing to do – hold our nerve.

We were directed from one street to the next, doubling back on ourselves, taking routes that made no sense whatsoever.

Finally we found ourselves walking up Gwendolen Road, usually bustling; today it was completely deserted. The silence hung heavy in the air. A car came out of nowhere, slowed down to a crawl as it passed, obviously scoping us out, then sped off.

I could feel Cate, who was as tough and resilient as they come, starting to get panicky beside me. Under her breath she whispered, 'Neil, what the fuck are we going to do?'

The truth is I had no idea. But I did know the one thing we couldn't do. We couldn't run. That's what had doomed the cop in Leeds. He had panicked and tried to escape – he had abandoned his cover story. And in undercover policing, your story is all you ever have.

'Just front it out,' I whispered, 'no matter what they do, no matter what they say, don't break character. Just front it.'

Turning a corner into one of the council's recently blocked off through-roads, we were immediately faced with a gang of seven well-known Highfields gangsters leaning against a wall.

My eyes flicked from one side of the alley to the other, looking for possible escape routes and trying to assess the situation. This group was made up of people from two different gangs – the only reason they would be cooperating like this was if they had put their heads together and picked us out as potential narcs. I could see JB at the end of the line, furthest from me, shifting from one foot to the other with nervous, belligerent energy.

But somehow, a little voice in my head told me to stay calm. If these guys had known we were cops, then we would have been battered into a bloody mess long ago. The only answer must be that they had suspicions, but hadn't yet made up their minds. This was an investigation, not an execution. Everything depended on our reactions, on how well we could hold our grit and remain in character.

The dealer I was originally meant to score from was closest. My eyes locked with his, and he jerked his head down to the ledge next to him. Lying there was the wrap of heroin I had been after. But there was something wrong. One look and I could tell it was fake. Wraps of crack and heroin come in sealed plastic, so that dealers can carry them in their mouths and swallow them if they get stopped. This wasn't plastic-wrapped, just twisted in a scrap of paper.

My mind spun into overdrive. This must be the test. They're looking at how I react to this fake bag of gear. For a moment my mind went completely blank. Cate and my safety, perhaps our lives, depended entirely on my reaction to this trial.

The only problem was, I had no idea what the correct reaction should be.

Should I kick up a fuss, and demand real gear? Should I try to curry favour, and come on extra-obsequious in that way addicts do when they need a score or think they're in trouble? All this flashed through my head in a single second. I could feel the gangs' eyes burning a hole straight through me.

Then from nowhere, I had it. If I didn't know the answer they were looking for, I would give them no answer at all.

I would deny them any useful information from my words or body language. If I couldn't satisfy their paranoia, at least I might be able to confuse them enough to let us walk away.

I dropped my gaze to the ground to hide any involuntary twitch or flicker of my eye. Making the absolute minimum movements necessary, I set down £20 on the ledge next to the dealer's right hand, and swiped the little paper wrap with my own.

We started to walk away, setting our pace as slow as possible. Everything depended on keeping up the appearance that, in *our* minds, everything was absolutely normal. The atmosphere was charged with such an oppressive, knife-edge tension that it took measures of discipline that I never knew I had not to panic and sprint off. I could feel Cate almost vibrating with nerves beside me.

Then I heard the shouts.

'Yeah, and don't you fucking come back here. You come round here again, you're dead – you're fucking dead!'

Just keep walking, Neil, just keep walking, I told myself over and over, the sweat beginning to bead on my skin and run down my backbone.

Then JB's voice rang out. 'Yeah, actually come back here. Fucking get back here a minute.'

This was it. There were seven of them against myself and Cate. I tensed to run.

Then Cate saved the day. She spun towards me and said, 'Just leave it Zack, it's not bloody worth it, yeah – just leave it.'

I don't know where she got that, but it was inspired. It was perfectly in character, and could have come out of any scene of street aggro in Britain – the girl telling her fella to 'just leave it'. It also gave her the perfect excuse to grab my hand and pull me away. I didn't look back.

Cate and I made our way back through town, both seriously shaken. All we could imagine was some other undercover team being sat down by their own DS and briefed about two operatives in Leicester who had blown their cover and been beaten into a broken mess.

We made it back to HQ and, backed up by Cate, I announced that this operation was over. The brass threw a little tantrum, but we brooked no argument. We were the ones risking our lives on the street while they sat in their offices worrying over stats. And when we described the scene we had just been through, even they had to admit that things had become too hot.

In my opinion it was the bosses who were at fault. They had pushed too hard. If they had shown a little more patience, and a little more willingness to listen to the people in the field, we could have kept that operation going a lot longer.

As it was, I had been deployed in Leicester for several months and was more than happy to see the back of Highfields. And, as I looked around at all the whiteboards set-up around EMSOU HQ, with their interconnected photographs and Intel notes, I did feel a real sense of pride. Out on the street, I hadn't realised exactly how much ground we had covered. I was certain that as we moved into the arrest phase, we could take down a lot of really nasty characters.

But there was still one last piece of unfinished business to be taken care of before I wrapped things up in Leicester. Digsy.

Carl called me into the briefing room for a sit-down with Jim Horner. They explained that the bosses at EMSOU were amazed at what we had achieved, and that Cate and I would both be receiving Chief Constable's Commendations. We had gathered enough evidence to directly charge OCGs operating right across the country. There was one target remaining, however, that had the potential to unlock a slew of other ongoing investigations.

Carl pointed up at one of the whiteboards. There was Digsy's picture, with a network of strings spidering out, linking him to OCGs from Glasgow to Manchester to London. Through intelligence sharing with other agencies, Digsy had been connected to several high-level investigations. The brass believed that if we could lay a serious charge on him, then he could potentially be flipped, become an informant and give us the dirt on a lot of very major-league gangsters.

'I totally see all that,' I replied, 'and when I first met him, Digsy actually seemed reckless in that he was willing to sell to me on the street. But since then he's just refused to come out. I've tried repeatedly, but he's lying low.'

'Look Neil,' Carl cut in, 'we know Digsy has withdrawn from active dealing lately, but is there anything – anything at all – you can think of that we could use to draw him out?'

I thought hard. I was more than a little tired of this operation, and looking forward to putting Leicester behind me. But I took Carl and Jim's point. If there were any way to turn Digsy into an intelligence asset to lead us on to bigger fish, then we should certainly take it. But how? If he was refusing to even sell me a single bag of smack, what was I meant to do? Coming on overly persistent would just arouse his suspicions – this town was already rife with rumours of undercover operations.

But I couldn't resist the challenge. This seemed an impossible nut to crack, and in those days I found that irresistible. So I cast my mind back, taking apart every interaction with Digsy in forensic detail. What made him tick? What could I use? Where was that little flaw that I could exploit?

I turned to Jim Horner.

'Do you know anyone at Customs?'

'I beg your pardon?' he responded.

'Do you know anyone at Customs and Excise? Can you make a call?'

'Look,' I responded to his expression of utter incomprehension, 'I first picked Digsy out of the crowd because he was wearing a shiny new tracksuit. Every time I've seen him, he's been wearing flash, expensive clothes. His thing is style, right?'

'So...we find someone at Customs who can give us some fancy clothes from their Seized Property locker. If Digsy won't come out to sell me drugs, I think I can tempt him with some flash "stolen" clobber.'

So, a call was made and a few days later a box of Stone Island bomber jackets was dropped off at HQ. Someone had once tried to smuggle these into the UK; now they were going to be used to catch a gangster.

'All right Digsy, it's Zack. Listen mate, I've just got a load of Stone Island jackets – off the back of a truck, like. Real good stuff man – thought you might be interested.'

Even I was surprised at how enthusiastically Digsy jumped at it. We agreed to meet the next night in a Burger King car park near the Leicester Ring Road.

We had one day to formulate our plan and run through every possible scenario. The first thing we did was put in an order for the 'flash' EMSOU tech apparatus that everyone had made so much fuss about.

It was laughable. There was an audio and video recording device the size of a brick, meant to go in my trouser pocket, with a wire running up to a camera poorly disguised as a button on my jacket. The button looked about as real as Michael Jackson's nose, and I thanked God that baggy rave trousers were still acceptable fashion in Leicester, otherwise that brick would be visible a mile off. All it would take was one pat-down, one close inspection or accidental contact, and I was a dead man.

I had a real moment of internal crisis about this. Digsy wasn't some scatty, desperate user-dealer. He was an experienced streetwise career criminal with a history of violence who was already paranoid about sticking his head above the parapet.

I came within a hair's breadth of walking out on the whole operation. But, once again, I'd come this far and I needed to finish the job.

Then, Cate burst in. 'Boss, we've got a problem. The Beaumont Leys team have just moved into their arrest phase.'

Jim Horner slammed his fist down on the table in rage. Richard's team in Beaumont Leys had been advised that we had one more ongoing enquiry. Unless an emergency arose, they were to wait for our word before starting to make arrests. But I knew the rivalry that underpinned this operation. It was no surprise to me that some kind of 'emergency' had presented itself. His squad had started kicking in doors the day before.

This was too much for me. With people getting busted in Beaumont Leys, word would be spreading like wildfire. Any gangster nursing suspicions about undercover operatives had just had them spectacularly confirmed. If Digsy had been paranoid before, now he would be manic. And I was meant to meet him in some car park, strapped up with this ludicrously antiquated recording equipment?

'I'm not doing it,' I announced. 'No way. They've fucked it.'

But Carl and Jim had an operation to wrap up. 'Neil, we've got everything organised. All we need is this one last piece of evidence. These people are responsible for murders, for rapes – and you can take them down, right here, right now.'

They appealed to my sense of honour, to that inner need to get the job done. They knew that if I walked away, some part of me would always feel that Digsy had won. I can't blame them, looking back; they were just doing their job. But it was me who had to actually go out on the streets and face the danger.

This is exactly the point where, under the EMSOU concept, Rajesh could have stepped in. The Cover Officer's job is to protect an undercover not only from their superiors, but also from themselves. But this operation had become like a boulder rolling down a mountain, sweeping every one of us along with it.

The car park was deserted when I turned up half an hour early, clutching my box of 'stolen' jackets. I did a careful circuit, checking for escape routes. We were isolated, but I could see signs leading out to a pedestrian underpass, and the lights of the ring road twinkling in the distance.

As I was taking a mental note of all this, I heard the revving of an engine. Digsy pulled up in a four-door Audi. He wasn't alone. In the car with him were two other men. Even though both were sitting, I could see at a glance that these guys were built like brick shithouses, with shaved heads and proper *don't fuck about* grimaces. I took a deep breath.

'All right mate,' shouted Digsy, swinging open the car door, obviously a little high himself, 'let's see these jackets then.'

I handed Digsy one of the bomber jackets, and was quite pleased that I had been able to guess his size from memory.

'Yeah man – this is ace,' he exclaimed, 'I'll give you two bags for that – your usual, yeah?'

He reached into his pocket and pulled out two perfectly wrapped and sealed baggies of heroin. As he handed them over, he added, 'You aren't looking for anything else, are you?'

I did a quick risk calculation in my head. I had Digsy handing over heroin on camera and wanted to get out of there, but I also thought that if he was offering crack, I might as well get him on the hook for that as well.

'Well mate, if you've got any white, I'll take a bag of that too, yeah.'

Without a word, Digsy walked round, opened the boot of his car and lifted out the biggest block of crack I'd ever seen. This was several ounces in one huge brick – a serious load to be driving around with in the Leicester estates. No wonder he had his bodyguards with him. Digsy pulled out a large butterfly knife, flipped it open and started chiselling off a little corner.

As he did so one of the bruisers from the car got out and approached me. Christ – I hadn't clocked quite how massive these guys really were. 'How long you known Digsy, then?' he demanded.

'Ages man, ages,' I improvised in a hurry, 'how long's it been, Digs?'

Digsy was still fiddling with his brick of crack, and absently muttered, 'Yeah, ages mate.'

Then everything went to shit.

I was keeping my eyes low, trying to avoid the huge guy's gaze. But I was tracking his every move.

I watched with horror as his eyes scanned over me – and locked on the camera-button on my jacket. His eyes widened in recognition. I felt my own breath involuntarily catch. Our eyes locked. There was a split-second of silent, invisible communication.

Then he grabbed my chest and slammed me against a thick concrete pillar, knocking the wind completely out of me.

'Fucking hell,' the guy shouted, 'he fucking is as well. He's fucking Five-O! He's fucking Five-O. Digsy man, he's the fucking heat.'

I was pinned against the pillar, struggling to get my breath back as the guy grabbed my jacket, staring straight at the camera-button.

For one of the few times in my career I genuinely panicked. Usually I was able to maintain a cool head and think my way out of situations. Now, trapped against the concrete, I went into pure flight-or-fight mode. And with the guy's elbows pressing into my chest, flight wasn't exactly an option.

Physically I stood no chance – this monster could have broken me in half. My only hope was to come on so aggressive that he might think I was actually crazy.

'What the fucking hell are you on about?' I yelled straight into his face. 'You fucking calling me Five-O? You fucking picking at my clothes? Who the fuck are you, mate? Who the fuck do you think you are? Digsy – your mate's a fucking dick.'

I unleashed a torrent of abuse, slipping into hyper-aggressive northern invective. The guy seemed genuinely taken aback. For a split-second he relaxed his grip. I immediately twisted out and put some space between us. I could see him hesitate, reading his thoughts as he considered whether he might have actually got it wrong. I used the moment to steady myself.

'You know what,' I declared, 'I don't need this shit. Calling me fucking Five-O...seriously, fuck this.'

I bent down and picked up the remaining jackets, moving as calmly and purposely as possible. I had to be seen to be storming off, not running away in a panic.

I stalked off with the jackets under my arm, acutely conscious of the weight of the recording equipment in my pocket. The giant bruiser seemed confused enough to let me walk off, but I knew that if he came after me and bothered with even the most cursory pat-down, then I probably wouldn't make it out of that car park alive. I kept my eyes forward, my heart pounding in my chest.

Then I heard the steps behind me. It was unmistakable – someone was running after me. I clenched my fist. Maybe, just maybe, if I threw one hard punch I could buy myself enough time to sprint away. I tensed and spun round.

And there was Digsy, jogging up with a shit-eating apologetic grin on his face.

'Mate, mate. Really sorry – that guy's just a dick. Don't mind him. Here, I've got your ting.'

He held out a generously proportioned rock of crack, crudely wrapped in a king-size Rizla. This was too much. All I could think was, *you have to be kidding me*. It was all I could do not to burst into laughter. I grabbed the rock and handed him £20, all perfectly framed and captured on camera.

'Yeah, all right mate, no worries,' I heard myself saying as if in a dream, 'he is a bit of a dick though – anyways, see you later.'

Once again I walked off, desperately forcing myself to keep an even pace. There was about thirty metres to go, then I would be out of their line of sight and could get the hell out of there.

I heard voices shouting behind me. A heated argument. I had no idea what was happening, but I could hear Digsy's voice, and that of the hard-man who had thrown me against the pillar. My heart rate started increasing again. *Just keep walking, Zack, just keep walking*, I kept telling myself over and over – referring to myself by my cover name to stay in character.

Still listening to the raised voices, I eyeballed the distance to the exit. Eighteen metres...seventeen metres. I could see the lights of the ring road in the distance.

Then I heard the screeching of tyres. I snapped my head back round, only to see Digsy's Audi speeding straight towards me. There was no question – they were trying to run me down.

You can't talk down the front bumper of a speeding car. There is no 'fronting it out', no psychological weakness to be played on. Staying in character couldn't save me this time. My character was broken. I ran.

I sprinted towards the exit. The car was gaining on me fast. Over that distance I had no chance. The roar of the engine was pounding in my ears.

I could see the metal barrier getting closer, but I knew from my earlier reconnaissance that beyond it was a ten-metre drop. If I jumped I would break both my legs and be a sitting duck for Digsy's henchmen.

The car was almost on me. I clenched my teeth and ran from nothing but sheer terror.

Then, just as I could almost feel the heat of the engine on my back, I swerved right, onto the pavement, and sprinted down a slope alongside the barrier.

Digsy's car swerved as well, the tyres screeching. I have no idea how they didn't go straight over the barrier themselves. Now they were actually driving on the pavement, chasing me as I ran.

By making them swerve, I had bought myself a precious two metres. The car's engine roared and once again they were bearing down on me. But I could see over my left shoulder that the slope was taking me down; in a few more steps I'd be able to leap over the barrier – while they would have to continue following the pavement round to the right. But could I even make it?

I dug deeper than I knew I had, calling up every last atom of strength from my fell-running. I was hurtling down the slope, but the car was right behind me. Then, just as I could see my own shadow in the headlights stretch out in front of me, I hurled myself left, over the barrier.

I felt the rush and suck of the backdraught as Digsy's Audi raced through where I had been running less than a second before. Then I landed with a crash on my left shoulder and rolled to cushion the blow. I heard the car screech to a halt, the doors slam and Digsy's voice screaming obscenities. But by then I was gone, sprinting off towards the ring road and the safety of the crowds.

I shakily limped back to town and put in a call for pick-up. Then I collapsed against a wall and just crouched there with my head in my hands.

It was only then that I realised I was still holding the bag with the leftover Stone Island jackets. I hadn't lost a single one. They were important evidence, and I still remember the satisfaction I felt when they were produced in court months later.

But this time when I got back to HQ and declared the operation over, I meant it. I could still hear the roar of that car engine and feel the heat on my back. The dysfunction at the heart of this assignment had just become too much to take.

This feeling was not helped when, during our debrief with our intelligence officer, he breezily dropped into the conversation, 'Well, I don't know why they didn't just shoot you. We've just run the licence number for that car, and the intelligence indicates they were definitely carrying a gun.'

It turned out that the huge guy who had held me against the pillar was already on bail for murder. A few months later he would go on to stab someone to death over a gangland rivalry, and get sent down for a very long time.

With any job of this intensity and duration there was always going to be a period of mopping up. I spent several months shooting back and forth from Leicester, compiling evidence, giving statements and testifying in court.

There would have been some satisfaction in facing all the characters I'd encountered as a vulnerable junkie, but now being able to stare them down from the witness stand. But of course, with gangsters like this, I had to give my evidence from behind a screen for fear of reprisals.

Darren's trial, in particular, stood out. He turned out to be an especially vile character, involved in very brutal violence. He got nine years and deserved every minute of it. But through that one little rock of crack he'd sold me, we busted into a major international West Indian cartel. This led to dozens more high-profile arrests, actually putting a tiny and very temporary dent in the crack and heroin supply to the Midlands and north of England.

But with the drugs trade, one very quickly learns that taking out one OCG just leaves a vacuum to be instantly filled by another, or even more worryingly, a power struggle between several competing gangs.

Digsy's trial was also interesting. He got three and a half years. I'll never know whether or not the prosecutors managed to get him to flip and pass them information for a reduced sentence. One thing I do know is that he was only charged with drugs offences, and not for trying to murder me with his car.

Someone at EMSOU later told me that the bosses were very pleased that this charge had been dropped, as it meant the footage was kept out of the public domain. It was thought that if any cop ever saw it, no one would ever sign up for undercover work again.

But during this period I was also going through a trial of my own. Till now I had been unconsciously holding on to the hope that I might be able to salvage my relationship with Sam – or at least make it amicable enough to be able to share the same house. But now the pressure of hiding my feelings was wearing me down, and worse, I couldn't help but feel it was having an effect on the kids. Sometimes I would catch a glimpse of sadness in their eyes that chilled me to the core. It deeply pained me to think that our unhappiness might be damaging them as well.

After months of shuttling between my undercover life as a junkie on the streets of Leicester, and the constant fear of upsets at home, I was exhausted. I had no more fight in me. This wasn't the day-to-day tiredness of a missed night's sleep, but an enduring, profound weariness that sat deep in my bones. I had been ground down. But once again, what was there to do? I said nothing, and kept my head down – throwing every ounce of energy I had into wrapping up the Leicester case.

Back at work, however, I did find the energy to make a stand.

I had just given my final piece of evidence against Digsy, and was having a beer with Jamie, our tech guy on the case, as we cleared the HQ. As the conversation progressed, he giggled. 'Yeah, I can't believe they sent you out with that old brick recording equipment... especially when they've got that amazing FBI gear just locked away.'

'What are you on about?' I asked, assuming he was joking.

'Yeah – they've got all this state-of-the-art kit they ordered from America but it's all under lock and key. And they sent you out with that clapped-out old rubbish.' He slapped me on the shoulder and started laughing hysterically.

'Wait a second, you're not fucking serious, are you? Tell me you're fucking joking.'

'I'm totally serious! Come on, I'll show you.'

Jamie led me back to our tech room and opened one of the lockers. He pulled out a tiny, sleek black rectangle, about the size of one of those business card holders from old-fashioned movies.

'See that – that'll record any sound in a twenty-five-metre radius, perfect quality. Here's the camera for it.' He held up a wire. Nothing more – just a wire. It was basically invisible.

Jamie thought I would be impressed, but I was raging. I managed to control myself in the moment, but at our final EMSOU debrief a few days later, it all came flooding out.

'You sent me out on operations that we knew were compromised – using a massive fucking brick of a recording device. And now it's come to my attention that the whole time EMSOU had top-shelf, FBI gear just lying around!'

The head of EMSOU gave a start. I was obviously not meant to know about this.

'Yes, well…we do have some more advanced gear from America,' he stammered, 'but…umm…we are about to deploy that for our Level 1 operatives, and in the meantime it is…uhh…operationally essential that the existence of this equipment remains secret.'

'Operationally essential? What the fucking hell are you talking about!' I shouted back. 'You directly put my life – and the lives of my fellow officers – at risk, in order to keep some kit secret? You must be fucking joking.'

'Well, Neil,' he faltered, 'it's...umm, it's a matter of strategic policy. Of course, we all very much appreciate – and
admire – the excellent work you've done on this case.' He did
at least look embarrassed.

'Well,' I spat, 'if you think you're getting any more excellent, admirable work out of me with shit gear – while you're
letting the best kit in the world gather dust...you can go fuck
yourself.'

I heard myself say it, and even I was shocked. I'd just told
the highest-ranking officer I'd ever met to go fuck himself.
But I couldn't help it. The last six months of tension, paranoia
and leading my double-life had just come pouring out. For a
split-second it hadn't been Neil the cop talking, it had been
Zack the street junkie crack addict.

But I meant it. When that car had been inches away from
the backs of my legs, I had genuinely thought I was about to
die. I had put my life on the line to bring down this target,
and all that danger could have been avoided simply by letting
me use some kit we already had.

I took a look around at the open-hanging mouths of my
colleagues. Then I pushed back my chair and strode out of the
room, slamming the door behind me.

As I walked away, I told myself that this was it – that I
was through with undercover ops. I would go back to 'normal'
detective work, and live a quiet life.

I filed a formal report and a long and detailed internal
debate ensued. The decision had been made based on a
larger safety consideration, the bosses said. Level 2 operatives were more likely to be searched and the surveillance
equipment discovered. The existence of this kit becoming

common knowledge would endanger Level 1 and Level 2s. To my mind it was being sent out with outdated boxy equipment that led to us being searched in the first place – their argument made no sense to me.

But EMSOU stood by their policy and I stood by my vow to walk away from undercover. Only the powers that be on the force knew me better than I knew myself. When they needed me again, they knew exactly which buttons to push to talk me round.

And it wasn't long before they came to me with the Nottingham job.

CHAPTER 12

NOTTINGHAM

They called it Shottingham.

The city was in crisis, racked with murder, street crime, drugs and gang warfare. The endemic violence, particularly gun crime, had spiralled to the point where Nottingham University was reporting falling applications and local businesses were finding it impossible to attract investment. In desperation, the politicians put massive pressure on the police to save their town.

Most of the chaos could be traced back to one man. Colin Gunn was a 6'4" skinhead bodybuilder, who had risen through the criminal ranks through sheer viciousness and brutality. He and his brother David ran the so-called 'Bestwood Cartel', seizing control of the city through a bloody war against some the hardest Yardie gangs in the country. Now they maintained their empire in the same way they had won it: with blood, bullets and beatings.

The Bestwood estate itself was completely under the Gunns' control, and virtually off-limits to the police. The cartel operated almost as a shadow government, enforcing an absolute code of *omertà* over the estate. If you had a problem or dispute, you went to Colin Gunn. Anyone who talked to the police would be beaten or shot, and possibly their families along with them.

Colin Gunn himself was a monster, capable of almost psychopathic violence. His favourite cocktail of drugs was a mix of cocaine and steroids, which is not exactly conducive to a balanced approach to life.

When a rival dealer was arrested after shooting one of Gunn's crew, the police placed the shooter in solitary confinement so that Gunn couldn't organise a prison murder in revenge. Gunn paid British Telecom engineers to find out where the guy's parents lived, sent his people to the seaside bungalow where they had retired and executed the two pensioners with sawn-off shotguns. When Gunn suspected one of his own lieutenants of disloyalty, he nailed the guy's hand to a bench, doused him in gasoline and flicked matches at him till he confessed. That was how Gunn ran his own crew, and the atmosphere of violence, intimidation and terror filtered down to infect the entire city.

But, as ever, the entire criminal empire was founded on drugs. Only the narcotics trade can generate that kind of money; no other branch of criminality comes anywhere close. So, that is where the police intended to strike.

That meant a reconciliation with EMSOU.

After Leicester, I had sworn that I was through with undercover work. Not only did I feel betrayed by them sending me out with dodgy kit, but I had begun to question the entire logic of the drugs war itself. In any case, after telling the head of EMSOU to go fuck himself, I thought they might be through with me as well.

But Jim Horner had other ideas. He sat me down, explained the urgency of the situation and proposed that, if I were willing to undertake the mission, then he would make things right with EMSOU.

At first I didn't want to know. I told Jim I'd meant what I said. I wasn't going out with substandard gear, and fuck them for asking me. Jim assured me that if I took on this assignment he would do everything in his power to ensure I received the support I needed. But even so, I was reluctant. I had seen how the War on Drugs functioned, and I wasn't sure I wanted to be part of that arms race any more. I had joined the force in order to fight the good fight, but I was beginning to doubt whether this battle was being fought in the right way, or was one we should even be fighting at all.

But Jim was smart. 'Neil, we need you. This situation is desperate and you're the only person in the country with the experience to do this job right. We have the support team in place and another undercover lined up as a partner.'

Then, ever the showman, Jim paused for effect before sighing and saying, 'I mean, I suppose if you really won't do it, we could try sending Jackie out on her own? She is very good – even if she is quite new to undercover ops.'

There it was: the covert police officer's talent for manipulation. Of course Jim knew that by threatening to send a woman out on her own, that he would trigger my self-image as a chivalrous, honour-bound protector figure. What can I say? Maybe it was silly, overly romantic and ego-driven, but I was a sucker for all that. And Jim knew it.

He laid it on thick and wore me down. There was a meeting with EMSOU and peace was made. We were going to do our small bit to try to save a city.

Jim introduced me to the team. Within seconds I could tell that these guys were real police.

The DI, Patrick Denny, and my Cover Officer, Simon Levy, were both strategically minded, ethically serious detectives who exuded professionalism and commitment. My partner for the assignment, Jackie, also immediately impressed me with her acuity and sharp judgement. There wasn't a hint of the dysfunction that had so nearly derailed the Leicester job.

But I wasn't taking any chances. 'All right, I want same day lab results.'

'Wait…you want us to get evidence to the lab and back the same day? You do know the lab's in Birmingham, right?'

'Yes – but I think if I score a bag of crack and do an evidence drop, there's no reason we can't get the product down there, then they can phone the results back.'

'All right,' Patrick replied thoughtfully, 'give me a minute.'

He left the room, returning a few minutes later. 'OK – same day lab results. It's arranged. Anything else you need?'

I was impressed. Same day lab results would be useful, but more importantly, I had wanted to make sure that when Jim said we'd get support, the others would follow through on his promise. This time, it seemed they were serious. We got down to business and Patrick and Simon outlined our strategy.

The Gunns were surveillance aware and security conscious. They knew police tactics and ruled their territory with an iron fist. There was no way we were going to catch them handling drugs, and no one was going to testify against them.

Our mission was a long-term commitment, building a picture of how the drugs trade functioned, from the ground up.

Jackie and I would be inserted into Mansfield, a town affectionately known as 'the boil on the arse of Nottingham'.

There were other operations taking place around the city, but Mansfield was exclusively our territory. Interestingly, the new EMSOU strategy was explicitly not to share intelligence with us. The idea was that evidence would carry more weight if we figured it out ourselves, and along the way we might pick up bits and pieces to corroborate other investigations, or uncover whole new leads ourselves.

Our backstory was that we were a junkie couple from Humberside. Jackie's ex-boyfriend had battered her, she had gone to the police and his family had become threatening, so we had been placed in Mansfield for our own protection. This is fairly standard procedure. If a witness is considered under threat, the force can get in contact with the authorities in a neighbouring town and request temporary use of a council flat.

A few years previously all we would have had to do was work the story out and drill our lines. Now though, things had changed. The gangsters knew our plays. We couldn't just show up in town asking about dealers – we needed deep cover.

False case reports were drawn up, and new documents arranged through the Home Office and DVLA. Then we put on our junkie outfits and were escorted to the council offices in our undercover identities by uniformed police.

EMSOU had to work on the assumption that the Gunns wouldn't have informants only on the streets, but also working for the council. It was essential that our story checked out all the way down the line. As far as anyone was concerned, we were just another junkie couple on the run. We were assigned a council flat, and picked up some bedding and second-hand furniture to make the place seem believable.

EMSOU also gave us a car. This was actually a pretty cool piece of kit. Battered and run-down on the outside to look like a motor that a couple of addicts would drive, inside it was fitted with two pinhole cameras to capture the front and back seats, which I could control with a tiny switch just by the steering wheel.

So, briefed and kitted up, it was time to hit the streets.

Mansfield was a heroin town. I'd never seen a place so awash with the stuff. It's easy to spot a junkie when you know what to look for: the way they walk slightly too fast when they're looking for a fix, and slightly too slow when they've just had one. The eyes that stay fixed on the ground, the skin ghosted a shade too white. In Mansfield, they were everywhere.

I paced the streets with Jackie for days; just keeping my eyes open and waiting for the right person to cross our path. Finally, I settled on a little clique of guys I called 'the gang', who hung out on some park benches across from the town's main market square. This lot stood out from the other junkies because, while they were clearly addicts, they didn't seem to also constantly have cans of Special Brew in their hands. It's hard enough to deal with smack- and crackheads, but when you throw booze into the mix, people just become too erratic and unmanageable.

I made my approach in the usual way: picking out the deepest addict of the bunch and sidling up just as he's starting to rattle, offering to share a scrape of my bag if he can organise a score.

Of course he jumped at the chance of some free gear, and introduced himself as Davo. It wasn't long before I had fallen in with his little crew.

Like most addict communities, people drifted in and out, hanging around the benches then disappearing for a while. But the core of the gang revolved around three close mates who I came to know well.

Davo had the longest habit of the bunch. He was a terminal junkie who lived purely from one fix to the next, but he was also a generous-spirited guy who meant no harm to anyone. Gary was the joker of the group, also a long-term smack user, but with a heavy crack habit to boot.

Then there was Cammy. He was slightly younger than the other two, about my own age, though he seemed twenty years older. I don't know what it was that he was running away from, but it was obvious he was using dope to self-medicate for some profound trauma. There was a sadness about Cammy, a kind of brokenness that it was impossible not to feel for. Looking at him was like staring at a parallel version of myself had things just gone a little differently.

But I wasn't there to help these guys fix their lives, I was there to make buys and gather evidence. I knew the rules now – as in Leicester, these guys were terrified of their own dealers. There was no way I could just start asking for phone numbers. I had to establish trust. I had to make myself part of this community.

That meant shoplifting.

We hit everywhere. Boots, Dixons, HMV, Homebase, Oddbins, JD Sports – you name it, we nicked it. We went through Mansfield like locusts, taking everything we could get our hands on.

By far the best though, was Woolworths. They had no stock-checking system whatsoever. You'd nick something, and they'd just pop another one back on the shelf. I saw Gary, by far the most prolific thief in our crew, nick the same PlayStation Memory Card three times in one day. He'd grab it, flog it, wait two hours for it to reappear, then steal it again.

There is absolutely no doubt in my mind that Woolworths went out of business because of all the smackheads pinching their stock. It was an open secret in the heroin community that if you really needed to get ten quid together for your next score, then Woolworths was the place to go.

I quickly discovered I had a talent for shoplifting. After years of covert police operations it wasn't exactly difficult to evade in-store security guards. I was able to keep up with my new 'friends' from the very beginning.

But I wasn't officially stealing. To come under the legal definition of theft, there has to be 'the intent to permanently deprive'. Whenever possible I made sure that what I nicked got passed to EMSOU, who had a system in place for getting it back to the store.

I also had another very useful resource with which to impress my junkie mates: the Seized Property locker. I could turn up with six copies of *The Lion King* on DVD and go, 'Oi, look what I got from HMV,' and they would all be incredibly impressed. Gradually I started winning not just their trust, but their admiration too.

My access to the police locker also allowed me to win them over through little gifts. One morning I came upon Cammy sitting on the benches alone, completely dejected. 'What's up, mate?' I asked, genuinely concerned.

'Ah man, I'm just on my arse. I don't know what's going on in my life, I'm just on my arse mate.'

'Hey, chin up.' I lamely tried to talk a smile out of him, not knowing what else to say. 'Tell you what... I've just nicked these hats off JD Sports, but I can't shift them. You want one?' I held out of one of the Kappa baseball caps I had taken from lockup that morning.

'What, you mean, just *have* it?' he asked in disbelief, giving me a look of utter gratitude as if he'd never been given a present before.

'Yeah man. I can't sell 'em. You want it?'

Cammy took his own cap off. It was so threadbare and filthy that it was barely in one piece. He looked at it for a moment, then flung it into the bushes. Then, with great care, he slowly placed the new one on his head. He turned and gave a smile that lit up his face in a pure, childlike way I had never seen before. It was just a man putting on a ten-quid base-ball cap on a park bench, but the gesture took on an almost biblical significance.

From that moment Cammy became a firm friend. He began to open up and tell me his story. He had set himself up as a user-dealer, working for low-level criminals to finance his own habit. He had been getting by quite well like this, but then he'd been busted with a quarter-ounce of brown. He was now on bail, so he couldn't risk dealing – meaning he had to go back to begging, shoplifting and scrabbling around for his daily £20 bag like the rest of the junkies.

But it was the way he reacted to the hat that really struck me. His expression of pure joy seemed so out of proportion to such a tiny gesture. But this was the condition in which these guys lived. They stayed in squats or run-down council flats, and spent every waking moment in a grinding, desperate search for their daily £20 bag of gear. It is a world of unimaginable harshness and insecurity that eventually breaks anyone who is forced to live in it too long. Just getting a new cap put a smile on Cammy's face and a spring in his step for the next three days.

And of course, as a cop, I took note. I had discovered a new way to work myself into their network. Time was dragging on this operation – I needed to convince one of these guys to overcome their fear and introduce me to a dealer.

It was Davo who broke first. I had always known it would be. He had the most serious habit and needed that extra bit of money so I kicked in for his score. I finally managed to get a number for Chris, his main dealer.

When I tried to score off Chris on my own, however, he had a test for me. 'Yeah OK, tell you what, you go down the needle exchange and pick me up some new sharps and I'll sort you out, yeah.'

'Umm all right,' I agreed, a little mystified.

'I want the long orange, yeah. Last time they gave the short blues – I fucking hate short blues. I want the long orange. Which ones do I want?'

'Uhhh…the long orange?'

'That's right. Don't fuck it up. Tell them Chris from Pleasley sent you.'

So, I walked to the local needle exchange and told the lady there that Chris from Pleasley had sent me to pick up his needles. 'Oh yeah, he can never be bothered to bloody come himself can he?' she joked, sliding a bag of sharps under the metal grille. I checked to make sure they were the ones with the long orange caps, and brought them back for his approval. Only then did he sort me out with some gear.

When I mentioned the incident to Davo the next day, he explained, 'Oh yeah, Chris makes everyone do that. It's his little test. He thinks if you know where the needle exchange is then you're obviously not a cop.'

I'd been posing as a junkie in this town for weeks, of course I knew where the exchange was. It felt almost insulting to be so underestimated.

As we chatted I noticed Davo was looking happier than I'd ever seen him. I gave him a friendly pat on the arm. 'You look fucking chipper mate, what's going on?'

'Ah Cookie, man,' he beamed, using my undercover nickname, 'I'm having a great bloody day mate – there's this vein in my arm that's been dead for years, and this morning it just opened up again… great bloody day.'

I realised this was the first time I'd ever actually seen Davo smile.

This was the squalor and deprivation in which these people lived. For Davo, Gary and Cammy the only sources of joy were a dead vein reopening to squirt more poison into, or someone giving them a shitty stolen baseball cap. It took me a moment to process this.

'Well, come on,' continued Davo, 'let's go get ourselves a little something.' I snapped out of my reverie, and we went to make another score.

But on the way back from Chris's place, we got a shock that wiped the smile off Davo's face. As we strolled along the high street, two policemen burst out of Marks & Spencer. Between them was Gary, handcuffed and grimacing in discomfort as they bundled him roughly towards the car. Just as they swung the door open and pushed him inside, he turned and for a second we locked eyes. He gave me one sorrowful shake of his head, then he was gone.

Cammy and Davo were fatalistic. Neither had much hope of seeing Gary again; they were sure he'd pushed his luck with the shoplifting too far this time, and would be sent down for sure.

But, about a week later, who should reappear but Gary himself. Somehow, despite all his previous convictions, he had been let off, on condition that he begin a course of Suboxone, an opioid inhibitor used to treat heroin addiction.

'Yeah mate,' he laughed stoically, 'pushed my luck robbing M&S – should've stuck to Woollies mate...should've stuck to Woollies.'

Gary immediately replaced the smack with Special Brew to give the Suboxone an edge. He'd get us all laughing, saying, 'Yeah, it's weird – with the subbies instead of the skag, I'm getting horny thoughts again. It's like my dick's been cut off for five years and suddenly it's back...and back with five years of rent due. I'm going bloody mad here!'

But as ever, there was a tragic undercurrent to his one-liners. Aside from his daily dose of the subbies, he received no other support. So, he just kept hanging out on the benches, nursing tins of high-strength lager and gazing after us with forlorn envy every time we went off to score. He lasted about two months before slipping on his bail conditions and drifting back onto the skag. It was the only life he knew.

Cammy was crying.

He was leaning against a wall, his head in his hands, tears streaming down his face. I immediately raced over to ask what was up.

'Ah mate, it's just this friend I had years ago, when I was a kid – before all this – he was my best mate, my best friend...I just heard he died. He wasn't like us – he was clean, y'know. But he was playing football and just had a fucking heart attack.'

'Ah mate, I'm so sorry. Is there a funeral or something?'

'On Tuesday,' sighed Cammy.

'Well, at least you'll get to say goodbye.'

Cammy turned and gave me a look as if I'd lost my mind. 'I'm not going to the funeral. I wouldn't do that to his family. The last thing they want is some dirty junkie turning up and ruining everything.' Once again he buried his face in his hands.

I just stood there looking at him, thinking back to that NA meeting in Manchester all those years ago. It was there I had first realised that fighting drug cartels meant understanding people. Well, here was the human face of our war right in front of me. No matter how society may condemn and look down on the addict, it is never, ever as low a view as he has of himself.

I desperately wanted to help Cammy, to offer some comfort or advice that might push him to rebuild his life. But that would have meant breaking character. I was Cookie the junkie. I couldn't step outside the role, no matter how grindingly miserable the heartache got.

But by this point, I was having my own troubles. The investigation couldn't get past the street-level dealers. People were just too paranoid. I could score off Chris from Pleasley as much as I liked, but that wasn't going to help us bring down any real criminal empires.

Patrick and Simon at EMSOU maintained absolute professionalism, and never put pressure on me personally, but undercover operations are expensive. To justify continuing, we needed to show progress.

The break came from the most unexpected place: McDonald's.

In the early 2000s, McDonald's brought out one of their new ice-cream fudge sundae monstrosities, which was served with a little plastic spoon. That spoon just happened to be the precise size and shape to measure out a perfect 0.1 gram, £5 dose of heroin.

So, to save them from having to carry scales around, smack dealers just started carrying these little spoons. They were everywhere, becoming part of the standard paraphernalia of the British drug user. That spoon even became part of my own standard set of junkie props, as much a part of the costume as my filthy beaten-up Reeboks, torn bomber jacket and packs of Rizla with the corners torn off.

But dealers were using these spoons to evade searches. So, I took a whole box of them from a McDonald's outlet at home in Buxton, and brought it in to Jim Horner to explain the situation. Jim made some calls to the corporate bigwigs at McDonald's UK, and they actually agreed to change the spoon's design.

These spoons were so useful to the dealers, though, that all that happened was a new black market developed, trading in the old McDonald's spoons. Dealers would offer junkies free bags of gear in return for a 'Mickey D's spoon'. It got to the point where spoons were going for upwards of forty quid – a lottery jackpot in the world of the street junkie.

By sheer good luck, I still had that full box of spoons that I had brought in for Jim Horner, sitting in our evidence locker. Suddenly I became 'the spoons guy' in Mansfield. Word got around. All of a sudden, I wasn't having to work the streets to worm my way in with dealers – they were coming to me.

That's how I met Emma and Jason.

They were another couple of user-dealers, but several rungs above the likes of Chris from Pleasley. Jason was a dour, miserable scally with anger management issues, and Emma was about the same in female form. Together they ran a crack and heroin racket out of their low-rise council house, and were connected to the serious Nottingham gangs.

I got to know them trading spoons for skag, and gradually made them my main connection. I was able to listen in on their endless bickering, and began to pick up scraps of information about how the drugs trade between Mansfield and Nottingham functioned. One name seemed to pop up again and again: 'Stitz'. I got the sense that this was the boss who Emma and Jason worked under.

They were incessantly angry, paranoid, awful people to spend time with, but somehow I knew these two would lead me on to something big.

Mansfield had been dry for crack for almost a week. My gang from the benches were going out of their minds with desperation. I volunteered to go and see my new dealers to see if I could beg any scraps.

By now the gang trusted me. Thanks to our same day lab results, I always knew who was selling the purest gear. It became a running joke: 'Well, if Cookie says it's the bollocks, then it's definitely the bollocks.' After a dry spell, though, they would smoke or shoot anything they could get their hands on.

'Yeah, all right, get in mate,' snarled Jason, pulling the door shut behind me. 'We ain't got nothing on us mate, fucking nothing. Gotta go into town to pick it up, innit.'

That's when Emma piped up, shouting from the next room, 'He's got a car ain't he? He can bloody drive us.'

Jason looked at me. 'Wanna earn a ten-rock?'

I just nodded. I'd be only too happy to drive these two around and figure out where they got their product.

We piled into my car and drove out to a run-down estate on the outskirts of Nottingham. I noted the address, and stayed in the background as they negotiated with two huge, rough-looking geezers. Six ounces of crack – half in cash and half on tic. This was a serious deal by anyone's standards.

The second they were in the car Jason whipped out his crack pipe and flick knife, and started carving himself off a chunk of one of the huge white blocks. The entire car quickly filled with the industrial, alkaline stink of crack smoke.

The moment that smoke hit his lungs, though, Jason was completely transformed. In an instant he was no longer his aggressively miserable self, but a hyperactive kid clowning around in the passenger seat.

He thrust the pipe in my face. 'Have a toot, bruv. Have a fucking toot.'

'Mate, I am driving.' Jason gave me a look like I was some sort of Victorian prude, and went back to huffing on his pipe.

Then, unable to sit still, he whipped out his mobile. 'Stitzy mate, I've got the white-ly-ite, I've got the white-ly-ite.' He was half-singing in a gleeful crack nursery rhyme.

This made me sit up and pay attention. I made a mental note of the time of the call, so intelligence could cross-reference his phone records. But then he proceeded to make six or seven more calls, getting more and more excited each time, squealing, 'Mate, I've got the white-ly-ite', 'Guess who's got the white-ly-ite?'

It was all I could do to resist singing along, 'Yeah, the white-ly-ite, it goes really well with browny-wown.' But I restrained myself and just concentrated on snapping pictures with the car's pinhole cameras, as Jason and Emma passed the crack pipe back and forth.

They were getting stratospherically high, lolling around the car, almost vibrating in their seats. Then Jason went suddenly quiet. He reached into his pocket and pulled out a black and white photo, shoving it in my face as I did my best to stay on the road.

'That's me, that is,' he slurred through his crack mania.

The photo showed a young boy, perhaps four or five years old, smiling in a paddling pool. A slice of nostalgic childhood bliss that seemed an impossible world away as we rumbled through the Nottingham sink estates enveloped in a fog of crack smoke.

'That's me when I was a kid,' Jason continued, his voice trembling as he reeled between existential despair and crack-induced euphoria. 'It's me...that's me...' he kept mumbling over and over, holding the photo like a religious artefact. He'd long since stopped communicating with me, and was just desperately trying to hold on to whatever thread remained to that smiling young boy in the picture. His head lolled forward in a twitchy stupor. All I could do was try to keep my eyes on the road, and my finger on the switch that controlled the camera.

Demand was high after the dry spell. Emma and Jason sold and smoked their way through their big score in lightning speed. By the time I tried to score off them again a week later they were sold out.

Seeing my forlorn expression, Emma blurted out, 'You know who might have a bit left is Stitzy—'

She suddenly stopped herself, realising she had gone too far. She glanced nervously over to Jason. He seemed to be back to his usual grumpy self, but gave a dismissive nod. I suppose our episode in the car must have earned their trust. I tapped Stitz's number into my phone.

I was told to meet him on a patch of isolated wasteland beside some derelict railway arches. The light from a few tower blocks shone in the distance, but the place itself was deserted. Stitz's black Toyota sat stationary beneath a sickly yellow-grey Nottingham sunset; families of rats scattered from discarded bin bags as I approached. I began the mental calculations of how long it would take an ambulance to reach this isolated spot.

The car door swung open and Stitz motioned me near.

He was a vicious-looking skinhead hard-man, with a violent look in his eye and classic scally-gangster chic – white tracksuit, Reebok classics and big gold rings. Beside him in the passenger seat was a boy, probably around twelve or thirteen, and very obviously Stitz Jr. He was a carbon copy of his father, a little scally Mini-Me in an identical tracksuit.

I walked up and leaned on the roof over the open door. 'Who're you then?' snarled Stitz.

'I'm Cookie, Emma's friend.'

The move was instant and violent. Stitz's left arm shot out, wrapping round my neck and pulling me down. I saw something flash in his right hand. Then I felt the knife.

It was pointing straight into my crotch, just hard enough that I could feel the point on the base of my penis.

'I said who the fuck are you?' His voice dropped to a poisonous rasp.

'Mate, I'm Cookie. Emma sent me. What the fuck?'

My entire consciousness zeroed down to the tip of that knife. Fighting the good fight was all well and good, but I wasn't getting my cock sliced up for it.

'Where the fuck you from?' Stitz gave the knife a twist to punctuate the question.

I could almost smell the aggression coming off him. My brain was spinning like a fucked record.

'I live in Sutton,' I gasped as Stitz squeezed my neck tighter. The Mini-Me in the passenger seat started giggling.

'What the fuck d'you mean you live in Sutton?'

'I just live in Sutton. With Jackie – maybe you know her,' I pleaded. 'I'm just a mate of Emma's, she said to call you.'

'Well I don't know you... I don't fucking know you.' I felt the knife twist again in my groin. Mini-Me was still cackling in the passenger seat like a demented scally gargoyle.

My mind went blank – I had nothing left.

'Well...I've only just met you as well,' I heard myself saying weakly.

Then I felt his posture relax. I saw the knife move away, though my brain could still feel it pressing on me, like a phantom limb. Stitz's arm slid back from round my neck, allowing me to breathe. Mini-me stopped his giggling – I guess the show was over.

'What you want, then?' spat Stitz.

'I'll take one bones and one brown, if you got 'em.'

Stitz snorted, handed me a rock of crack and a wrap of heroin, snatched the money from my hand and slammed the car door. As they pulled away I could still feel the point of that knife, pressing just hard enough to send a shudder of terror snaking up my spine.

I made it back to 'our' flat, and collapsed on the sofa. Jackie immediately rushed over, but it took a few minutes before I could even speak.

I put a call in to HQ to organise an evidence drop. I told Simon what had happened and the line suddenly went silent. After a few seconds, he said very quietly, 'I think the two of you had better come in.'

The entire team sat across the briefing room table, as Jim Horner began, 'I know it's EMSOU policy to restrict the intelligence you're given, but in light of what you've reported there are three pieces of information it would be a dereliction of duty not to share with you.' Jim stood and began to pace the room as he spoke.

'First, this character, Stitz – we know him. He's one of Colin Gunn's main lieutenants, and runs all his operations north of

Nottingham – all the way up to Sheffield. That phone number you gave us may well lead us straight to Gunn himself.

'Second – you should be aware that Colin Gunn has put an order out to his entire crew that any undercover police who are discovered will be killed, without question or hesitation.

'Third – your man Stitz is a fucking knife-happy psychopath. Word on the street is that he was slicing so many people up that it was drawing police attention. So Colin Gunn took him to a field, stripped him naked, stuck a shotgun in his mouth and told him to mind his manners. Judging by your meeting, he hasn't taken the advice to heart.'

Jim sat back down across from us, and finished quietly and seriously. 'You two bloody watch it out there, all right?'

I was moving up in the world of Mansfield junkies. But, my main set of connections in the town was still very much the gang from the benches. And things there were falling apart.

Davo liked to pepper his heroin shots with a bit of crack to make a speedball. It's a recipe for serious trouble. When he began feeling the pain in his leg he just loaded up on more smack to get himself through. Within weeks he collapsed and had to be rushed to the hospital. The paramedics rolled up his trouser leg to reveal a virulent, pus-spewing abscess the size of a tennis ball.

Following surgery, Davo was held at the hospital in Nottingham for a few days. Jackie and I figured the NHS dosage of painkillers would never be enough for an addict like Davo, and he'd probably have a dealer coming through the hospital. So we picked up some petrol station flowers, and visited our friend in the recovery ward.

Davo had never had anyone visit him in hospital before. The fact that we'd spent £3.99 on flowers for him, instead of on drugs, made his eyes go moist. I could see his heart melting right in front of us as we made small talk, and he showed us the hole they had cut out of his leg. It was big enough to fit your fist through.

And naturally, amidst all this outpouring of emotion, I leaned in and said, 'Hey Davo, all our guys are dry. If you've got a number, we've got a bit of cash. We could all share a couple of bags.' Davo's eyes lit up at this expression of true junkie friendship. Of course he had a guy. Of course we called him in. And of course Jackie and I took his number to pass on to EMSOU.

This was our job. We visited people who thought of us as friends, at their most vulnerable, lying in a hospital bed, and manipulated them into gaining us intelligence for the fight, the War on Drugs.

As we walked away after divvying up the score, Davo's eyes were still glowing at the idea that he had friends who cared enough to visit him.

As we left the hospital Jackie mentioned she needed to leave early. I told her not to worry, she could head off and I'd organise the evidence drop. To be honest, I needed the time alone. Something about what we had just done felt dirty. I needed a solitary walk to process all this, and began trudging back through town to our drop-off point.

I wandered past the council estates and boarded-up shops, weaving my way through the shambling smackheads, broken-down drunks and packs of predatory kids in hoodies. Then I caught a glimpse of my own reflection in a betting shop window. My breath caught in my throat. That wasn't me.

That wasn't Neil. That was a fucked-up, overly skinny, sallow-cheeked skag addict. I hadn't realised how deep I had gone.

That's when I heard her.

'Sex for sale...Sex for sale...'

She was threading an unsteady path down the high street, clutching a can of K Cider, nothing but tracksuit bottoms and crop top against the evening chill, her straggly blonde hair pulled back in a tight bun. She couldn't have been older than twenty-one. Once upon a time she must have been a very pretty girl. I had rarely seen a junkie so desperately rattling for a fix. Sweat was pouring off her as the can of cider shook in her hand.

'Sex for sale...Sex for sale...'

She was shouting like a market trader flogging baskets of fruit. I watched as she staggered down the street, and other people walked straight past her – as if they could pretend there wasn't a young woman trying to sell her body for a £10 wrap of skag shouting in their faces.

I was overcome by a wave of pity and rage. My entire being screamed to just take that girl by the hand and drive her to a hospital, a rehab centre, anywhere she might get some help. Had I not joined the police to help the vulnerable? Was she not exactly the kind of person I should be reaching out to? Why were we throwing thousands of man-hours and millions of pounds at catching dealers, while leaving this poor girl walking the streets?

But of course I couldn't do it. I had to protect my cover. In fact, it was worse than that – in the eyes of the law she was a criminal, a drug addict. The only contact I could ever have with her would be if I arrested her and slung her into a concrete cell to sweat out her rattle, surrounded by other people whose disease had turned them into outlaws. All I could do was watch as she swerved erratically along the road, shouting her grotesque bill of fare.

'Sex for sale...Sex for sale...'

Then, just as she was passing me, she paused, and for a split-second our eyes met. She looked me up and down, then almost questioningly cried, '...cheap sex for sale?'

I almost burst into laughter right there on the street. For all my patronising flights of fancy about wanting to help her, all she saw in me was a street junkie so ragged and destitute that he wouldn't even be able to afford the prices she was selling at. I smirked with quiet gallows humour, and moved off down the road. But that image of desperation, pain and squalor stuck with me. I found that woman flashing into my mind again and again for years after.

Cammy got busted. He wasn't shoplifting or dealing; it was just a couple of cops who thought he looked sketchy, searched him and found a tiny wrap of heroin in his shoe. It was leftovers, barely enough for a shot, but on top of him already being on bail, the whole gang were sure he'd go down for a couple of years.

But then, only the next day, who should rock up to the benches but Cammy himself? We all leapt up to congratulate him on getting out, but he was ashen-faced.

'It's all fucked man. I'm totally fucked.'

'What are you on about, mate, you got off,' scoffed Davo.

'No man, you don't understand, it's the cops, it's the fucking cops.' Cammy slumped onto the bench with an expression of utter despair.

'What happened, mate?' I asked, in horror that one of my colleagues might have given Cammy a kicking at the station. It turned out to be so much worse.

'They took me in this room, and said I had to tell them where I get my gear. Of course I'm not gonna fuckin' tell them. I'm no rat, and it's not worth my life if any of the cunts I buy from finds out – I'd rather do the time inside... But then they say, well if you don't tell us, we're going to spread the word around the streets that you did anyway.'

He looked up in terror. 'If they do that, I'm dead – I'm fucking dead.'

'What the fuck?' I gasped in outrage, 'were they fucking Drugs Squad? What department were they?'

This was beyond the pale. That kind of blackmail was such an egregious breach of ethics that my only thought was finding out who had done this and getting them booted off the force. But Cammy had other things on his mind.

'I don't know – it was just a couple of cunts in suits... but I don't know who they're working for, do I?'

'What d'you mean?' I asked in incomprehension, 'they're cops ain't they?'

'Fuck off man.' Cammy looked at me like I was an idiot child. 'They could be working for any gang in the city – fucking Colin Gunn, anyone. For all I know they're working for Gunn and just testing me to see if I'll snitch.'

Now the blood drained from my own face as I realised the true horror of the situation. The idea of my fellow cops blackmailing Cammy was awful enough. But to Cammy, there was every possibility that those cops were being paid by the gangsters to do their own spying.

My mind couldn't even process the ramifications of all this. What the fuck was happening? Had the arms race of the drugs war spiralled so far that cops would spread the word that someone was a snitch, knowing it could get them killed? Had the gangsters got so paranoid about police tactics that they'd just started hiring the cops as employees instead?

I didn't know which option depressed me more. Both represented a profound moral corruption of what our mission as police was meant to be. And both made me ask questions about my own role in this battle – and I didn't think I had the courage to face the answers those questions demanded.

It felt like there was no solace whichever way I turned. Each night that I returned home from my life on the streets I would stand with my key in the door, frozen on the spot, terrified of what might be waiting for me inside. It became a traumatic evening ritual.

Between the situation with Sam and the pressure of the job, things were becoming impossible. So, with nowhere else to turn, and not feeling any support or comfort at home – I searched for it elsewhere.

Meghan was a kind, beautiful and intelligent woman. She was a uniformed police officer, but before joining the force she had worked as a teacher. As things spiralled from bad to awful at home, Meghan offered me not just sympathy, but practical advice and strategies on how to cope with my situation.

But, for all her kindness, the combined pressure of work and marriage kept building. Cracks and sores started appearing on my face and lips. Bouts of severe abdominal pain started to come and go with no rhyme or reason. I began suffering from severe sleep insomnia, just lying there night after night, my heart nervously racing.

I suppose the sores and fissures must have been quite good for my role as a street-level drug addict. But I was in a bad way. I booked a doctor's appointment to see if there was anything to do about the stomach pain. She examined me, listened to my symptoms and declared very matter-of-factly that I was suffering from severe stress-related disorders. She advised me to take Milk of Magnesia and avoid stressful situations. She didn't know the work I did.

Three days later I was sitting in the car with Simon, my Cover Officer, driving back to HQ after another day out on the street. I felt that familiar white-hot spasm of pain twist through my stomach, and doubled over, grimacing in agony, until the moment had passed.

'What the fuck was that?' demanded Simon.

'Ah nothing mate, I'm just getting these weird pains in my belly. The doctor says it's just stress though.'

The car jolted as Simon swerved and pulled to a stop. 'Right,' he said decisively, 'the job ends now. We're pulling you out.'

'No mate, you can't do that,' I pleaded. 'We're close. I only need a few more scores to put these fuckers away. Seriously, I'm fine.'

'Neil, look at yourself. Your face is all fucked up – you're covered in sores. It's not right.'

Simon was doing exactly what he was meant to. His job was to look out for my welfare, even when I wouldn't. But I didn't want this investigation to end. I was too close and had worked too hard. I couldn't let the gangsters win.

Eventually I argued Simon down. We sat down with Jim Horner and the EMSOU brass, and agreed to continue the case, as long as I was signed off by an Occupational Health Officer.

It took about thirty minutes.

She opened her clipboard and read out a series of yes or no questions. Do you have thoughts of suicide? No. Do you self-harm, or think about self-harming? No. Do you use illegal drugs? No. At the end of the list she simply said, 'I think you're all right to continue working, just try and watch the hours.' The boxes were ticked, and I went back to work.

As it happened, we only needed a few more buys off Stitz anyway. Each encounter was uniquely unpleasant in its own way. Stitz was a paranoid, hyper-aggressive bully, who maintained control by constantly acting as intimidating and violent as possible. I gritted my teeth, logging every detail as evidence. This case had become personal. I was going to make sure this guy was taken off the streets.

But as we moved into the arrest phase of the operation, I was to once again have my faith in the entire project shaken to the core.

The investigation had gone on for so long that our support team had to be rotated to take time off. Simon, my Cover Officer who had been so consistently dedicated and professional, was moved on, and command sent us a new guy.

I walked into the briefing room and shook hands with the newbie, who introduced himself as Charlie Fletcher.

Something immediately wasn't right.

To this day I have no idea what gave it away. The way his eyes darted to the right? The way he ran his tongue over his teeth as I held out my hand? There was just something off. After years of undercover work you learn to trust your instinct.

Without saying a word I walked straight through into Jim Horner's office.

'I want him out.'

'I beg your pardon?' Jim replied in surprise.

'This new guy. Something's not right. I don't want him in our briefings. I don't want him knowing my identity. Tell him to wait at the station, and we'll call if we need to – tell him anything you bloody want, but get him out of here.'

Jim started to respond. Then he looked at the expression on my face and trailed off.

'All right Neil, if that's your judgement. Wait here.' He went through into the briefing room. When I came back out, the guy was gone.

Two years later Charlie Fletcher was arrested for being a spy for the Gunn crime family. He had been personally recruited by Colin Gunn to join the force, and paid £2,000 a month on top of his salary to pass on information regarding any relevant investigations. And he'd earned it. He'd smuggled out reams of intelligence that allowed Gunn to stay ahead of the law for years.

Had I not gone with my gut instinct in that briefing room, or had Jim Horner not taken me seriously, there is no telling what Gunn might have found out about this operation, or what might have happened to me or my family.

But when I talked to my superiors, they just shrugged. 'Of course it happens, Neil. With so much money in the drugs business how can it not happen?' This casual acceptance that the War on Drugs made corruption not only likely, but inevitable, was perhaps the final nail in the coffin of whatever naïve belief I had once held in the value of the campaign we were waging.

It was one thing for the police to be locked in a fruitless, destructive arms race with the gangsters, but at least we knew we were *the police*. I was a cop – that was the one thought that had seen me through. If the drugs war meant that even the idea of *being a cop* was under threat, then what was the fucking point of any of this?

We came down hard in a broad sweep of the city. Everyone got picked up: from Stitz to Chris from Pleasley and every other chancer I had met along the way. From the intelligence we generated, over sixty arrests were made.

Stitz got five years, Jason got four, and Emma three and a half. But crucially, through tracing Stitz's phone records, the intelligence crew were able to begin serious investigations into the Colin Gunn empire. Gunn was eventually sentenced to thirty-five years for multiple murders, then had seven years added to his sentence for police corruption in the Charlie Fletcher case.

But despite these successes, for me there was no happy ending to this operation. Every single member of my little gang from the park benches was arrested and charged as well.

Cammy and Gary both got two years. Davo got five.

The idea that Davo, who was an addict but meant no harm to anyone, could end up with the same sentence as the knife-wielding career criminal Stitz, was sickening. But, in the eyes of the law, that little gang were criminals the same as any other. They were just more statistics for police department reports, EMSOU budget allocations and politicians' soundbites.

Something felt so profoundly wrong in all this. We were fighting a War on Drugs – but against whom? Gangsters like Stitz and Colin Gunn were obviously the enemy, and we needed to take them down. But was the law so blunt a tool, and were the police so blind, that they couldn't distinguish between violent murderous criminals and guys like Cammy?

It made no sense. I'd joined the police to protect the weak and vulnerable – and to fight against those who victimised them. Yet the most vulnerable people I had ever met were now being turned into criminals and sent to prison. If we were fighting a war, then these were the exact people we should be fighting to protect. And if we weren't, then what were we fighting for at all?

But I couldn't just blame the system. I had to take some personal responsibility. These people had trusted me; I had used and manipulated them – and I had put their lives at risk. When they wound up in prison, it would be common knowledge that they were the ones who had led an undercover cop to the gangsters. I made sure that Jim Horner wrote an official letter requesting that they be sent to minimum security prisons on the other side of the country, where they would be unknown.

I had devoted my professional life to fighting the War on Drugs. I was now discovering that, like every war, the people who suffered most weren't the combatants, but the civilians caught in the crossfire.

Once again though, I wasn't quite ready to follow these thoughts to their conclusion. I was still a cop. I was a soldier in this war, and I wouldn't let my comrades down. I would march and keep order, and do what I could to keep fighting.

But nothing I had seen so far could prepare me for what was to come next. I was about to discover the grotesque, terrifying reality of what the arms race of the War on Drugs truly meant.

CHAPTER 13
NORTHAMPTON

They were using gang rape as a method of control and intimidation.

For years this gang had kept entire districts of the city terrorised with beatings, stabbings and shootings. Now they were intensifying the violence. The threat to women was made grotesquely clear through a series of savage, brazen public attacks. Any man who spoke to the police, or stepped out of line, would know they were putting their wives, girlfriends or sisters at risk.

Police forces and hospitals began receiving appalling cases of these 'punishment-rapes'. Knowing that most sexual assault cases don't even get reported, we could only assume the situation on the street was exponentially worse. Reviewing the evidence of these investigations gave one a sickening sensation akin to vertigo.

I had never seen Jim Horner like this. There was none of his usual roguish humour or clownish schtick. Even the most hardened officers had been shocked by these developments. Jim sat with an expression of hard-lipped severity and introduced me to our new targets.

This was a gang I had heard of. Anyone working in UK law enforcement would know their reputation as one of the most infamous mobs in the country.

The Burger Bar Boys took their ridiculous name from the fast food joint on Soho Road, Birmingham that served as their unofficial headquarters. Their decades-long turf war with rival gangsters the Johnson Crew had left a string of bodies in its wake. But they had exploded into the national consciousness with the murders of Letisha Shakespeare and Charlene Ellis, two innocent teenage girls gunned down in a gangland drive-by shooting gone horrifically wrong.

The Letisha Shakespeare case, as it was known by the press and public, ended with four gang members being sent down for between twenty-seven and thirty-five years each. But even that high-profile investigation had almost collapsed due to witness intimidation. Out of the 355 statements the police had originally taken, only ten people had agreed to testify. Such was the terror the Burgers exerted over the population of Birmingham that an unprecedented level of anonymity was granted to witnesses who testified.

Now the Burgers were expanding into Northampton. After a brief but brutal war with the local gangs, they had taken over the city's drugs trade. Northampton had already been in the grip of a crack and heroin epidemic, but within a year crime rates had shot up and overdose deaths were through the roof. The city was slipping into the same state of terror as those parts of Birmingham the Burgers controlled. My mission was to drive them back.

Once again, I was being asked to take over an ongoing investigation that had ground to a halt. Pat Shaw, my former partner from Derby, had been leading an undercover team in Northampton for a couple of months. But the unit couldn't seem to penetrate anywhere above street level, and certainly nowhere near the Burger Bar Boys.

After my experience in Leicester, I didn't like the idea of taking over another investigation not knowing what mistakes had already been made. Before I agreed, I laid down a condition: I wasn't going in blind. EMSOU would have to set aside their methods and let me see every piece of intelligence they had.

It was a very repetitive story. Pat's team would make a few buys, but the second they'd enquire about the Burgers, or any other real gangster, they'd hit what Pat's notes described as a 'wall of *fuck off*'. The Burgers knew our tactics – they weren't letting anyone get close.

According to Intel, a team of six Burgers had come up from Birmingham, led by a heavy-hitter gangster named Jackson. Jackson's name had come up in several major investigations and been placed by witnesses in the car when Letisha Shakespeare and Charlene Ellis were gunned down. But he had never been convicted.

As I read the file I resolved to myself that it was time this foul bastard was put away. But this crew were ruthless, brutal, professional criminals. I would have to work this hard, from the gutter up.

It was desolate. The casualties were everywhere, staggering around like the walking wounded, frantically trying to beg, steal or scam their way to the next fix. But there was something else at work here, something darker even than what I had seen in Nottingham or Leicester. I walked the streets for days just trying to figure out why these streets seemed so creepily isolated and desperate.

I was trudging through a park, stepping over discarded needles, when it hit me. I couldn't spot a single little gang, as I had in Mansfield. The street addicts here worked alone. They walked fast, keeping to themselves, their eyes fixed on the pavement. This isolation infected the whole city with a rank air of nervous paranoia.

It also made it hard to establish any kind of initial contact. One day followed another and I couldn't see any way to even start a conversation that wouldn't immediately mark me out as a suspicious outsider. It was one thing to walk up to a group of guys who were already hanging out and chatting, but here no one stayed in one place long enough for me to make a realistic approach.

But I couldn't just hang around observing people. The investigation had to move forward. The DI for the case was an excellent detective named Max Copeland, but the Cover Officer, Gino Rossi, had a real push to *get the job done*. I could sense a growing impatience, and knew I had to show some progress.

I decided to play rattling. A junkie desperate enough for a fix will approach anyone. I would just have to get the body language exactly right: the shortness of breath, the hands fluttering with nervous energy, the eyes darting around for any scrap of opportunity.

It still took me hours of watching and waiting, but finally I spotted my mark.

He was yellow. Literally. His skin was bright, Bart Simpson-yellow. One look and you could tell he was an intravenous heroin user. This was liver damage caused by hepatitis C from a dirty needle. I could also tell he was on his way to score. There's a walk that junkies do when they need a fix, a sort of intense, focused stride, trying not to draw attention, but also desperately trying to move as fast as possible towards the gear.

'Oi mate – mate – you going to buy?' I rasped to him in my junkie whisper.

Yellow Man just kept on walking, his eyes tracking the pavement. I had to jog to catch up.

'Mate, it's just I need something, know what I mean? If you can sort it, I'll give you half my bag.'

He stopped dead in his tracks. 'Half a bag?'

'Yeah man, yeah – I just need something, y'know?' I rubbed my hands together and fidgeted on the spot, simulating the ragged nerves of the junkie rattle.

'All right, yeah,' he muttered under his breath. 'It's a bit of a walk, but I can sort it.'

But then, just as we were moving off together, another bloke appeared from round the corner and walked straight up to my new friend. 'We going to get this gear, yeah...fuck the trek across town, I'll pay a taxi.'

This was weird. This new character wore a white knitted jumper, with a tidy crew cut and trimmed goatee. He was obviously no street junkie, but there was an intensity about him, a frightening kind of hyper-focused energy that only really serious addicts can attain.

Then the situation got even stranger.

Crew Cut turned and bellowed at the top of his lungs down an alley, 'Oi, you fucking coming or what?' Another figure crept up. This guy was deep into his rattle. He was so cramped up he was having trouble walking straight and his clothes were drenched in sweat. Without a word he joined our group, and off we went.

I didn't like anything about this. We were a freak show of four obviously drugged-out basket cases in a town where the junkies kept themselves purposely isolated. But dropping out now wasn't an option. No addict backs out on the way to a fix – and I had already waited too long to make a connection in this city.

So we piled into a taxi, Yellow Man up front and Crew Cut, Rattler and I crammed in the back. There was something about Crew Cut. I recognised him. I'd seen him before. But where? It must have been another drug deal in another town, but by now I'd done too many to be sure.

I could see his eyes flicking over to me as well. This was grim. In my line of work having your face spotted by the wrong person means a bullet.

Eventually the tension became too much to bear. 'Oi mate', I said, leaning over, 'don't I know you from Leicester?'

Crew Cut's head snapped round. 'No names,' he snarled, 'no fucking names.' Then, almost under his breath, he growled enigmatically, 'Yeah, I've been to Leicester.'

And that was it. The two of us sat in dead silence, eyes straight ahead, for the rest of the journey, as Rattler slumped between us trembling in the cramped personal hell of his withdrawal.

We piled out, Crew Cut paid the fare and the three of us waited while Yellow Man disappeared to make the score. Crew Cut said he knew some disused toilets, so our ragged band set off once again.

On the way, I managed to get Yellow Man chatting. 'Yeah, I've not scored around these parts for a while. I've just been on remand for a week – all my usual guys already changed their numbers.'

'Fuck, you've just come off a week's remand? So, you've done your rattle?'

'Aye, I've done the rattle...but you know what it's like.'

This was worrying. Most heroin overdoses occur in the first week after withdrawal. People's tolerances are down, but they shoot their usual dose anyway and their systems just can't take it. The last thing I needed was for this guy, already weak with hep C, turning from yellow to blue and overdosing on me.

Finally, we crossed a scraggy patch of grass and made it to the derelict toilets where we were meant to do our business. The thick layers of dust couldn't camouflage the decades-old stink of stale piss. Yellow Man, Crew Cut and Rattler sat straight down and started cooking up. I ended up standing between them, awkwardly explaining how I was going to smoke my bit at home.

At the same time I had to make sure that Yellow Man took his half of the wrap *before* he handed it to me. If I took my half and then gave the rest to him, it could be argued that technically I had supplied him with drugs, and thus my evidence was obtained illegally.

Just as I was finessing this arrangement, Yellow Man piped up, 'Ah fuck man, we've only got two filters.'

Crew Cut just shrugged. 'Nah man, I'm fine without.'

Now I was genuinely stressed. Smack addicts cleanse their gear by sucking it through a cigarette filter. Shooting with no filter very quickly leads to blood clots and strokes. So, not only was I now worrying that Yellow Man was going to OD, but also that Crew Cut was about to give himself a pulmonary embolism. In my head I started doing the maths on how long it would take me to sprint back across that patch of wasteland and flag down an ambulance.

Yellow Man and Rattler sucked massive shots through their filters, tapped their veins and slammed their needles home. They were both squirters. I had to sidestep as two jets of blood arced out, splattering on the floor. Each fat drop of blood caused a little puff of dust to rise up, swimming and circling in the grimy half-light.

Then I watched in horror as Crew Cut sucked his own dose right off the spoon, dropped his pants and shot straight into his femoral vein.

When you shoot into the femoral, the wound never heals. It just forms a kind of valve, and you can keep shooting into the same spot again and again. This is convenient as it means there are no track-marks or dead black veins running up and down your body – but it also means that any potential septicaemia or embolism is going straight to your brain. To do a femoral shot with no filter is Russian roulette – there's about a one-in-six chance you're going to die.

I kept my eyes fixed on Crew Cut as he held his penis aside and slid the needle into his upper thigh. He wobbled, but didn't fall. Then his arm shot out and he steadied himself against the cubicle wall.

It was only then that I could exhale in relief. The most disturbing thing was that I could tell he knew exactly what he was doing. There was an element of death wish about this guy that was terrifying just to be around.

I turned round just in time to see Yellow Man and Rattler both lolling into full-on heroin nods, every muscle in their bodies turning to cottage cheese. But as he slipped away, Yellow Man managed to drag his hands, still covered in blood, all over his face.

'Uhh mate...I think you've got a little something there'. My gallows humour got the better of me.

Rattler looked up and slurred out his first words of the entire afternoon. 'Fuuuuck maaan...your face – it's got all blood on it...'

Yellow Man was so high he could barely talk. He just lifted his palms and, in a slow, smacked-out parody of washing, smeared the blood all over himself. He ended up with a grotesque marbled effect of pink blood on yellow skin.

'Yeah mate, that's a bit better,' I said, trying to comfort him.

He immediately fell back into a deep nod, and I had to just stand there for fifteen endless minutes, watching these guys float away while making sure that no one stopped breathing. Eventually I got them to their feet and we all walked back towards town with Crew Cut still giving me the evil eye, and the other two doing the classic heroin zombie shuffle.

We parted company outside the station. As I walked away I realised I hadn't even managed to get a name, let alone a dealer's phone number.

Thinking back now, I have no doubt that every one of those three is dead. Yellow Man with his hepatitis, Crew Cut with his death wish, and Rattler sucking such gratuitously huge shots into his needle. That's what the War on Drugs had turned Northampton into: a city thick with fear, exploitation and death, where the most vulnerable people were forced to isolate themselves in the shadows.

This was the city I was now trying to infiltrate.

It was desperately hard going. People in Northampton knew that to introduce the wrong person to a drug dealer meant getting beaten, shot or worse, so they had become suspicious of any unfamiliar face. In my early jobs I could make a connection in days; now it took weeks of slow legend-building and trying to establish trust.

Very gradually though, I began to weave myself into the life of the city's drug-addict underworld. Working out of a shabby ex-local authority flat, rented under a false name by EMSOU, I spent day after day begging and shoplifting my way into friendships with several local characters.

There was Joni, the *Big Issue* seller who we all called Uma because her only outfit was a bright yellow tracksuit, like a street junkie version of Uma Thurman in *Kill Bill*.

There were Ned and George, a young gay couple in their early twenties who had run away from home in North Wales to be together, but ended up addicted to smack in the squats of Northampton.

There was Ellie, a gentle, intelligent woman who worked out of a flat with no heating or hot water, selling the only thing she had left to feed her all-consuming habit.

As before, I worked my way in with the odd gift of a DVD or pair of trainers; I'd say I'd nicked them but couldn't sell them on. I soon realised that I also needed to target a very specific sort of person: the kind ones.

Anyone selfish or hard-nosed was useless to me. They acted in their own interests, and were too afraid of the gangsters to even talk to me.

What I needed were the generous ones – the people whose resolve would break when I played rattling and they saw another person in pain. Every addict knows the coruscating agony of withdrawal, but only some will reach out a helping hand. My job was to identify those with a generous, sympathetic streak to their characters – then to ruthlessly exploit it.

This was how I got in with Angus and Sara. They were a sweet couple, locked together by addiction but also by genuine love. She got up at dawn to grab the best pitches for selling the *Big Issue*; he walked with a cane from childhood polio, so begged and hustled as best he could. They were exactly the type of soft touches that I could play on to make the connections I needed.

They were also in trouble themselves.

As a result of his disability, Angus had been given a car by the local authority. Being drug addicts, they immediately decided to fund their habits in the most effective way possible, and started using the car to do a bit of dealing.

But of course, you can't just pick up and start dealing in a town run by gangsters. It wasn't that Angus and Sara were ever going to become rivals to the Burger Bar Boys – the threat came from their own customers.

Imagine you're an addict. Now imagine you get arrested for possession. The cops offer you a deal: they'll let you off – if you give them information on your dealer. Now you have a choice – you can grass up the Burger Bar Boys and get shot, or you can rat on Angus and Sara, the sweet couple with the red Ford Cortina. The police don't care – either way it's an arrest and their monthly statistics look a bit rosier.

Angus and Sara lasted two months before they were ratted out and busted. They were on bail when I met them, terrified of being split up when they inevitably got sent to prison.

This was yet another archetypal War on Drugs story. A tactic is developed to catch gangsters, but ends up directly protecting them, and targeting low-level users instead. The cops don't even care that they're being played – on paper they're still making busts.

But I was able to use Angus and Sara's worries to gain their friendship. I played even more down-and-out than usual and appealed to them as a fellow sufferer. I knew I was manipulating them and putting their lives at risk. But this was a war, and I had a mission.

I also had commanders – and they were becoming impatient. Max and Gino wanted to start seeing results. As much as I tried to explain that I could buy off as many other users as I wanted, but it wouldn't get me any closer to the Burger Bar Boys, Gino didn't care. He wanted to see numbers. How many buys was I making? How many contacts was I picking up?

Gino was a brash, laddish guy who had watched too many movies before joining the force. He was pure Midlands Miami Vice, with a confrontational, hard-man sense of humour that too often blurred the line between 'banter' and simply 'being a prick'. He also liked to drink. Every time I saw him break open that cheeky 5 p.m. can of lager, I knew I was about to get a wave of pressure about the case, accompanied by a string of rubbish, off-colour jokes.

But no matter how much Gino blustered, there was little I could do to speed things up. Gradually, score by score, I was working out how the system in Northampton worked.

The Burger Bar Boys weren't stupid. What they had done was to insulate themselves with a layer of small-time user-dealers. They would offer some addict a few extra bags to courier their product to other junkies in town. While the police were kept busy busting these user-dealers, the Burgers were essentially shielded, and could just sit back and rake in the money. All they had to do was to beat, shoot and rape enough to terrify anyone out of ever testifying against them.

It was a smart move. It was also the inevitable response to police tactics – yet another example of how the arms race worked directly to target the vulnerable, while actually protecting the real gangsters.

The key to cracking through this layer of user-dealers was Angus and Sara. Their stint with the car had lifted them into a slightly higher echelon. I would occasionally hear them refer to 'the Brummies' in conversation. All I had to do was work out how to manipulate them into putting their own lives on the line by offering me an introduction.

It was all in the timing. I waited till I knew they were going to be out of town for a few days, then turned up at their door, with tears in my eyes. 'Ah pet, what's wrong? Come in.' Sara rushed me into their living room.

I needed a sob story – so I stole Cammy's.

I directly lifted his tragic moment from the benches in Mansfield. My best friend from childhood had suddenly died, and I was beside myself, not even wanting to go to the funeral out of junkie self-loathing. Then I looked up through tear-stained eyes. 'I just really need something right now, y'know – something to get me through... And you guys are leaving tonight... I don't know what I'm going to do. Is there anyone you can hook me up with? I just need something for the next few days.'

It felt dirty then. It still feels dirty now. But that was the position in which our war put us. The ends had to justify the means. The Burger Bar Boys needed to be caught, and this was the only way the job was going to get done.

And it worked. Sara stroked my head with almost maternal care, looked over to Angus and said, 'Don't worry pet, we'll introduce you to the Brummies.'

'Right, we've got to get our story together'.

Angus was shitting it. I could feel the tension coming off him as he started throwing out questions for us to review: where had we met? Who did we score off? What shoplifting had we done together? It was exactly the same work we did as police when putting together an undercover identity.

The Burger Bar Boys had set up their base at a snooker club in Castle Ward, right in the middle of Northampton city centre. Angus exchanged a nod with a huge geezer in a black bomber jacket. This guy, obviously the security, turned and gestured to a group of six or seven hard-men, lounging in a cloud of smoke in a back corner, illuminated only by the glow of the fruit machines.

One of this gang motioned Angus and me to follow, and led us into the toilets. My heart beat faster as I recognised Jackson.

We followed Jackson into the men's room. The five other geezers who had been sitting at his table trooped in after us, and I was quickly surrounded by these five huge guys, in their matching black jackets, leering down at me.

'Who the fuck is dis then?' barked Jackson.

As if on cue, the five bruisers immediately started walking a tight circle around me, closing me in.

'It's Woody man...he's cool, he's been around here for ages,' Angus stammered from the corner, using the ironic nickname I had chosen for this operation.

Then Jackson turned to me and shouted, 'Who's his fucking bird then?'

'It's Sara, I've known them ages.' I tried to keep my voice low and humble. 'I just wanted—'

BANG. One of the guys circling me lashed out. The head-butt wasn't hard enough to knock me down, but it sent me staggering to the side, only to be pushed straight back into the centre of the circle.

'Where he live, then?' barked Jackson.

'Out in Kettering,' I cried back, in a rising panic.

BANG. BANG. Another headbutt, followed by a hard shoulder-slam into my back. I reeled one way, then another.

'Who you fuckin' score your tings off?'

'Uhh...I know Mike from Abington...and Jamie from down St. Crispin—'

BANG. BANG – BANG. BANG.

I was cut off by another rain of blows, coming in from all directions as they continued to pace their tight circle around me.

BANG. BANG. BANG. The shoves and headbutts kept coming, harder and more violent.

'I know Ellie, the working girl from Bridge Street,' I cried in desperation, feeling immediately guilty for endangering her by dropping her name – but by this point I was frantic.

'Yeah, all right,' Jackson growled.

And with that one phrase, the guys stopped circling. Without a word they trooped back out the door.

Jackson loomed over me. 'What you want, den?'

'Uhh…just a one and one,' I stammered.

'Yeah, all right.' He reached into his pocket and held out a rock of crack and a wrap of heroin.

'Gimme the money, gimme the fuckin' money,' he snarled, and snatched the twenty quid out of my hand.

Then he got close, right in my face, his voice dropping to an exaggerated growl, 'You talk to the pigs – we kill you. You talk to some other cunt that talks to the pigs – we fucking kill you. You fuckin' get it, bruv?'

I just nodded.

Jackson turned to Angus, still standing in the corner. 'Give him the fucking number.'

As we walked out of the snooker club Angus turned to me. 'Don't fuck about with them lot – they're wrong'uns, mate…They're just fucking wrong.'

I knew Angus wasn't speaking for my benefit. Any infraction I committed against the Burgers would rebound onto him and Sara. I made a promise to myself that I would do everything in my power to protect them from any repercussions.

But I was soon to find out just how *wrong* the Burger Bar Boys could really be.

I tried the number Angus gave me, and was told to go to an isolated spot near the Racecourse, a scraggy bit of parkland that had become an open-air shooting gallery for the city's junkies.

A black car with tinted windows rolled up. Out stepped Jackson's second-in-command, a huge bruiser who everyone just called D, along with another geezer in a black jacket. acting as bodyguard.

D gruffly sold me a two and one – two bags of heroin and one of crack. Then, just as I was handing over the money, he grabbed me by the collar and violently yanked me forward. 'Don't fuck with dis,' he brayed in my face.

I just nodded, trying to communicate utter subservience. He pushed me roughly and I staggered back. 'I mean it. Don't fuck with dis, bruv,' he snarled again. Then he very deliberately lifted the bottom of his jacket.

There it was: the black chrome handle of a US police standard issue Glock 9mm. I took another step back, keeping my eyes on the ground and raising my hands to my chest, palms out in a gesture of total surrender. D just smirked with a venomous mix of malice and contempt and slid back into the car.

Of course I didn't write up the handgun in my evidence book. By now we all knew how the system worked.

I had to give the Burger Bar Boys credit though. Their crack came back from the lab 92% pure, and their heroin around 60%. This was by far the best product any of us had ever encountered. To be shifting gear like that meant they had to be plugged into some major international networks.

But in addition to targeting the Burgers, I was trying to build a broad picture of how the entire drug scene functioned in Northampton. That meant carefully and patiently maintaining my network of underworld junkie contacts.

This led to problems with Gino. He wanted results fast; and his gung-ho attitude only got worse if he had had a pint or two with lunch.

I would do an afternoon score and call in for a pick-up, only to have him order me to stay out and make another buy that evening. I tried to explain that this was unrealistic behaviour – a junkie would do his shot, then need several hours to ride out the high, then beg or steal enough money for the next fix. If I charged around making several scores a day from different dealers, I might as well print myself a T-shirt saying 'Undercover Cop'.

It got to the point where one afternoon I got into the car, only to have him snap, 'No, no – we're not leaving yet. I want us to do another buy. We're going to get an evening one today.'

I could smell the beer on him, and even wondered for a moment if he was fit to drive. 'Gino, listen mate, it's not the right move. I've been out all day, trust me – I know the situation.'

'No, you listen, Neil!' he shouted in pent-up frustration, 'you don't know everything, yeah. I'm telling you we need another bloody buy today.'

This just wasn't worth the hassle.

I got back out of the car and stood on the pavement, pretending to punch a number into my mobile. I held it to my ear and counted off fifteen seconds before giving Gino a fatalistic shrug. 'Nah man – gone to voicemail – nothing to be done.' Gino bought it, but the entire way back to headquarters

I couldn't stop thinking that I shouldn't have to be pretending to make calls just to get my own Cover Officer off my back. This was simply not how an operation should be run.

The Burger Bar Boys had one mobile number they shared between them – a tactic to frustrate efforts to gather evidence on any specific gang member. Every time a different voice would pick up with, 'All right Woody,' and I would receive instructions about where to make the deal.

I always dreaded it when D answered. Scoring from the Burgers always meant some form of unpleasantness, but he was by far the worst. This particular evening he had a particular edge in his voice as he ordered me to come all the way across town.

He didn't pull up in his usual sports car, but in a large minivan, along with four guys I'd never seen before.

D started walking around me, like a military sergeant doing an inspection. Then he turned to one of the other guys and grunted, 'What you think then?'

Without a moment's hesitation the guy immediately yelped back, 'I reckon he's fucking Five-O.'

The rest of the group immediately exploded into shouts of 'Yeah, he's fucking Five-O, bro...fucking do him, bro...just fucking kill him now, bro.'

D stepped back to his group. He then reached round his back, and out came the Glock. He stood, arms crossed, slowly tapping the gun against his left shoulder. 'Take off your shirt.'

I carefully removed my torn jacket and charity shop jumper, and stood there shivering and thanking God I wasn't wearing a wire.

'Fuckin' do him...Just fuckin' shoot him, bro,' the gang brayed like a pack of hyenas.

D looked on, impassive. 'Your pants,' he commanded.

I slid my trousers down to my ankles. 'I said your fucking pants,' snarled D. The gang went suddenly quiet.

My underwear followed my trousers down round my shins. Now the hyenas exploded in laughter. 'Look at de little white boy...'rah mate, look at dat, he actually fuckin' did it 'n all.'

Now I was getting annoyed. I've never had any problems in that department, and I needed to let D know that even as a junkie, there was only so far he could push. 'Yeah, all right, it's fucking cold, y'know.'

The gang seemed to respond to that expression of male defensiveness – maybe they could relate. 'Ah, put yourself away, man,' sneered D, obviously satisfied I wasn't wired up. I hurriedly threw my clothes back on and proceeded to buy three bags of heroin and two of crack, making myself a mental promise that I would take this fucker down.

All across my Northampton addict network things were in crisis.

George died of a heroin overdose. His boyfriend Ned woke up to find his lover's body lying on the floor of their squat, blue and cold, the needle still stuck in his arm.

Ned called the emergency services in an anguished panic, and was promptly arrested for possession with intent to supply. He was twenty-two years old. He and George had run away from home to be together, and now he was trapped in the justice system, utterly alone.

There was nothing I could do. I heard the story on the junkie grapevine as it was passed from street corner to street corner. I immediately rushed back to HQ to see if there might be any leeway. Ned was no dealer, but Northampton police were looking to nail him as having supplied George with the skag that killed him. It was a disgrace. But the EMSOU brass were clear; they couldn't be seen to be meddling in Northamptonshire Constabulary affairs.

A week later, Ellie got battered by her pimp. She turned up to score with a split lip, and appalling yellow-purple bruises darkening each eye.

'Fucking Christ Ellie, what happened?' I gasped in shock.

'Just someone being a prick,' she answered fatalistically.

'Yeah but I mean...did you tell anyone?'

'Woody, who the fuck am I going to tell?' She seemed surprised at my naïveté.

'Am I supposed to go to the cops and say *my junkie pimp beat me and raped me?* What the fuck do you think will happen? They'll arrest me and then he'll cut my face up when he finds out.'

She grimaced in pain, and put her head in her hands. 'What the fuck...let's just score, yeah? I fucking need something right now.'

I let her keep almost the entire bag, keeping only the bare minimum I needed to present as evidence to Gino. But I was crushed. I had already, of course, begun to feel deep misgivings about the way the War on Drugs was being fought, but Ellie's complete and automatic distrust of the police spun me round.

How had the system become so twisted that instead of protecting people like Ellie or Ned and George, they were forced to live outside it? They weren't just terrified of their own dealers, but also of the police – the very people they should have been able to turn to for protection. All I could see around me was our own tactics being used against us while we busted vulnerable people on meaningless charges.

'Woody, hey Woody,' a voice called from behind me.

I spun round to see Joni, my *Big Issue* seller friend, in her usual *Kill Bill*-yellow tracksuit.

'Fuck, are you all right?' she gasped.

I was playing rattling that day – like a junkie in serious need. I'd made my eyes red and watery, I was walking with a cramped stoop and had quickened my breath into a shallow rasp. From Joni's reaction, I guess my act was working.

'All right Uma?' I put an extra little tremble into my voice and used her street nickname. 'You don't fancy getting a bag do you?'

'Ah I can't, love, I've got to sell the magazines.' She looked at me sympathetically. 'But you're really hurting aren't you?'

Without waiting for an answer she held out a five-pound note. 'Here, sort yourself out. I'll be fine selling these, you look like you could use some help.'

Joni needed that fiver. She had a serious habit; in a few hours she'd be rattling herself. But she believed I was in trouble *at that moment*, and needed the money more. By the standards of the civilian world it was a tiny gesture, but for a penniless addict it was an immeasurable, profound act of kindness.

What could I do? I didn't want to take her cash. I was pretending to rattle for effect – Joni used heroin to self-medicate for her horrific childhood. But no junkie in history has ever turned down free money.

As I walked away with the fiver in my pocket I almost burst into tears. Maybe I was vulnerable and strung out, but the fact that this junkie – considered the lowest of the low by the rest of society – would perform such a massive act of compassion made me question everything I was here to do. Why was this person considered a criminal? Why couldn't she turn to the system for help? There was nothing morally wrong with her, so why was she considered beyond society's pale?

I still needed to take the Burger Bar Boys down – there was no doubt about the pain they caused. There was still a battle to fight, and I was still a soldier. But as I crept along the streets of Northampton in my worn-out trainers and torn jeans, I was forced to ask myself once again if we were even fighting the right war at all.

It's a four-hour drive between Northampton and Buxton. As the operation dragged on, I began stopping over more and more often out of sheer exhaustion.

As a reward for good work – and an incentive for more – Max and Gino started booking me into a posh hotel outside the city. The place had a five-star restaurant, armour on the walls and gold-plated taps in the bathroom. But I never felt right there.

I would come in straight from the job and have to walk through that fancy lobby still in my trackies and baseball cap – still inhabiting my street personality. I could feel the eyes of the other guests burning through me. I shouldn't be here. I didn't belong. Those nights were spent anxiously turning in the embroidered Egyptian cotton sheets, wondering what the hell I was doing there.

It was on about my fifth stay there that I cracked. I had spent most of the day chasing a crack-addled user-dealer around derelict Northampton council estates with Ellie, the bruises from her attack still vivid on her face. Now I was sitting on my own in one of the fanciest restaurants in the Midlands, listening to 'tasteful' piano jazz while chubby executives tried to impress identikit skinny blondes in too much make-up.

My food arrived. I stared down at the glistening veal chops, smothered in some sort of redcurrant gravy, and thought back to the empty Pot Noodle cartons, used needles and burned-up sheets of tinfoil that littered Ellie's flat.

I looked around the restaurant again. The soft pink of the meat in front of me perfectly matched the pink in the artsy photographs of African sunsets hanging on the walls. I cut into a chop, raised a morsel to my mouth, then put it back down and pushed the plate away in disgust.

I walked to the bar and ordered a double Scotch. Two more quickly followed. Why not? EMSOU were paying.

Even here I couldn't find any peace. The drinks were all served with little individual napkins under them. What was the point of that? What was the fucking point of all this useless shit when a woman like Ellie was beaten and raped, but couldn't turn to the police for help? What was the point when every tactic we used to catch gangsters was turned back round against the people we should be protecting?

'Can I get you anything else, sir?' asked the kindly old bartender.

'Sir?' I laughed in disgust. 'Who the fuck are you calling *sir*? I'm not your sir. *I'm not your fucking sir!*'

I realised I was shouting.

I swivelled on my barstool. The entire room had gone silent, staring at me in open-mouthed horror. What was happening? This wasn't me speaking, this was some unhinged council-estate street junkie.

'I'm . . . I'm sorry,' I whispered to the bartender, then slid off my stool and staggered out.

That night I slept in my tracksuit on the hotel room floor.

The next day Gino picked me up for my morning deployment. 'Don't ever put me there again,' I said, the second I got into the car.

'You what?' he blustered.

'Just don't put me in that hotel. I can't hack it there. Find somewhere as simple as possible, or I'd rather just sleep on the couch at HQ.'

Gino went into a sour little sulk for the whole journey back into town, but at this stage I didn't have the energy to manage his mood swings. I just didn't ever want to see that hotel again. The chasm between that and my life on the streets was just too wide, the disconnect too much for me to handle.

But as conflicted as I had felt at that hotel, nothing was as bad as actually having to go home.

Whenever I walked into our once cosy family home I'd feel like I'd stepped straight into a sullen, hostile war zone. Sam become unrecognisable to me, and the acrimony and shouting sessions were escalating.

My affair with Meghan had ended. She had met someone else, and I had no right to hold her back. So I needed a new form of solace. I wasn't an alcoholic – I dealt with addicts every day of my professional life – I know what that looks like. But, once you start using booze as a coping mechanism, there's only one way it can go – and it never ends well.

There had been a rape. Someone had defaulted on a crack debt and their girlfriend had paid the price. Nothing was officially reported – sexual assaults rarely are, particularly when the perpetrators are ruthless gangsters – but we had received urgent intelligence that the previous evening five of the Burger Bar Boys had thrown a woman in the boot of a car, driven to the outskirts of the city and each raped her in turn.

Max, our DI, was an extremely dedicated, ethically serious police officer. To him, doing service to a rape survivor took precedence over all other operational concerns. Our mission here as he saw it was to act ahead of the game, to gather whatever evidence we could, just in case anyone was to come forward in future.

'Woodsy, we need you to get yourself into a car with the Burgers today. There's a chance – a slim chance, but a chance – that whatever car they're driving today is the same one they were using last night. We'll organise an immediate pick-up for your clothes afterwards – you may well be covered in DNA evidence.'

When the Burgers pulled up in their jeep that morning I immediately threw open the door and slid into the back seat, not giving them the chance to get out and do my deal on the street. The two gangsters up front turned in irritated surprise, but I launched into a volley of, 'Ah mate, mate – thanks for coming out –I just, like, need a bit y'know. Just a bit for the morning, y'know how it is.'

I talked fast, like any desperate, rattling junkie. They'd seen it all before and sold me my bag of smack.

I jumped out of the car and raced round the corner to where a forensics team was waiting to put my clothes in sterile evidence bags.

But, just as they were finishing bagging everything up, we got a radio from HQ. The car that had actually been used for the rape had been discovered burned out on an industrial estate outside of town. It was a grim moment. But if anything, it strengthened my resolve to let these bastards know that they couldn't get away with it. As much as they might cover their tracks, I was going to put them away.

But that would take time and work; and once again, the painstaking, patient process of building a major case didn't sit well with Gino.

The only word he understood was *more*: more buys, more evidence, more results, more feathers in his cap. As much as I explained that more evidence didn't mean better evidence, he didn't want to hear it. As the case dragged on, he hit the booze ever harder, and got ever more aggressive.

It got to the point where I was regularly faking phone calls and evidence runs, just to get him off my back. Each time felt worse than the last. I was the guy who would take the bullet if I weakened my cover by making too many buys. Why should I be having to pull fake deployments like a schoolkid in order to mollify my own Cover Officer – the guy whose sole job was meant to be to protect me?

Eventually I snapped. I'd been out on the streets for eight hours. I was exhausted and cold, thinking about the drive home and what might be waiting for me when I got there. And now Gino was on the phone telling me to stay out and make another buy that evening.

'No Gino, I'm not doing it.' I kept my voice calm, but firm.

'Neil you have to bloody do it,' he snapped back.

'No. No I don't. This is my assignment, and I'm coming in now.'

'No, no, no! These are orders from the DI, Neil. He wants another buy today.'

'Well, tell you what – you get the DI on the phone and he can tell me himself, yeah? Now listen – I'm coming in right now. You either come and pick me up, or I'll get a taxi and bill it to EMSOU.'

The phone went dead. By the time I made it back to HQ in my cab, Gino was fuming. I could smell the beer on his breath.

'What the fuck was that about?' he stormed.

'Gino, listen. I'm the guy out on the streets. It's my call when to make a buy or when to come in. I just need your support on that, all right?'

'No Neil, no!' He was actually shouting now. 'You need to learn how to fucking follow orders. I'm going to take this to bloody EMSOU.'

'Well fucking take it to EMSOU,' I replied flippantly, 'I have a feeling they might just take my side over yours.'

'Oh fuck you Neil. You know what your fucking problem is?' He jabbed his finger into my chest. 'You're just not committed. You've just got no fucking commitment, Neil.'

This was too much. I could take people shouting at me – God knows I got plenty of that at home. But after the things I'd been through on this case – after the guns, the beatings, the death, the rape, the squalor – to be told I wasn't committed was a bridge too far.

I squared up and hissed straight into his face. 'Listen. I don't know what your problem is – but why don't you go out, get pissed, pick a fight and work it out with someone else?' Then I turned and strode out of the room.

Unfortunately, that's exactly what Gino did. He went out to a club, got raging drunk and picked a fight with the bouncer. He came off worse, and ended up repeatedly calling the guy a 'fucking black bastard'. Someone reported him, and he was immediately suspended.

I never saw Gino again. I have no idea what happened to him, but his brand of cocky racist bullshit has no place in the police force. After all the madness, dysfunction and mistrust of the police I had experienced recently, it was reassuring to see the system actually working for once. His replacement was a woman named Natalie, who was as brilliant and responsive a Cover Officer as one could hope for.

This relief was quickly undercut when the entire regional police force was rocked by scandal. Johnno got busted with cocaine.

He had obviously developed a taste for the stuff, and had started buying significant quantities from the same people he had once investigated. He was sent to prison for a year, and – obviously – never worked in law enforcement again.

This arrest of an elite Drugs Squad officer threw the entire force into disarray. Suddenly everyone was under surveillance. Even my old mate Steve, the expert Level 1 undercover, almost lost his pension over a few crumbs of hash.

I felt awful for Johnno. He was an excellent cop. He'd been my observations officer on several deployments, and had shown more concern for my well-being than probably anyone else on the force. Did it make sense that his life should be ruined over snorting a few lines? The propaganda of the drugs war casts all users as inherently morally deficient. What did it say about that attitude if genuinely dedicated, talented cops were starting to use these substances that were supposedly only for 'criminals'?

As the case moved on, things moved from the terrifying and dysfunctional to the downright surreal.

I had started wearing a wire with the Burger Bar Boys. I felt I had gained their trust enough that even D wouldn't force me to strip at gunpoint again. EMSOU came through this time. I got a recording device about the size of a ten-pack of cigarettes, hooked up to a tiny pinhole camera.

Usually the Burgers ran a tight ship. They were careful on the phone and always on the lookout for police surveillance. This time however, when I swung open the car door I was hit by a solid wall of dank ganja smoke. My eyes immediately began to water as I peered through the haze to see Jackson, obviously high as the clouds, lolling in the back seat with flaming red eyes and a massive grin on his face.

'Woody man... come in, man.' I slid into the back, doing my best not to cough my lungs out as the gang continued to pass around a spliff about the size of a car exhaust.

'What you wantin', Woody man?' asked Jackson, his voice slow and hoarse with smoke.

'Uhh... I'll take a two and one mate, if it's cool?' I replied, trying to work out if my camera was even going to pick up Jackson's face through all the smoke.

'Yeah man, it's cool... it's cool'. Moving in stoned slow motion, Jackson handed me the gear and took the cash.

The deal done, I moved to get out. But just as I was turning to open the door, Jackson grabbed my sleeve. I froze in dread, my mind flashing to the wire running up my torso.

'Woody man,' he began in a stoned slur, 'Woody man... why dey call you Woody, man? Is it... is it because you look like Woody Allen, man?'

I almost lost control and burst into hysterics. I was a skinny, six-foot bloke from Derbyshire, currently dressed like an inner-city street junkie. It's safe to say I didn't look anything remotely like Woody Allen. And the fact that the most dangerous gangster in the South Midlands was even talking to me about Woody Allen was just bloody weird. Not to play into cultural stereotypes, but Jackson didn't exactly come across as the *Annie Hall* type.

But I was getting a bit high myself off of all the smoke in the car. 'Nah mate, it's not that... I'll tell you what it is, though.'

'Yeah?' replied Jackson, leaning forward, his face rapt with gurning fascination.

'Well, you know the movie *Toy Story,* yeah?'

'Yeah.' Jackson nodded enthusiastically.

'Well, you know that bit where the kid takes Woody, the cowboy doll, and burns a hole in his forehead with the magnifying glass?'

'Yeah, yeah...yeah...'

'Well, when I was like fourteen, I had skin cancer on my forehead, and they had to burn it away with a machine. And after that, all the other kids called me Woody, because I was like Woody from *Toy Story* with a burnt forehead.'

Jackson looked at me with an expression of profound, almost childlike sadness.

'Aaah maaan,' he murmured slowly, 'that is rough...that is so rough, man...that is roooouuuughhhh.' He trailed off into his own silent meditation on the tragic story. I thought he might burst into tears right there.

So, there I was with a multiple murderer and crack-lord of Northampton, looking at me with dewy-eyed sympathy for my imaginary teenage trauma. It was just too weird. I left him there lost in his trance, and raced back to HQ to check I'd got the whole episode on tape.

From around that score on though, things became easier with the Burgers. Maybe word had filtered down from Jackson not to fuck with me too much; anyway the constant threats and intimidation cooled off a little.

I saw my opportunity and began wearing the cameras in earnest, catching each and every one of them on tape selling me crack and heroin. I reintroduced Pat to the mix, and he managed to make some buys as well, corroborating and strengthening the evidence I gathered.

When the bust came down, we went through the city like wildfire – something like ninety-five arrests were made.

But the real prize was always the Burgers. On the day itself, I was assigned to do a buy-bust on D. It gave me extraordinary satisfaction to meet him in a downstairs car park, record the buy on camera, then just watch him drive away and listen for the screech of tyres and shouts of 'Stop, police!' from the street.

The Burgers all got eight or nine years apiece. To my mind they deserved even more. The drug dealing was the least of the brutalities they were involved in.

But as ever, fighting a war means collateral damage. To make the evidence against the Burger Bar Boys stick, every single one of my contacts had to get written into the story. They all got caught in the net.

On top of their previous charges, Angus and Sara got three and a half years each. Ellie, the addict sex worker who had already suffered so much, now had to add prison to her list of troubles. Even Joni, the *Big Issue* seller who had given me her last fiver, was arrested and found her small act of kindness used against her.

This was nothing I could take any pride in, but also nothing I could do to stop. The war machine was in motion, and I was just a tiny cog in the apparatus.

With EMSOU there were never any big celebratory drinks. Even when the operation was wrapped up my identity had to remain protected. So, Max, Natalie and I ended up at the pub doing a staff party, undercover-style.

They were both in backslapping mood. 'You'll get a Chief Constable's Commendation for this Neil,' Max said. I raised my eyebrows and sipped my pint in silence. *Yep, another one to throw on the pile.*

'Come on Neil, cheer up,' giggled Natalie, 'you've just helped put a serious dent in the Northampton drug supply...for about seven minutes.'

I had to laugh at that one – old-fashioned police gallows humour at its best. But it was also the truth. Even as we ordered our rounds at the bar, a new set of gangsters would be rushing in to serve the market the Burgers had left open.

Later that night, though, as I sat on the sofa at home with a tin of lager, the joke kept replaying in my mind.

If this operation had been such a success, why did it feel so wrong? I thought back to Leicester and Nottingham and got the same sense of profound unease. Don't get me wrong – I got a rush of anger every time I thought about the Burger Bar Boys, and what they had been able to get away with for so long. I still wanted to crush their horrible little empire with every fibre of my being.

But that was the thing. The guys I busted in Northampton were second-generation Burger Bar Boys. It had started with their fathers fighting for control of the drugs trade, and been passed to Jackson and his crew through their older brothers. The gang was set deep in the life of the Midlands and a new generation was already stepping in to take their place.

So, while I may have put a few of the gang away for a while, I had done absolutely nothing to address the situation that actually gave them their power. And along the way, I had made a lot of vulnerable lives even more unbearable.

As a cop fighting the drugs war, I was caught up in the arms race just like everyone else. Surely there had to be a better way? But if there was – at this point at least – I just couldn't see it. What was there to do but to keep fighting, battle by bloody battle, and just accept that each one would cost a little more in brutality and human suffering than the last?

Even now, I wasn't able to follow these doubts and questions to their inevitable conclusion. I wouldn't be able to make that final leap until I had witnessed the endgame of the drugs war arms race with my own eyes.

And I saw it on the streets of Brighton.

CHAPTER 14

BRIGHTON

I n Northampton I had seen the bloody trenches of the British War on Drugs. In Brighton I saw the dead zone.

When you walk the streets of any city there are two populations. There are those who pass through on their way to work, home, the shops, the pub, the station. Then there are the people *of* the street: the cleaners, the *Big Issue* sellers, the bin-men, the drug dealers, the buskers and, of course, the homeless. These are the ones for whom home and work *are* the streets. The people of the street can become invisible. You step over the beggars, you skirt around street cleaners – to you they are just vague shapes at the edge of your peripheral vision, abstract obstacles in the urban landscape. But they see you. They watch you go by, and they know that you are just a tourist in *their* world. The world of the street is always there, beating its rhythm all around us. It has its own rules, its own opportunities, its own dangers lurking in the shadows – which, most of the time, you won't even realise are there.

By now I had become attuned to the world of the street. In any new town I immediately noticed the homeless, the addicts, the hustlers, the beggars. I could spot a junkie on the way to meet their dealer – I could tell when someone was trying to keep a lookout for the cops. Over time one becomes sensitive to the patterns, and can pick up the atmosphere just by walking around and noticing.

Brighton was rotten.

Within hours of starting to walk those streets I could tell something was deeply wrong in the homeless community. At this point it was just a sense – something in the way that people hurried past, something about how they avoided eye contact. It was as if every street person was carrying the same horrible secret, and they didn't dare speak to anyone for fear they would let it slip.

There was something sick here, something profoundly different from anything I had seen, even in the squalor and violence of Northampton, Leicester or Nottingham. I returned to headquarters after that first walkabout deeply disturbed. Something was going on in this city – and I was going to uncover it.

Brighton police had been one of the first forces in the country to start running Level 2 operations, and had one of the UK's most extensive covert policing programmes. Yet for the past year or so, they hadn't managed to catch a single significant gangster. Having helped write the book on undercover tactics, I was invested. If something wasn't working, I wanted to help fix it.

But there was something else that sparked my interest in this operation. Brighton had by far the highest rate of heroin overdoses in the UK. The previous year had seen fifty-four deaths – more than one a week. As a per-capita rate, that was shockingly higher than any other city in the country. With my growing empathy for vulnerable addicts, this was not a statistic I could turn my back on.

The first briefing was a nightmare.

Within minutes my impression formed that for all their supposed experience – and all the funding they'd received – these people seemed incapable of structuring a targeted, intelligence-led investigation. From where I stood, I could see none of the EMSOU discipline and professionalism. Instead, all I felt were all the worst hallmarks of police culture gone wrong: arrogance, brash insensitivity, idiot machismo and the chasing of statistics over the welfare of victims.

The DI was a hulking blowhard who appeared to run his team like a pack of wolves, each one snapping at the others, trying to raise their place in the pecking order.

When I began asking questions about the city's awful rate of heroin overdoses, one of the younger officers immediately chimed in, 'Yeah, we had fifty-four last year. This year we're already on thirty-six – fuckin' hell, looks like we're going to beat our own record!'

The room immediately erupted in raucous laughter and mocking high-fives. It only got worse from there. Every opportunity for a gag at the expense of a dead homeless person was exploited. The briefing fell apart in a storm of shitty jokes, as they all tried to out-banter each other.

Don't get me wrong; I like cop humour – I'd held my own with Bomb Damage and the Derbyshire boys for years. But in Brighton it was something different. I felt the job was actually suffering because of this team's internal squabbles.

The one solace was that at least I knew I'd been brought in to sort out this mess. I had been sent down as an expert troubleshooter, and if nothing else, it was clear that I was in charge of my own operation and they would respect the way I did things.

Or so I thought.

That consensus didn't last beyond my first deployment on the street.

The first thing that struck me was the sheer number of homeless addicts in the city.

Brighton is usually thought of in terms of British seaside kitsch: Victorian piers and slot machines, stony beaches and the slate-grey sea, fish and chips and mushy peas. But those are the associations of the people who walk the streets on their way to warm, cosy homes. The people *of the street* view this city in a very different light.

My theory is that most addicts are running away from something. They run and run, then they hit the sea and there's nowhere left to go. It's something I've observed in seaside towns across the country. Brighton was simply the largest.

As usual, I made no buys at first. I didn't even attempt to strike up a conversation. I was just observing, taking the city's ragged pulse. Again I felt the overwhelming sensation that the entire homeless community in the city was suffering from some deep collective trauma. There was something sick about this city, something festering, secret and vile.

When I got back to HQ, the wolf pack turned on me.

'What, you didn't buy anything?' The DI gasped incredulously.

'Well, no. I'm observing first. I'm building a picture of how the city functions. That's how good undercover work happens.'

'I thought undercover work meant buying bloody drugs,' he replied. The rest of the room broke into guffaws.

'Yeah, but you haven't done any undercover work, and I have. So why don't you have a sit-down and I'll explain it you, yeah?'

I knew instantly that I'd fucked up. I'd let myself get angry.

'Ooh, touchy,' mocked the DI, mimicking the voice of some neurotic housewife.

The entire squad tittered. They reminded me of a group of kids encouraging a playground bully in the hope that he won't turn on them.

I forced myself to take a breath. I'd faced down speed-addled gangsters with samurai swords; I'd sent ruthless gun-wielding thugs to prison. I wasn't going to let this lot get under my skin. I flashed the DI a condescending smile, turned and left the room.

Out on the street I stuck to my own schedule. That pack of desk police at the office could run their operations however they wanted – I was the guy in the field.

I spent several more days just watching from street corners and shopfronts. Looking at how the city functioned. It wasn't until a few weeks in that it felt right to approach Frank.

He was a *Big Issue* seller who held the prime pitch in town, just under a pedestrian footbridge on the slope up to the main station. He rocked a wild ginger Afro and, like Ali up in Leicester, had a charming salesman's patter.

It turned out he had once been a successful club promoter, making his name in Ibiza as part of the mid-90s rave gold rush. But he also suffered from childhood trauma. Ecstasy was his first self-medication of choice, but he soon followed the well-worn path towards heroin, and had drifted in and out of prison before washing up on the streets of Brighton.

As well as English, Frank spoke five languages fluently. He sold his *Big Issues* in French, Spanish, Portuguese, and Italian. He was in the process of learning Polish and Latvian from a couple of newly arrived homeless guys in town. Once again I was overpowered by the thought of what a guy with this intelligence and creativity could have achieved if he had been given a little support instead of turned into a criminal.

After he sold out of magazines we shared a couple of cans of lager on a bench looking out over the sea. I carefully let him draw from me that I was an on-and-off junkie who had dropped out of art school, got busted shoplifting and was now back living on a court-ordered Subuxone prescription with my dad in Southwick.

After a couple of hours, and a few more cans, I thought the time was right.

'So, mate,' I ventured timidly, 'you think you could help me out getting a bit of brown?'

Frank just rolled his eyes and gave a disappointed sigh. 'Oh, so you're a cop, then?'

It was enough to almost make my heart stop.

'You what?' I sputtered in feigned incredulity.

'Come on mate, I know the drill,' Frank intoned, more in boredom than in anger. 'Some new bloke shows up and wants a bit of gear – then it turns out he's a cop and you go to fucking jail.'

'Mate, mate, that's not me – seriously. Look, don't bother if it's a hassle.'

'Uh huh.' Frank just sipped his beer in total indifference.

I pleaded my case, filling in any weak links in my story and dropping in details that only a real junkie would know.

My head was spinning. Had the Brighton team overused undercover operations to the point where any new face in town was automatically assumed to be a cop? Was that even possible?

Eventually I did manage to win Frank over, but more out of his own nihilistic fatalism than any genius on my part.

'Look,' he explained, 'I'm about ninety per cent sure you're not a pig...but, to be honest, I don't fucking care. Put me in jail. I don't give a shit – you might just save my life...Another winter sleeping in the underpass will probably kill me anyway. At least in prison it's warm.'

There was no melodrama in his voice, no sense of exaggeration or self-pity. His rational calculation was simply that it was September, cold weather was on the way and he was probably too weak to survive. The uncaring, blasé tone in which Frank discussed his likely death was as horrifying as anything I'd heard or seen as an undercover.

Frank told me to wait on a corner, then disappeared for fifteen minutes before returning with the gear. Obviously, this was useless to me. I needed to at least catch a glimpse of his dealer. But having already raised suspicions, I couldn't afford to press the point. I told myself that once again I would just have to patiently build trust and wait for the right moment.

We went off to a deserted bit of scrubland so he could fix up. I was able to claim that I was waiting till my Subuxone had worn off, otherwise it would block the skag and the gear would be wasted. This was completely legitimate junkie logic, and actually served to back up my story.

I held a lighter so Frank could aim properly as he spiked his vein, then watched his head roll back in pleasure and relief. As he collected himself, he leaned forward in a smacked-up haze.

'Listen,' he mumbled, 'I don't care if you're a cop or not, you're a nice bloke. I don't want you to fucking die, so listen – I'm gonna tell you how it works.'

He proceeded to lay out, in skag-slurred speech, the appalling reality of exactly how the street drugs trade in Brighton operated.

There had been so many undercover operations in the city that the gangsters had developed a failsafe system to thwart them. Each dealer would choose one or two addicts as a designated point of contact, and conduct all their business through them. If anyone else wanted to score, they had to go to that one courier. No one else would ever even see the dealer.

This was why the Brighton cops had stopped being able to catch real gangsters. They could arrest points of contact all day long, and never get close to a real criminal. The gangsters didn't care. As soon as one point of contact got busted, another would step forward to take their place. No resource is more expendable in the War on Drugs than the life of an addict.

Every suspicion I'd ever had about how the drugs war functioned as an arms race was being confirmed right in front of me.

But the real horror was still to come.

Frank pulled me close, slurring into my ear. '...And if you fuck with the system they kill you. If I was to even bring you within sight of a dealer, I'd be fucking dead. No questions – nothing – just fucking dead.'

'What?' I gasped incredulously, 'they shoot people just for letting someone see them?' I pointed my fingers at my own head, miming gunshots.

'Nah...They don't bloody shoot you. It's fucking easy to get rid of a smackhead, isn't it – they just give you a bad shot...they let you do it yourself.'

I suddenly felt nauseous. It was like the ground had fallen away and suddenly I was staring into the dizzying abyss. In a flash everything I had felt about Brighton made sense. This was pure horror. It was no accident that there were so many heroin overdoses in the city. It was murder by narcotic.

From the gangsters' point of view, it made perfect sense. Make it look like an accidental overdose and the police will never even investigate. Make the addicts live in a constant state of terror that their fix – the one thing they need more than anything else in the world – might kill them, and they become your slaves. You instantly create an entirely obedient, terrorised population.

Now I knew I could put a name to that deep, fundamental *wrongness* I had sensed in Brighton. It was fear. The addicts couldn't stop using, but they had to deal with the continual knowledge that each shot could be their execution. The entire city was rank with terror.

It was all I could do to nod along as Frank spoke. My mind was racing. I needed to investigate this – I needed to uncover real evidence and break this whole scam open. And to do that I would need support.

It quickly became clear I wasn't going to get any.

'You want us to do what?' roared the DI. I saw his face reddening in astonishment.

'I need you to help me go through the files on every overdose death you had last year. There are indications that at least some of them may have been murders.'

'Aren't you undercover agents supposed to bring back drugs?' he smirked. Once again, I heard a round of mocking sniggers sweep across the room.

'What I've just brought you is the single most important piece of operational intelligence of your career.'

'Yes well,' he responded in what seemed a mock-serious tone, 'that's duly noted. I'll inform the higher-ups and we'll see what we can do, yes?'

I knew a bureaucratic brush-off when I heard one. This was hopeless. I rolled my eyes, and went back to trying to actually get things done.

I scored off Frank several more times. He never let me anywhere even near the line of sight of a dealer. Rules were rules, and inasmuch as Frank valued his own life, he stuck to them.

All Frank's friends were dead. He had no doubts whatsoever that they had been murdered by overdose. He was just waiting his own turn – marking time until he slipped up and transgressed some unwritten rule he didn't even know, and the gangsters decided his time had come for a dirty shot.

Homeless people survive by forming tight-knit networks, little gangs like my park bench crew in Nottingham who can help each other out, and sleep in pairs for security. Frank had seen his entire network picked off one by one, and it had broken him inside. Behind the snappy show he put on to sell his *Big Issues*, there was a fathomless sense of despair that sometimes made him hard to even look at.

One time he had the possibility of getting some sheltered accommodation in Hove. The train fare to do the preliminary interview was £5.40, but he just couldn't see the point. He needed that cash for his smack and Special Brew, and he assumed he'd be dead in a matter of months anyway, so why waste the money? There's no other way to say it – it was fucking heartbreaking.

In the end though, what stopped me from hanging out with Frank wasn't existential despair; it was my own bosses.

'Time to move on now, we've got him, don't we?'

'What do you mean *we've got him?*'

'This guy, Frank – we've got him. We've got enough evidence to arrest him.'

'And why would we want to arrest him?'

'Well…he's a drug dealer.'

'Is *that* what you call a drug dealer?' I asked in disbelief. No wonder these amateur-hour play-police weren't catching any real gangsters.

'Well…he sold you drugs.'

'No. Frank's not a drug dealer. Frank is a user who has been coerced into supplying other addicts on the street. If you want to arrest an actual drug dealer, you don't arrest Frank – you use him to get to a gangster.'

'Yeah, but he sold you drugs – he's a drug dealer. If we arrest him, we've arrested a dealer.'

I sighed in defeat. This was useless.

'All right, do whatever you need to do. Just don't arrest him until I say, yeah. Right now I need him on the street.'

I wanted no part of this. I needed the bosses off my back, but I also didn't want to give them any more evidence against the poor guy. Frank deserved better than that. From then on I just tried to avoid him as much as possible.

But, to keep the mission going, I would need some new targets.

I moved through the city's homeless like a lab-rat through a maze, covering a lot of ground but always hitting the same dead end. Everyone was happy to take money off me to score, junkies always are, but no one would let me anywhere within eyeshot of a dealer. No matter what manipulations I tried or tricks I pulled, it was just never going to happen. These people were terrified. In any case, most of them weren't even scoring off gangsters, but off other addicts who had been designated points of contact.

My primary concern was corroborating Frank's allegations about people being murdered by overdose. I was a detective and I knew one homeless addict's theory wasn't enough to build a case on.

Every single person I encountered repeated the claim. It was just a simple fact of life on the street – even a suspicion that someone had transgressed the gangsters' law meant they would be found dead with a needle in their arm. Everyone had at least one friend they knew for certain had been murdered.

I had seen the knife-edge existence of the addicts in other cities, but this was something else. The sheer tissue-thin fragility of these peoples' lives, the corrosive underlying terror in which they lived, the casual and matter-of-fact assumption of their own execution, was appalling on a fundamental human level.

The psychological pressure was only increased by the weird juxtaposition of this pretty seaside town – full of tourists and rich Londoners down for a lark – and the grinding daily horror endured by the city's underclass. Seeing these two worlds coexist in the same space day after day was not just unsettling, it was a form of cultural schizophrenia that ran like a seam through the entire city.

There was one couple who made a particular impression. When I first met Sophie and Gregg, she was living in a women's shelter and he was sleeping rough. Somehow they managed to get hold of a tent, and pitched camp together in a little copse of trees on one of the green spaces near Union Road. Gregg was a point of contact for one of the local gangs, and they supported their habit by scoring for other users.

They were completely head over heels, and very protective of each other. The first time I scored with them, Gregg slipped the gear out of his mouth and into my hand. Sophie immediately sprang up and grabbed my arm. 'Now you put it in your mouth.' She wouldn't let me leave until she saw the wrap under my gums.

She was making sure that if I was arrested, Gregg's DNA would be covered by my own. Those were the rules. The gangsters made every point of contact mouth-carry to cover their DNA, and Sophie was protecting her man in the same way.

I had to take that wrap, which had just been passed from the mouth of a drug dealer to the mouth of a homeless smack addict, and place it in my own. A wave of disgust scudded through my guts at the taste of stale beer and cigarette ash.

But for all that, there was still never any question of Gregg introducing me to a dealer. The few times I even hinted at it, Sophie would immediately cut in. 'No way! Just no – I don't want him to die…I need him.' Then she'd give a weak smile and tousle his hair. The way they protected each other was deeply touching, but heartbreaking – it was as if they both knew their days were numbered, and yet they held together, each one counting on the other for survival.

Week after week I tracked the city, moving from false start to dead end, making endless scores from vulnerable addicts that would never lead me any closer to an actual gangster.

Essentially, I was becoming just another Brighton under-cover operative.

This wasn't what I had joined the force to do. It simply wasn't what I thought of as real police work.

Eventually, I just stopped.

I started going out looking only for intelligence. Occasionally I'd make a buy, but mostly I would just talk to people, trying to figure out if there was any angle, any tactic, that could actually open the investigation up.

I knew that any user I scored off would be classed as a dealer and slung in prison. What was the point when they weren't leading us to real criminals? It's one thing to claim the end justifies the means, but here there wasn't even an end – just more misery for vulnerable people. That being the case, I chose not to keep buying drugs with police money.

Of course, this created problems with the squad.

'Aren't you supposed to be making some bloody buys?' the DI demanded.

'Well – yes and no. What I'm meant to be doing is laying out an operational strategy that might lead us to some real criminals. When that involves making buys, I'll let you know.'

I could sense that the DI didn't appreciate the challenge to his authority, particularly in front of the other guys. A few days later, I walked into headquarters to see two new faces. 'Oh hi, Neil,' he said. 'We saw you were having some trouble, so we thought we'd bring in Sandra and Mike here to help you along.'

On her second deployment Sandra actually managed to speak to a user-dealer one tiny step up the food chain. This involved her being dragged into a disused warehouse, strip-searched and assaulted. She had been trained for this, and there was a backup team nearby, but she still returned to HQ badly shaken. I couldn't help feeling the DI and his team were secretly pleased – *see, a girl managed to do it.*

I just stood there and watched the scene, thinking to myself, *yep – just wait and see what happens when you get out on the street again tomorrow.*

Of course she never got anywhere near that user-dealer again. The strip-search was just an initial test to see if she was wearing a wire. From that point she was thrown back into the same mix as the rest of us. The entire ordeal had been a complete waste of time.

As the weeks dragged on, the situation became ever more depressing and hopeless. There was no way this strategy was going to take us anywhere, and the atmosphere among the team was becoming intolerable for me.

So one night I sat up all night alone in our HQ, trying to figure out a new way.

The next day I presented my ideas to the team.

'OK look. The gangsters in this city have figured out our tactics and they've taken countermeasures. We're never going to get anywhere near them by coming up from the gutter. They've got their system sewn up, and the population completely terrorised.'

I was met with a wall of blank stares.

'So let's try a new tactic. Let me rent a van, and fill it with seized goods from customs. Furniture, computers, TVs – stuff like that. I'll drive into town and reinvent myself as a medium-level house burglar from Manchester, looking for proper connections down south. I reckon it will take me three months to work my way into the scene, at which point I can legitimately try and buy a weight of cocaine and we can make some meaningful arrests.'

'Three months?' cried the DI. 'What do you think this is, a bloody ocean cruise?' I heard the obligatory round of mocking sniggers ripple through the room.

'No. What I think this is is a poorly thought out, shitshow of an operation – and it needs someone with actual experience on the street to sort it out.'

This was getting resolved right here, right now. The DI leapt to his feet, his voice rising in fury. 'What – and your solution is to fuck about for three months in a van? You're meant to do as you're told and buy bloody drugs, mate!'

'No', I replied coolly, 'the idea of the van is a stopgap. Because you've overused undercover tactics so much by now they're basically useless. After we pull the van stunt, the gangsters will have worked that out too – it's just a last throw of the dice to save this operation.'

I paused before continuing, enjoying the looks of gawping astonishment from the team.

'The real solution here would be to re-examine those fifty-four heroin deaths you had last year.'

The DI slammed his hand down on the table. 'Do you really expect us to take fifty-four accidental deaths, and stick them back on our books as unsolved murders? For a bunch of fucking smackheads?'

Then one of the younger members of the team piped-up, 'Yeah, a dead junkie's a dead junkie, innit. One less to bloody worry about.' This provoked a round of approving mutters across the room.

For me, this was beyond the pale. I knew the *junkies* that little brat was talking about. I lived with them. I scored dope with them. I had seen the deprivation in which they lived. No cop should ever talk like that about the people he is meant to be protecting. Looking around the circle of smug grinning faces, I also realised that not one of the addicts I knew, no matter how much they resented getting busted, would ever have said anything so abysmally callous about the officers sitting in this room.

But in that moment I had other worries. I had challenged the DI and now he needed to show the wolf pack he was still the boss. He stepped out from behind his desk and squared up.

'You know what your problem is?' I saw his face twist and his breathing grow heavy. 'You're just fucking scared. You're a coward, and you're too scared to do your bloody job – so you just try to faff about with vans and reopen old cases.'

This was too much. I felt myself go icy cold. After the things I had done, he was calling me a coward?

The room hushed as I stepped forward. I saw his eyes flicker as if even he knew he'd gone too far.

I saw his chubby little face floating in front of me. The DI had been sitting at a desk for too long – I'd been out on the street. I knew I could drop him with a single punch. Right in the throat. I felt a white-hot spike of rage shoot up my spine. For a split-second I was no longer Neil – I was Zack, Cookie, Woody, Danny – every codename I'd ever used to become a desperate, ravening street addict who would stick a knife in your belly for a twenty-quid bag of gear.

Then I came back.

I stepped forward, dropping my voice to a low, purposeful hiss. 'Don't you ever call me a coward. You haven't done the things I've done. You couldn't do the things I do – you'd fall apart in thirty seconds. I'm a hundred times the cop you are – and secretly – you fucking know it too.'

I turned and slowly, deliberately, walked out of the room.

I had no idea where I was walking, but I knew I wasn't going back to that office. Whatever it this team were doing, it wasn't police work as I understood it.

Inevitably, it being Brighton, I ended up at the seafront, watching the waves crash on the rocks. Not sure if I was acting as the Neil the cop or Woody the addict, I ducked into a corner shop and bought myself five cans of strong lager and a pack of cigarettes. It's the only relapse into smoking I've ever had. Then I found a bench on the promenade and sat down to think things out.

I was a mess – a million thoughts flashing at a thousand miles an hour, and none with any clarity or coherence. Of course I was angry. But the DI and his crew were just a bunch of incompetent pricks, and I'd dealt with incompetent pricks before. Of course I was disappointed – but by now I should have been used to the idea that sometimes operations just failed. This was something else, something much deeper.

I sat there on that bench wrestling for a grip on the feelings raging inside me. I sucked down my beers and smoked like a forest fire. My fists clenched and unclenched compulsively, my heart shuddering in my chest like a freight train.

What was it? What was I looking for? Why did I feel these electric currents of panic shooting through my mind and body?

Then, staring out at where the black sea met the grey sky, from one moment to the next, I realised exactly what was going on.

There was no mystery here. There were no unanswered questions. Not only did I know exactly what was troubling me, but really, I'd known for a long time. I just hadn't been able to admit it to myself.

The War on Drugs was wrong. This battle, which I had been fighting for so long, which I had poured so much of my life into, was a massive, glaring, futile, stupid failure. It wasn't the tactics. It wasn't the strategies. It wasn't the momentary lapses and inevitable mistakes. It was the War itself.

This was a truth that I had seen long ago, but been afraid to truly accept. The internal contradictions had been tearing me up inside, and now I felt a wave of peace wash over me – I could just let them go.

If I was honest, it all went back to that one night during the Leicester job, sitting on my sofa watching Cold War documentaries and realising the inevitability of the drugs war arms race. The truth had been right there; I just hadn't yet had the courage to face it.

Undercover work is the most aggressive, intrusive and potentially damaging tactic in the police arsenal. In the street-level War on Drugs, it's the nuclear option. Well, we had gone nuclear, and the gangsters had not only worked out how to deflect the weapon – they had redirected its explosive power onto the very people we were meant to be protecting.

Each job had got tougher, each story I encountered more brutal and horrifying. I had fooled myself into believing that the arms race was just a regrettable by-product of our tactics and strategies. I now realised it was written into the script. There was never any potential for de-escalation – never any possibility it could go any other way.

It is an incredibly difficult, but strangely liberating, moment when you realise the battle you have devoted your entire professional life to has done more harm than good.

I could now cast a cold eye, and see how the people who had suffered most through my operations weren't the gangsters I hated, but the civilians and addicts I was trying to protect. By fighting this war, it was us who had placed innocent people in the firing line. We hadn't meant to, but it was the inevitable result of our actions. The road to hell is always paved with good intentions – but there does come a point when you can stop and think about the direction you're travelling.

Don't get me wrong. I had seen the havoc that drugs could wreak, and I still wanted to destroy the pushers and gangsters who ran the trade. I simply now understood that law enforcement wasn't the tool to fix this problem. We had tried, and we had failed. We were always going to fail. Now it was time to try something else.

And, in that instant, the sense of hopelessness left me. I knew what I had to do.

I was still a cop. I was a detective with multiple commendations and an expertise in the narcotics trade that was unique in the force. I still wanted to fight the good fight – that wasn't ever a question. I just wasn't going to waste my time chasing homeless addicts – I was going to change the system.

I would go back to my detective work and keep fighting gangsters and murderers. I would build my reputation and expertise, advance through the force and influence policy from the inside – away from the narrow mentality of the War on Drugs, towards a solution that might actually work.

It would be a long hard road, but I had never shied away from a challenge. In fact, it's what I lived for. To me, this was just my next operation.

The job I had always wanted in the police force was Detective Sergeant, running a team of detectives, structuring complex, intelligence-led investigations. With my experience I knew I could achieve this. Jim Horner advised Chief Constables on drugs. If I got the same profile maybe I could do the same, allowing me to influence policy.

All I have ever needed in life is a mission. Now I had one. With this new sense of purpose, I felt the war that had been raging inside me begin to subside. It was only then that I realised just how long I'd been harbouring this inner conflict without even knowing it. I felt lighter and happier than I had in years. It seems the truth will set you free after all.

I flicked the cigarette I was smoking out onto the stony beach and gave the greying horizon one last glance. This mission was over.

I didn't even stop by Brighton HQ to pick up my stuff.

CHAPTER 15

BUXTON II

I came so close to making it work.

I moved back up to Buxton and threw myself into my work with renewed vigour, eventually making it to Detective Sergeant, the job I had always aspired to on the force. I was engaging with the aspects of police work I truly believed in: directing complex, structured investigations into powerful organised crime groups.

At the same time I was educating myself. I spent every spare moment turning myself into an expert on the roots, function and implications of drug enforcement policy, both in the UK and across the world. I had to be absolutely sure that my ideas on the drugs war were not just an emotional reaction to my own experiences. I was a cop – I needed evidence.

And the evidence blew my mind. I became a statistics machine, reeling off numbers, facts, analysis. I pored over the data, weighing and dissecting each conflicting viewpoint like any sceptical detective should. The conclusion I came to was indisputable. My epiphany on the Brighton beachfront had been correct – the War on Drugs was a harmful, counterproductive misadventure. The catastrophic failure had always been a foregone conclusion.

The illicit durgs trade in the UK alone is worth roughly £7 billion a year. To put that in perspective, total annual spend on unemployment benefits is around £4.9 billion.

That is seven billion pounds transferred straight into the pockets of the gangsters I had spent my life chasing down. It is the financial base on which all other forms of organised criminality rests. Even worse, the costs of policing drugs are an additional £7 billion per year – £7 billion taken straight out of investigations into murders, rapes, robberies and other violent crime.

I knew this message might be unpopular among certain sections of the police hierarchy, so I took things step by step, making sure my credentials were absolutely in order.

Jim Horner had been appointed to the influential Association of Chief Police Officers (ACPO), as a specialist drugs policy advisor. I knew by this stage I actually had more specialist knowledge than he did; and if I played my cards right I could eventually make it there too, giving myself the chance to make a real impact on policy.

My first move was to become an accredited Drugs Expert Witness. I began travelling the country providing expert testimony at trials, attending seminars, getting myself onto committees and making contacts in the field.

Eventually I found myself giving presentations to three hundred specialist drug officers at the National Conference, teaching them about the implications of *R v. Moon*, a stated case in European law mandating that police forces must take into consideration when an addict has been selling in order to fund their own habit. Obviously I cared deeply about this; I had seen the difference between user-dealers and real gangsters consistently ignored in pursuit of stats.

By the end of that conference I had been appointed to the board of the Drugs Expert and Witness Valuation Association

(DEWVA). The head of DEWVA also served on the Serious Organised Crime Agency (SOCA), and had direct access to politicians. I was making progress.

At the same time, I ran a tight team as a DS, bringing in a steady stream of convictions against serious OCGs. Rookie detectives I tutored routinely came back with the highest detection rates in the county. This is the type of stuff that establishes a reputation in police circles.

But as much as I had personally vowed to take no further part in the drugs war, that was always just a fantasy. The narcotics trade permeates every level of organised criminality. There is more money in drugs than every other criminal enterprise combined. In fact, now there is virtually no organised criminal activity that isn't in some way drug-related. We would scratch the surface of a murder and almost invariably find a turf war between dealers, or a gang protecting their supply network. In policing organised crime, all roads lead to dope.

At this point in my career, things had also settled down at home. Sam had changed jobs and was working long hours, which suited me as I had the house to myself most evenings and I could get on with taking care of the kids. They were growing into wonderful, intelligent children who I loved spending time with. For a few years I had the quiet, focused life I needed.

Then the nightmares started.

It was a sword at my throat. It was a glowering face forcing me to take amphetamine. It was a woman clutching a can of Special Brew, walking down the street shouting 'Sex for sale'.

I would wake up screaming, soaked in sweat, with the kids at the door asking what was wrong. But I couldn't sleep. Sleep was where they were.

I would zombie my way through work the next day, my mind fixating on the moment that night when I would have to close my eyes again. Eventually the horrors began creeping into my waking life. The tiniest throwaway remark could trigger my heart rate – suddenly I would be back in Northampton, forced to strip at gunpoint. I'd have to excuse myself and lock myself in the toilet until my breathing returned to normal.

And just as I was struggling to deal with this growing mental instability, my relationship with Sam once again began to spiral into chaos. For years I had been using under-cover work as an escape from the situation at home – literally the chance to become somebody else for a few hours. Now, without that release valve – and terrified even of sleep – I medicated in the only way I knew how. Once again, three cans of lager at night became five. But I always paid the price for this momentary relief in hungover paranoia and self-doubt the following day.

My work began slipping. It began slowly: a lost file here, an un-followed piece of evidence there – nothing that would raise eyebrows from the bosses. But I always knew when a day's work didn't come up to my own standards. By now I was a survivor, able to get by under stress and paper over the cracks to fool the world. But I couldn't fool myself.

And just as my night terrors were spinning out of control, and our home life was nearing the point of collapse, I began work on what would be my last major case on the force – a case that would give me one final chilling illustration of the corrosive effects of the War on Drugs.

The target was Kenny McMinn, a lieutenant of the infamous Manchester gangster Arran Coghlan. Coghlan was called the 'Teflon Don', as it was widely known he had got away with murder three times after witnesses refused to testify, or cases collapsed in dubious circumstances. The investigation into McMinn was part of an ongoing campaign against Coghlan's criminal empire.

When we sat down for our initial briefing, the very first order our DI gave was that under no circumstances were we to speak to anyone from Greater Manchester police. In fact, if anyone from the Manchester force contacted us, or even mentioned the case in any way, we were to immediately inform our commanders.

The younger detectives in the room didn't understand. Surely, they asked, sharing intelligence between departments could only be a good thing? The more experienced investigators got it immediately. Manchester police leaked like a sieve. We had to assume that the gangsters had moles throughout that force, and any information we passed on would go straight to our targets. Just as with my previous experience of criminal infiltration in Nottingham, the fatalistic response was simply, 'Well, with this much money involved, how can corruption not happen?'

No one seemed to be drawing the blindingly obvious conclusion – why not take the narcotics trade out of the gangsters' hands, and actually deprive them of all that money? But this briefing didn't seem to be the ideal moment for me to suggest the legalisation and regulation of the entire drugs trade.

We worked the case hard, fighting our way through the standard drugs-war brutality and violence, and keeping our information flow as tight as possible to prevent leaks. Eventually I managed to flip one of McMinn's own user-dealers, offering him rehab and the chance of a new life in witness protection on the other side of the country.

As we were awaiting trial on the McMinn case, I was called to attend a crime scene in Hayfield, a posh town on the Cheshire–Derbyshire border. It seemed this site was connected to Arran Coghlan's drug empire, and may have some bearing on our investigation.

As I pulled up, I saw a large team from Greater Manchester police working the crime scene for forensics. My hackles went up immediately. Remembering our instructions regarding the Manchester force, I leapt out of my car, demanding to see the supervising DS.

But before I could launch into my tirade, the DS broke into a broad smile. 'Don't worry. We know the concerns regarding the Greater Manchester Constabulary – we're a special unit. In fact we were formed precisely because of those concerns.'

It turned out that he was the head of a team of twelve hand-picked detectives, specifically charged with dismantling the Arran Coghlan empire. This was their only mission, and they reported directly to the Greater Manchester chief constable – and only to him. The bosses in Manchester knew their department was so riddled with spies that this team had to operate entirely in secret, totally cut off from the rest of the force.

'So wait – there's twelve of you, yeah? So, you're basically the Untouchables.'

'Yeah.' The DS laughed loudly. 'But our guvnor says we're not allowed to call ourselves that.'

Now we both laughed. It was classic prohibition policing: form a special squad, but instead of sorting out the corruption that actually made it necessary, spend your energy monitoring what they call themselves.

I hung out with *not-the Untouchables* all afternoon, watching them work and getting their perspective on the war we were all fighting. I found the very idea that this squad was necessary – that out of the 11,000 or so police under the Manchester chief constable's command, he could only find 12 he could trust – completely insane. Once again, though, that fatalistic phrase kept cropping up, 'Look, with this much money in the game, how can corruption not happen?'

For them this was simply a bleak statement of the obvious. For me, it cut much deeper. On top of all my other doubts about the War on Drugs, we were now being asked to accept the inevitable corruption of the police force itself. Of course there have always been a few bent coppers, but it is only drugs that generate the kind of money that makes other cops just shrug and accept it as inevitable.

I had dedicated my life to the police. Despite everything, I still absolutely believed in the essential necessity of our mission as cops. The one thing I could not stand was the thought that the police themselves were becoming warped and tainted by the war they were being forced to fight. I drove home that evening in a fury, more convinced than ever that the War on Drugs must end, and that protecting the integrity of the police itself meant that I must do my part to bring this about.

But it was getting harder just to maintain my own work, let alone fight a crusade for policy reform in my spare time.

Each day the exhaustion made it harder to maintain my focus. I would sit at my desk, staring at the patterns in the styrofoam ceiling, while the telephones and office chatter faded to a dull hum, miles away. I fell so behind on my paperwork that I began having to bring files home, catching up in the witching hours after I'd woken from some awful nightmare and couldn't go back to sleep.

And now the situation with Sam reached a crisis point.

The real collapse began one morning after we had dropped the kids off at school. The second they were out of the car the shouting began. I tried to stay calm and maintain focus on the road – but there was always that voice in my ear – louder, louder, louder. It felt like it was never going to stop. Something inside me snapped. I couldn't take it anymore.

I slammed on the emergency brake, sending the car screeching to a halt in the middle of Buxton market. Then I pounded my fists onto the horn and just held them there, the blaring of the horn giving some momentary relief from that voice.

I slowly turned my head to look at Sam, my eyes actually beginning to fill with tears. Was I actually losing it? Actually going mad?

Slowly the world swam back into focus. I could hear the shouts and beeping of the drivers stuck behind us. Summoning every atom of self-control that I'd developed over years of undercover work, I restarted the car and drove off.

That moment stuck with me. I would slump exhausted over my desk at work, going over and over it in my mind. It felt like Sam was purposefully pushing me towards the edge. Surely she couldn't be doing it on purpose? It sounded ludicrous to my rationalist, police-trained mind. It must be me. I must be losing it. It's a terrible feeling to imagine you are losing your grip on reality.

I was lucky that my uniformed inspector at the time was understanding. A few years previously he had needed to take six months off himself due to stress. He frequently let me know that his door was open if I needed to talk. Looking back, I wish I had taken him up on the offer.

Not that it would have made much difference when the break finally came.

The situation couldn't last. I had been pushed beyond my breaking point, and needed to escape from the shell of my marriage. I had originally stayed to protect my children, but now I realised they were old enough to make their own decisions, and maintaining the façade of this relationship was doing them more harm than good.

Sam must have realised it too. I was about to head off on a two-week Detective Sergeant's course, and we decided we would drop the kids with my parents, and she would use the time to find a new place. Tanith and Gareth were to stay with me.

An indescribable weight had been lifted. I went off to that DS course feeling reborn. I couldn't remember a high like this since I had heard the handcuffs click on Danny Anderson at the end of my first undercover job.

But I shouldn't have fooled myself. It was never going to be that easy.

The day I got back from the course I went straight in to work. That evening I signed out a CID car in order to drive through to Matlock Station, where my own car was parked. On the way down I thought I'd pop into the house for a quick shower and change of clothes.

Of course she hadn't moved out. The shouting started the second I opened the door. It was as if our previous conversation had never even happened.

At that moment, something inside me broke. Every memory of blades and guns, squalor and savagery from my years on the streets came exploding through my brain at once. I couldn't breathe. I gasped frantically but no air seemed to come. My chest felt like it was being pounded by a sledgehammer. For a moment I thought I might actually be having a heart attack.

I sank to my knees, the tears streaming down my face. I didn't know what to do. My mind was white noise. The only thought I had was that I had to get away. Still blinded by the tears, the only vision in my mind was Kyle from Stoke holding his samurai sword to my throat, I crawled on my hands and knees under the kitchen table. I curled up in a ball and sobbed.

*

That's where I woke up the next day. I groggily opened my eyes, only to realise someone was banging on the front door. I staggered up and opened it, only to see my own DI standing there on my doorstep. His eyes widened when he saw the expression on my face.

'Neil...Woodsy...what the hell is going on?'

I couldn't even answer.

Of course the CID team at Matlock had come in that morning and wondered where their car was. It was my name on the sign-out sheet.

The DI didn't press me. He put his hand on my shoulder and gently asked, 'Neil, do you need to go sick for a bit?'

The words wouldn't come. All I could do was nod in abject relief. That afternoon I pulled myself together, ran the CID car back to Matlock and phoned into the station from the car park to tell them I was taking leave.

Of course Sam did eventually move out. There had never really been a question.

Between the time off from work, and the time off from the relationship, I began stitching myself back together as a human being.

For the first time in my life I went to see a counsellor. Within two sessions of describing the nightmares, panic attacks and trouble focusing, she had diagnosed post-traumatic stress disorder.

At first I had a hard time accepting the idea. To me, PTSD was for guys coming back from Afghanistan and Iraq, not Leicester and Brighton. I also pointed out that I had mainly felt very calm and rational during most of these actual encounters.

'Neil, I've treated many patients with PTSD – both military and non-military. You have a severe case. You need to take this seriously. It's not necessarily the fear you feel at the time that causes this type of harm; it's the fear you don't even know you're feeling – the fear that gets repressed till years later.'

My counsellor also talked through the history of my relationship with Sam, forcing me to undertake a process of completely re-evaluating everything I thought I understood about marriage and what love and partnership really mean.

There is no figure in society more abject than the junkie, no character more degraded than the addict who will crawl on their belly and endure any humiliation in order to get their fix. Somehow, I was able to relate. Or, to put it another way, you know your home life has become unmanageable when your coping mechanism is going out every day and pretending to be a homeless crackhead.

Gradually things began to piece themselves together. The Police Federation got me two weeks' rehabilitation at Flint House, a law-enforcement convalescent centre in Hertfordshire. The staff there were amazing, and helped me finally kick booze. I began exchanging emails with my DI, arranging my return to work.

But the return never came.

Sam and I were never going to have a clean, easy break. Between the kids and the fraught emotional complexities of our relationship, it took months of toing and froing, picking up and dropping off, arguments and lawyers' letters. Then, one day in late April, when Gareth and Tanith were both away, she called and brusquely told me she was coming to pick up her table.

I knew immediately what she was talking about. Sam had brought the beaten up old coffee table with her when we first moved in together. To be honest, the thing had always slightly annoyed me. It was too small to actually use, but big enough to make any room feel slightly awkward, and the chunky edges had a sharpness that stung like a whip when you inevitably stubbed your toe. The wood was chipped and ugly, and I was more than happy to see it go.

It was only as I was carrying it out to Sam's car that I realised that this was it – this was the last of her possessions gone – the final physical trace of how her life had imposed itself on mine. The kids were old enough to come and go between our separate places, but now she would have no reason to come inside – there would be no ghostly feeling of her still weighing down on me in my own living room.

Walking back into the house, I was immediately swept with an almost uncontrollable rush of exhilaration and joy. But there was also another emotion, something unrecognisable, an uncanny sensation that I couldn't place or name even as it flooded through my veins. I spent hours just padding from room to room in a sort of daze, trying to put the right word to this exotic new feeling.

It took hours before it came to me. I was walking down the stairs from my bedroom to the kitchen, when I stopped dead in my tracks. Safe. That was what I felt. For the first time in years I felt safe in my own home. It had been so long that I couldn't even recognise the sensation. I sank down to sit on the stairs and leaned against the bannister, letting the sense of release and weightlessness wash over me.

I stayed like that for what felt like hours, my head leaning on the bannister and my mind spinning as I felt years of fear and trauma beginning to wash away. When I came back to myself, I could see through the hall windows that it was now evening, and the entire house seemed bathed in the whisky-gold of a late-spring sunset. Almost on autopilot, I stood up and walked out the door to my car.

I had no idea where I was going. It just felt right to be on the road, driving with no set destination. For the first time in as long as I could remember the future seemed wide open, I could go anywhere and anything was possible.

I soon found myself deep in the Peak District, and pulled over at the top of a high ridge that was one of my favourite spots from my days running the Fells. Leaving the car behind, I walked off and sat down at the cliff edge, my feet dangling into thin air. The entire valley seemed limitless and glowing in the sunset. Two hawks wheeled around, lazily riding the warm currents of air as they circled the hills.

Looking out at this glorious scene I began to think about the future, about how I would return to my job as Detective Sergeant and rededicate myself more deeply than ever to the cause of reforming drug policy.

The question never exploded into my mind in some sort of momentous flash of inspiration. It was as if it had always been there, but only now could I actually hear it.

Why did I need to return to the police to pursue this reform? Could I not better serve this cause without the force's rigid institutional boundaries? I had put in my years with the police, I had more experience in this field than almost every other officer I knew – maybe it was now time to deploy that experience elsewhere?

I think at any other moment this thought would have been too shocking for me to even contemplate – being a cop was such a fundamental part of my identity. But, somehow after what felt like the final goodbye with Sam that day, everything felt boundless and infinite. Anything was within reach. Why not think about a life beyond the police?

For real cops, the police force isn't just a job or an institution – it's a way of looking at the world. Being a cop was in my blood, that training had formed my mind and taught me how to think. I knew that after all I had given to the force, and all the force had given me, I would carry that identity until the day I died. But somehow, I also knew that this wasn't where my immediate future lay. My priority – my new mission – was to work to end the War on Drugs. This was my purpose, my meaning. This was the legacy I wanted to leave to my own children, and all those who had suffered in this stupid, pointless, self-defeating struggle. To pursue this mission fully, I needed total freedom to operate. I needed to get political.

I took a deep breath, and went back to looking out over the valley, watching the hawks as they floated, wheeled and dove.

Then I walked back to the car, almost unsteady with the weightless thrill of my realization – but completely, finally, at peace.

The next day I tendered my resignation. That was that, I was no longer a cop.

CHAPTER 16

A THOUSAND WASTED YEARS

Over the course of my career, my drugs investigations put people in prison for a total of well over a thousand years.

For me, every single one of these is a year wasted. These are a thousand wasted years of human potential; a thousand wasted years of possible creativity, learning and exploration; a thousand wasted years of people languishing in tiny cells rather than contributing to the world.

Don't get me wrong – I haven't gone soft. A lot of these people deserved to be punished and definitely needed to be taken off the streets. People like Kyle in Stoke, Stitz in Nottingham and the Burger Bar Boys in Northampton had all committed vile, horrific crimes, and I take pride in having held them to account.

But it didn't need to be this way. There is a common thread to all these stories. There is an underlying condition that made their criminality not just possible, but virtually inevitable: the fact that there is a global illegal narcotics market worth £375 billion every year.

These were a thousand wasted years because people were born into a situation where selling drugs was the logical choice. It was the law that created this market. It was the law that ensured the addicts these people sold to were trapped, unable to seek help because they were now 'criminals'.

There is a mythology common in police circles that some people are just 'bad' – that if drugs were legalised they would simply find other forms of criminality. This line gets predictably trotted out whenever the current prohibition is challenged. It's drivel.

Most cops who toe this line only have experience of prosecuting criminals – I've lived among them. I spent fourteen years undercover, living with dealers, thieves, addicts and gangsters. I know their motivations. I can tell you categorically – the idea that most people commit crimes because they are somehow inherently 'bad' is mendacious, propagandistic bullshit.

There are extremely few genuine psychopaths in the world. The criminals I encountered in the drugs trade were business-people. They had made the decision that their best option for getting ahead in life was to sell crack and heroin to a captive market. Some of them were capable of disgusting, almost sociopathic violence, but they became that way through exposure to the drugs trade.

This isn't theory – I've watched it happen. The clearest example was JB's crew in Leicester. Those kids were eighteen years old. Over the months I was deployed there, I saw with my own eyes the process by which they were transformed from schoolkids into hardened gangsters. I could see each fork in the road in front of them, as day by day they were forced to learn that their only option was to become ever more violent and brutal.

To simply label some people as *evil* is a lazy moral choice. It's also a lie – and an evasion of responsibility. I will no longer even use the word 'junkie'. It's a word that stigmatises and condemns, when what is needed is greater effort to understand.

The fact is, we set up the conditions whereby these characters can make and carry through their decision to sell drugs. We declared some of the most vulnerable people in society criminals – turning them into hostages to their own dealers. We set the arms race of the War on Drugs in motion.

But, we can fix it. We can change course. We have the power to rationally analyse the evidence, and choose a course that will spare future generations the awful harm that prohibition does.

This change of course is the purpose to which I am now dedicating my life.

I left the police with a strange feeling of brokenness and liberation. For so long I had defined myself through this work. Being a cop wasn't just what I did – it's what I was. Now I had to discover a new role.

At first my only concern was to take care of the kids, and make sure to provide them with some stability through my divorce from Sam and change of career.

But after several months of intense reflection, I began to realise that, though I may no longer be a police officer, I still had a specialist knowledge of this field, shared by only a handful of people in the world. I could still put this to good use. The madness of the War on Drugs still had to end – and I could still play a part. In fact, I realised, not having to work within the confines of trying to advance my police career may even free me to operate more effectively.

I contacted a criminal justice organisation called Release, and they in turn put me in touch with LEAP.

Law Enforcement Against Prohibition (LEAP) was founded in the US in 2002. It is made up principally of members and former members of various enforcement agencies who, like me, have come to realise the utter futility and fundamental immorality of the War on Drugs. There are currently official chapters in twenty countries, from the US to Latin America, Europe and beyond.

It was incredible for me to discover this network of experienced, like-minded people. Before long I had joined as a chairman of the newly formed LEAP UK.

We campaign for an end to the War on Drugs, and the full legalisation and regulation of the illicit drugs market.

This may seem like an extreme position from someone who has dedicated so much of their life to putting drug dealers in prison, but I – like everyone else in LEAP – arrived at this conclusion based not only on my experience of fighting the drugs war, but also after rigorous, in-depth study of the larger issues involved.

This is not some naïve hippy, utopian movement. We're a bunch of cops. I detest woolly thinking and imprecise data. I'm into rigorous methodology and peer-review. Essentially, I'm still a trained detective – I'll only accept a piece of evidence if I believe it could withstand cross-examination from the best defence solicitor in the country.

So, when we at LEAP say the War on Drugs must end, it is based both on our hands-on experience and on deep, hard-headed analysis. We've lived this – and we've studied it. We know our business.

I still think like a cop. I still feel loyalty to police around the world. Other people have written volumes about the public health and policy issues of the War on Drugs; my specialist knowledge is in how it specifically affects law enforcement.

It's worth looking at the damage drug prohibition does to police forces themselves.

In January 2008, the internationally renowned professor David Nutt was appointed Chairman of the British government's Advisory Council on the Misuse of Drugs. He lasted eighteen months. He was sacked for arguing that drug policy should be based on scientific evidence rather than political convenience. Several other longstanding members of the Council resigned in protest.

One of the nice things about coming from a police background is that politicians have to at least pretend to listen to you. No one wearing a suit and tie in the House of Commons or in local government can accuse me of passing judgement from an ivory tower. I know about the fight against drug cartels; I've put my life on the line for that fight. I've earned my right to speak out on this.

The fact is, though, even most politicians realise that drug prohibition is a form of wasteful madness. In 2014 the British government released a major report, which, even after significant political fiddling, concluded that punitive measures have no actual impact on levels of drug use. Developed democracies with liberal drug policies have roughly the same or lower drug use than those with harsh laws.

The numbers are pretty simple. On average, about 10% of people who use drugs use them problematically. It's 6.8% for cannabis, 10% for cocaine, 10% for alcohol and 15% for crystal meth – with heroin as an outlier at 25%. This 10% figure is exactly the same for people who have a problem managing gambling problems, yet successive governments have actively encouraged the gambling industry and the construction of new casinos.

With 90% of users managing to consume drugs without wrecking their lives, it seems like an act of actual wilful self-destruction to spend £7 billion a year criminalising those who do have a problem – thus ensuring they are unable to get the help they need.

The evidence from around the world is fairly conclusive. Wherever drug policy has been moved away from law enforcement, the positive outcomes have overwhelmingly outweighed the negative.

In the year 2000, Portugal had both the highest drug addiction rate and highest rate of drug deaths in Europe. The country was in crisis. Some estimates put the rate of heroin addiction at 1% of the overall population. In response, the government convened a panel of experts, and took the extraordinarily brave step of resolving to actually follow the advice they were given. Against the usual outcry from opposition groups and sections of the security apparatus, Portugal decriminalised drug use, and shifted drug policy from law enforcement to public health.

Fifteen years later the country has been transformed. Portugal's rate of acute drug deaths per year is now three per million of population – the current UK rate, by contrast, is forty-six per million. Infection rates of HIV and hepatitis C are way down, as are both violent crime and petty crime rates associated with drug use.

Most significantly, there was no rise in the rates of actual drug use, despite the hysterical warning screams of the opposition. Casual drug consumption has remained fairly stable, with a significant dip in long-term heroin use.

In Switzerland they created a series of official injection centres in major cities, supplying clean equipment, medical advice and a space where addicts could inject safely. None of these places has ever seen a fatal heroin overdose. In addition, Switzerland uses Heroin Assisted Therapy – actually prescribing heroin to addicts – alongside various methadone programmes. HAT has an 80% success rate in weaning addicts off heroin, far higher than any other approach on record.

UK policymakers have a lot to learn. But they don't even have to look abroad.

In 1982 Dr John Marks began a massively important experiment in Widnes, Cheshire. Using a loophole in the law he began prescribing heroin to users, instead of forcing them onto methadone or other programmes.

The results were astonishing. First off, there was a 93% drop in the level of acquisitive crime such as burglary, auto theft and shoplifting. The manager of Widnes Marks & Spencer was so grateful that she reportedly donated £2,000 to Marks' clinic.

No longer having to scramble around for their £20 bags, Marks' patients began to stabilise and improve their lives. Street prostitutes were able to leave sex work; thieves and robbers were able to take on – and keep – regular employment.

The gangsters who had been running drugs in the town saw their market dry up, and drifted off to Liverpool.

Crucially, over those years Marks recorded a decrease in the number of users. There were no more pushers actively trying to get people hooked, and the number of addicts actually fell.

If the British government had adopted Marks' strategy, my undercover career would have been very short indeed. Unfortunately, it did the opposite. When Marks' experiment became public in 1995 he was vilified and blacklisted, and ended up having to emigrate to New Zealand to rebuild his life.

Within two years of the programme's cancellation, forty-one of Marks' 400 patients were dead.

I want to state once again that I am in no way downplaying the horrors and dangers of addiction. I have lived among addicts and seen the squalor and misery that the disease wreaks on their lives.

All I am arguing is that the police are not the correct tool with which to fix this problem. And unfortunately, just as in DIY, when you use the incorrect tool to try to fix something you can end up damaging the tool itself.

Put simply, drug prohibition is very bad for the police.

The key problem is that it's much easier to chase stats by busting low-level user-dealers than by hunting down real gangsters and solving serious crime. Not only does this serve to actually protect the big organised crime groups – but also, cops forget how to do real police work.

This process has played out most clearly in the United States. In the late 1960s the clearance rate in American murder cases was 90%. Then came the War on Drugs. By the mid-seventies murder clearances had dropped to 64%, and have flatlined ever since – and this in an era of vast leaps forward in surveillance, digitisation and DNA technology. Not to resort to cliché, but one in three of America's killers are getting away with murder.

The fact is, you can have all the tech in the world, but if you hand control of entire communities over to the gangsters, you will never be able to gain intelligence or find witnesses to testify. For all that policymakers can talk about preventative policing and 'Broken Windows' policies, once you lose the trust of a community you simply will not be able to solve serious cases. The arms race of the War on Drugs dictates that the more you go after the dealers, the more they will protect their market by brutally enforcing the code of silence on civilians.

And the arms race has another, even darker effect on the police.

I had brushes with corruption on the force over the years. My experiences with Colin Gunn infiltrating my own unit in Nottingham, and meeting the *not-the Untouchables* special squad in Manchester, both deeply shook my confidence in what we were doing.

But in both cases, the reaction was simply, *with this much money involved, how can corruption not happen?* That money only comes from one source, the drugs trade.

Those were two random examples, and that was ten years ago. Following the inevitable logic of the arms race, one can only assume that by now it is much worse.

There is a standing order from the Home Office to Chief Constables across the UK that their top priority must be to *maintain public confidence in the police.* The reasons are obvious: the moment people lose that faith, society starts to break down. As a result, there are constant hushed rumours in police circles of stories of corruption being buried and soft-pedalled.

In 1930s America, it was the stories of police corruption that really destroyed public support for Prohibition. My instinct is that if the public were to ever learn just how often current police forces are forced to shrug and say *well, how can this not happen?* then support for drug prohibition would disappear just as quickly.

With regard to my personal field, undercover work, I read the headlines about the manipulation of female activists by Mark Kennedy and Bob Lambert with utter disgust. To me, they symbolised another example of departments that had completely lost their moral compass. But, I tell you now – you should be much more worried about the stories you *aren't* reading.

The narcotics trade provides the financial basis for almost every other form of organised criminality. In Britain alone, remember, the market is worth £7 billion a year. It costs a further £7 billion in policing – and that's without the associated costs of imprisonment and public health and everything else.

Over fifty per cent of the inmates in British prisons are there for drug-related offences. Read that figure again. Let it sink in.

Not only is prison essentially post-graduate advanced training for criminals, but every one of those prisoners means a family without a father, mother, sister, brother, husband, wife or friend. These are people like Ali, Cammy, Ellie, Angus, Sara and Davo. They are you and me, had our lives gone in another direction – and I've seen just how knife-edge that difference can be.

Now imagine the good the police could do if drugs were properly reimagined as primarily a public health issue. Imagine if we stopped handing gangsters a £7 billion annual war chest with which to terrorise our communities and corrupt our enforcement agencies.

Though they're not allowed to say it publicly, many officers and detectives agree with me. Most police are good people doing a difficult job. Most of them didn't join the force in order to make the lives of the vulnerable even more difficult. Many resent being forced to do so.

The fact is, what we as a society are asking the police to do is to take care of our dirty laundry – out of sight and out of mind. Drug addiction is an issue that all aspects of society need to engage with. Outsourcing it to law enforcement alone is a simple act of moral laziness.

Every day that politicians continue the War on Drugs, it is not only a choice to make the vulnerable suffer for political convenience – it is also a direct betrayal of the police themselves.

In Bruce Lee's masterpiece kung-fu movie, *Enter The Dragon,* there's a scene where Lee is on a ship with some other martial arts experts. One of them, a hulking bully, confronts Lee, demanding to know what his style of combat is called. Lee replies, 'The art of fighting without fighting.'

The bully scoffs and challenges Lee to fight. Lee agrees, but says they need more space, and suggests they take the ship's dinghy out to a nearby island. The bully climbs down into the dinghy – at which point Lee simply unwinds the line-rope, so the bully is stuck getting dragged out behind the ship, soaking wet and at Lee's mercy. There you go – the art of fighting without fighting.

One of the phrases I often hear from my own allies is that the War on Drugs should end because it is unwinnable. I fundamentally disagree. The War on Drugs is eminently winnable. All we have to do is stop fighting.

We need to take a moment and just consider the possibility of not confronting the issue of drugs as a *war*. Legalise and regulate the supply of narcotics and at a stroke you deprive the most vicious gangsters in the world of the £375 billion annual income that enables all their operations. At a stroke you allow some of the most vulnerable people in society to seek help for their addictions, instead of being shoved into prison cells. And, at a stroke you allow the police to get back to doing the vitally important work they are actually trained for, and can take real pride in.

The drugs war corrupts everything it touches. It corrupts the addicts who are forced to live in the shadows; it corrupts the gangsters whom the arms race forces into depths of brutality even they wouldn't otherwise stoop to; and, most painful to me, it corrupts the police. You can't ask an army to fight a war it isn't meant for and doesn't really believe in, day after day, without moral rot setting in.

If you need a vision of where the War on Drugs is heading, just look at the dystopian brutality of the cartel wars in Mexico, a country where every level of civil society has been grossly and wantonly violated by prohibition.

Or, to put things in further perspective – a few years ago I tried a thought experiment. I attempted to add up the total amount of time for which all my operations taken together had actually disrupted the UK drug supply. The number I came up with – at a very optimistic estimate – was about eighteen hours.

Now, think back to the thousand years that I put people in prison.

A thousand years of captivity, so that a few addicts had to wait an extra eighteen hours for their fix. Does that seem a fair exchange to you? Does it seem wise? Does it seem just?

Or, does it seem insane to the point of actual immorality?

I'm aware that not everyone is ready to hear this message. But they haven't seen what I've seen. This isn't theoretical for me – I know where it leads.

Since I began speaking about these issues, there has been some kickback from sections of the police. Most of my friends from the force have been forced to distance themselves.

One very close friend completely disappeared from one day to the next. I found out from elsewhere that she'd been called into the DCI's office and ordered to delete my phone, email and Facebook contacts right there in front of them, or face career-damaging disciplinary action.

I half-expect that, when this book is published, some cops will accuse me of recklessness, or even betrayal, for exposing undercover tactics. Anyone who says this hasn't been paying attention, and needs to spend more time trying to catch real criminals. Gangsters learn fast. I stopped doing undercover work almost ten years ago, and my tactics were almost obsolete by the time I walked away. Anyone on the street who would still fall for my tricks now would be such a small-time no-hoper that chasing them would be a waste of resources.

In any case, I'm ready for the criticism, and for the larger battle of ideas. There is some way to go. There are vested interests in sections of politics, law enforcement, religious institutions, privatised prison industries and parts of the media that are heavily invested in the War on Drugs. I just happen to have seen these issues much closer-up than they have. All I can do is try to convince people, one by one.

And there are many hopeful signs. Governments from Ecuador to Colorado to Switzerland are catching up. If you had told me even a few years ago that cannabis would be legal in several American states, I would have assumed you had been smoking a bit too much yourself. I believe the tide is turning.

I also feel ready for this fight because for the first time in my life I feel supported. After my divorce from Sam I spent some time simply taking care of Tanith and Gareth, watching them both grow into incredible, smart, independent and generous people, whom I admire more with each passing day. Then I met Lynette. She is a wonderful, beautiful woman, a true companion for me and an amazing presence in the lives of the children. We married about the same time I began work on this book.

I've chosen to commit myself to ending the War on Drugs for many reasons. Partly it is about undoing some of the harm I have caused. I was part of the arms race like everyone else. I think back to people like Ali in Leicester; Cammy, Gary and Davo in Nottingham; and Angus and

Sara in Northampton, and I have to recognise that I used and manipulated them. And I must accept that in doing so, I put their lives at risk. If the gangsters ever found out it was them who introduced me, they would have been the ones to suffer, not me. But at the time, they were all considered acceptable losses in the war I was fighting. That war needs to end so that more people like them aren't put in harm's way by people like me.

Most of all though, it comes back to fighting without fighting. I want to end the War on Drugs because I want to win it.

I hate the drug cartels. I've seen their viciousness and brutality up close, and I despise them. I want to stop them. I want to end their savagery and take their power away. And they should fear me. I've done more than most to send them to prison. I know their weakness. Fighting to end the War on Drugs will do more harm to the gangsters than anything I ever accomplished as a cop.

For me, this is simply a new mission, a new operation – a lifelong deployment. And to undertake this work I no longer have to operate in the shadows. I can finally be who I am, while doing something I truly believe in.

This is an important, global battle and there are many others fighting it. If I can contribute in my own small way then I am glad to play a part. It might partly be a way to heal some of the harm I have caused, but mostly it's just the best way I know to make a positive change in many people's lives. And maybe, just maybe, it's simply a truer, better way for me to fight the good fight.

Because really, that's all it's ever been about.

ACKNOWLEDGEMENTS

In making the transition from cop to campaigner, I have been privileged to learn from so many brave, intelligent people. I hope you all know who you are, and that you have my thanks, support and respect.

There are some who deserve special mention: Jason Reed and Beccy Gardham of LEAP UK for sheer intellect, and for being such great, inspiring friends – and of course, Jason, for the fantastic film *The Culture High*!

Nicky Saunter and everyone else at Transform and the Anyone's Child Campaign – as a Detective Sergeant, it was the work of Transform that helped me see that change is possible. Niamh Eastwood and all at Release, whose work is so crucial. Steve Moore and the team at VolteFace – when change happens in the UK, you will be in the centre of it.

Dale Beaumont Brown and the rest at Elixir for the essential film *Grassroots: The Cannabis Revolution*. Johann Hari, for your tireless work and support, and the important and brilliant book, *Chasing The Scream*. Annie Machon for all your help, guidance and wonderful work; and all the people at Virgin who do so much for the international effort.

Particular thanks to Neill Franklin, Diane Goldstein and all other past and present board members of LEAP in the USA, for your inspired – and inspiring – leadership. Indeed, thank you to every LEAP member and speaker from Brazil to Germany, from New Zealand to Costa Rica. The spread of LEAP across the globe is going to be crucial in bringing about the change we need.

For bringing this book about, special thanks is due to Adam Gauntlett, who first saw that this story needed to be told, along with Jonathan Sissons and all at PFD.

Thanks also to Ciara Foley and all at Ebury, in particular Kelly Ellis, Liz Marvin and the legal team who guided us through the wrenching process of bringing our original text in line with the UK's absurd Libel and Privacy laws. These laws are a disgrace – credit to all those working to reform them.

JS Rafaeli would like to thank his family for their constant support and love, particularly Rafi for saying 'jump cuts' exactly when he needed to hear it. And, of course, Vera.